Praise for Jack Roney

'*The Angels Wept* is a book you simply won't be able to put down until the last gripping page. Heart wrenching at times but a must read... a magnificent ending to a thrilling tale.'
Goodreads.

'*The Angels Wept* is an edge of your seat, hang on for dear life thriller. The gritty descriptions and palpable tension will hook you in. You won't want to look away.'
J. Blackmon – Author.

'I kept telling myself, ok, just one more chapter, and then five more chapters would be done. This was one of those stories that wouldn't let me go and I'm still thinking about it a week after I finished it.'
S. Faxon – Author.

'A nail-biting thriller that unravels at just the right pace to keep the reader turning the pages. I read it in two days.'
G. Anderson – Author.

'Fast paced, with gritty action, frightening antagonists and a well-thought-out plot. Roney's experience as a police officer is evident in his writing. This book has everything a good crime thriller should have: a loveable protagonist, a psychopath killer with a superbly created motive, a ton of 'hold on to your seat' action and fantastic twists. There were parts when I held my breath, desperate to see what unfolded next.'
L.J. Duncan – Author.

A DETECTIVE JARROD O'CONNOR STORY

JACK RONEY

THE ANGELS WEPT

BOOK ONE IN THE SERIES

The Angels Wept second edition published in Australia in 2023 by Hawkeye Publishing.

The Angels Wept was first published in 2021 by BMAC Productions

Cover Design by Alex Jay MacDonald

NATIONAL
LIBRARY
OF AUSTRALIA

A catalogue record of this book is available from the National Library of Australia.

ISBN 9780645714913

Proudly printed in Australia.

www.hawkeyepublishing.com.au
www.hawkeyebooks.com.au

PROLOGUE

ROXY Stone cowered on the filthy living room floor, pulling her knees to her chest. Throbbing pain in her skull intensified. Her vision strobed with colourful spots and dizziness threatened to consume her. Blood gushed from her nose and into her mouth with each gasp of air. The coppery taste made her nauseous. She wheezed and coughed, winded from the blow to her abdomen.

Something crashed against the wall and the floorboards shook. Shards of splintered timber were all that remained of the shattered coffee table. The ashtray was sent flying, scattering cigarette butts all over the floor. Grey particles of ash and the scent of tobacco lingered in the air. Beer cans and whiskey bottles littered the cluttered room. A homemade bong lay on the couch, the sludgy water seeping into a cushion. Pungent burnt cannabis blended with other rank odours in the neglected house. The room was dark, the air thick and rancid.

A stuffed monkey with an unsettling smile sat upright in the middle of a stained quilt spread out on the floor. Other discarded toys were scattered nearby. A hovering fly circled over an up-ended baby's bottle, coming to rest to feast on the spoiled formula dripping from the rubber teat.

The beating Roxy had endured was more violent than ever before. This time, he was out of control. He stood over her, gazing down with rage in his eyes, fists clenched. His chest heaved with each ragged breath. She lowered her eyes to the floor, too terrified to make eye contact. Tears cascaded down her gaunt face. He had grabbed a fistful of her blonde hair when he hurled her to the floor, flinging her like a rag doll. The matted mess was now draped over her eyes.

Roxy summoned the strength to lift her slight frame onto her knees. She had been through this ordeal far too many times and couldn't take it any longer. She had to get away. She had to do something, or die trying. But she had nowhere to go; no life, no family, no friends, no lifeline. In her isolation she was cut off, unable to reach out for help. Living with him was a life sentence. He had taken possession of her soul.

His face contorted like a madman's. She turned her head away and closed her eyes tight as he crouched and pressed his face against hers. The coarse bristles on his rugged jawline scraped her cheek like sandpaper. She could smell him, alcohol leaching out with his sweat, the odour of tobacco in his clothes and in his breath.

'You're not going anywhere!' He raised his hand, threatening to backhand her again.

She shielded her face with her forearms. 'No, please stop.'

'You are *mine*. Do you understand me?' He brushed his mouth across his bulging biceps, using his sweat stained t-shirt sleeve to wipe away the spit. Fierce tattoos covered both arms. 'I will never let you leave me, ever!' he shouted.

Through the ringing in her ears came the muffled cries of her baby in the next room. Vincent craned his head and sprung to his feet. With his attention drawn to the baby, he backed away and turned towards the hallway.

Roxy gripped the arm of the couch and mustered her remaining strength to pull herself to her feet. 'Stay away from her, you bastard. Don't you dare touch her!'

Vincent halted and turned. He stormed back into the room and thrust his hands around her throat, pinning her against the wall. He lifted her off the floor, her bare feet dangling. She scratched at his wrists to prise open his vice-like grip. The muscles and sinew of Vincent's powerful arms were rock hard. As he squeezed, Roxy drifted into unconsciousness. Her hands slid down by her sides. She no longer cared if she lived or died.

He whispered in her ear, 'You live because I let you live. You can't take her away from me. If you ever try to leave again, I'll hunt you down and kill you. You know I will.'

Pressing his cracked lips against hers, he inhaled her wilting life-force. She choked until her eyelids drooped, her vision blurring into a foggy haze. Embracing the descending darkness, she tasted the sweetness of her imminent death. Yet Vincent was in total control, still playing his sick games. He released his grip as she teetered on the brink, denying her last bid for freedom. She slid down the wall, slumping onto the floor in a broken heap. Her throat burned as she gasped for air.

Vincent left her alone for a momentary reprieve. Roxy knew he was toying with her. She had to act now. It was her only chance. Through the corner of her eye, she watched him flop onto the couch and stare out the window, his drug-affected mind mesmerised by the tattered curtains swaying in the breeze.

Wincing in pain with every movement, Roxy crawled away, pulling herself to her feet as she reached the kitchen doorway. Dragging one foot in front of the other, she made her way into the kitchen, her eyes fixed on the carving knife in the sink. She reached in and gripped its wooden handle, leaning on the bench for support.

She turned, defiant. 'Vincent, you bastard. Do you hear me?'

Vincent said nothing. The silence from the living room stretched on.

'Do you hear me, you bastard?' she sobbed.

She heard the slow and deliberate thump of footsteps. He meandered into the kitchen, folding his arms as he leaned against the door jamb. He glanced at the knife and his eyes rose to meet hers. He gave a humourless laugh and rubbed a hand over his mouth and chin. His cold, hateful eyes narrowed. His hardened face became an angry scowl.

Roxy clutched the knife with a shaky grip, her body trembling. She summoned a steely determination. This was her final stand. She tried to speak but the words were nothing more than a hoarse whisper. 'I've got nothing left. You've taken everything from me. All those times you stuck needles in your arm, it made you crazy. It screwed you up, Vince. It screwed us both up. Why do you think I smoke pot? It's the only way I can escape from you and my life. You can bash me all you like. I don't feel anything anymore, but I won't let you destroy our baby's life as well.'

'You stupid bitch,' he mocked. The edges of his mouth widened to form an arrogant smirk. He casually stepped towards her, his arms down by his sides. Roxy cried out in terror, her breathing short and frantic. She jabbed the knife towards him with her dwindling strength, terrified it would fall from her grasp.

'You don't have the guts,' he snarled.

In three steps he was on her, lunging. With one powerful move his hand was around her throat once more. His face was twisted with madness, his eyes black and hollow. She knew he would kill her this time. He would squeeze the life out of her until her neck snapped.

With his other hand, he reached for the knife as Roxy thrust the blade deep into his abdomen. Vincent groaned and looked down at the protruding knife, eyes wide and bulging. He released her throat and stumbled backwards, dropping to one knee. Blood squirted from the wound. He wrapped his hands around the knife handle and peered up at her in disbelief.

Roxy stood over him. 'You won't hurt us again, you monster.'

Vincent gazed in astonishment at his blood-covered hands. His face turned pale and his body convulsed. 'You're nothing without me,' he sneered. Bloody spittle frothed at the edges of his mouth.

He collapsed onto his side, writhing in the expanding pool of blood. Roxy stepped over him and staggered towards the sound of her crying baby, her bare feet leaving a trail of bloody footprints. Vincent's eyes followed her as she left the room. She returned, cradling the baby in her arms.

Roxy watched as Vincent lay motionless, fading into unconsciousness. She was finally free.

~

Vincent opened his eyes, confused and disoriented. He couldn't lift his head. A man in a white coat stood at the end of the bed, examining a clipboard. The doctor lowered his chin and peered over his spectacles. 'Ah, Mr Miles, glad to see you're back with us. We almost lost you. You lost a great deal of blood.'

'Where am I?' Vincent asked in a barely coherent drawl.

'You're in hospital, but you'll recover in time. You've had surgery and blood transfusions. By some miracle there was no damage to any vital organs, however your bowel was perforated. Don't try to move, the anaesthetic is wearing off and you'll experience some discomfort.'

Vincent's eyes darted around the room to find his bearings. He was startled by the beep of a monitor beside the bed head. He studied the clear rubber bag hanging from a pole, his eyes drawn to the hypnotic dripping of fluid. One wrist was handcuffed to the bed railing. He rotated his other wrist to inspect the IV needle and flinched when it sent a sharp pain up his forearm. He ran his fingers over the padded bandaging protecting the stab wound to his belly.

'Where's Roxy and the baby?' he asked. The realisation of his situation was clearer. 'Why am I handcuffed to this bed?' he grumbled.

The doctor hesitated. 'Yes, well, about that... there is someone outside who needs to speak with you. Try to rest, Mr Miles.'

The doctor backed away and drew open the blue disposable curtains. He nodded at someone and disappeared. A smallish man stepped inside the cubicle, one hand bandaged. The fringe of his brown hair flopped over his eyes, his tired looking face unshaven. He wore jeans, brown boots and a crumpled shirt beneath a tweed jacket with patches on the elbows. A police issue Glock was holstered to his belt.

'I'm Detective Sergeant Jarrod O'Connor,' the man said, holding up his badge. He was holding a digital voice recorder in his other hand. 'I must warn you that you have the right to remain silent. You are not obliged to answer any questions. Anything you do say will be recorded and may later be used in evidence. Do you understand that?'

'What the hell do you want, filth? Did that bitch call you?'

O'Connor clenched his jaw with a look of disdain. 'Who are you referring to, Mr Miles?'

'Roxy, my woman. Where is she?'

O'Connor held Vincent's gaze. 'Roxy made an emergency call saying there'd been a murder. The paramedics arrived just in time to save your life.' A look that Vincent couldn't read flashed across the detective's face. 'When was the last time you saw Roxy and the baby?'

'Well, let me think, straight after the bitch tried to gut me and left me for dead.'

'Why did she stab you?' O'Connor kept his voice even.

'She had to be taught a lesson,' Vincent said, like it was obvious. 'She needed to learn some respect. She tried to take the baby from me. No way in hell was that gonna happen. She needed to be reminded who's the boss.'

'So who is the boss, Vincent?'

'I am!' he snarled.

'What did you do to her?'

'No comment, pig.'

The cop stared at him in cold-eyed silence. He slid a chair closer to the bed and sat down. The guy had balls. Given half a chance, Vincent could easily overpower him and rip his throat out.

O'Connor paused for a long moment, eyeballing him. 'Roxy and the baby are dead. We found them in your car in the garage. There was a hose leading from the exhaust. The engine was still idling when we arrived. The baby was in her arms.'

'You're lying!' The pounding of his heart roared in Vincent's ears.

'I saw their bodies myself. There was nothing we could do.'

'Bullshit! She wouldn't do that. She wouldn't hurt our baby. Why are you saying this? No way, man. It's not true, you lying prick!' Vincent shook his head, refusing to accept the news. His hands clenched into fists, the whites of his knuckles prominent as he crumpled the bed sheets, twisting and strangling them in his grip.

'She'd been seriously assaulted, Vincent. Did you do that to her?' the cop probed.

The rage surged from Vincent's gut and threatened to explode into uncontrollable fury. He was incapable of speaking, his temper on a hair-trigger.

'What happened, Vincent? You need to tell me,' demanded the cop.

'You... don't... know... anything!' Vincent spat with each jagged word.

The cop leaned forward. 'What don't I know? Tell me.'

'You're the devil! You did this, didn't you. You killed them!'

'No Vincent, I didn't. What did you do to Roxy? Why did she feel she had no other choice but to kill herself and the baby?'

'God will pay for this, you will all pay! Do you hear me? God will pay.'

'God had nothing to do with this, Vincent.'

'I should have killed that bitch, I could have. Many times. But no, I showed mercy. I'll find her. She can't hide from me.'

'They're gone, Vincent. You have to live with that.'

Vincent lunged forward in the bed. 'I'll kill you!'

7

O'Connor jumped to his feet, the chair clattering as it toppled over.

The sharp pain in Vincent's abdomen jolted him back onto the bed.

'No, no! My baby, not my baby. She killed my baby,' he cried.

He thrashed in the bed, screaming.

O'Connor leaned over him with his body weight, pinning his shoulders to the bed. A burly orderly bounded into the room and helped the cop pin him down. Searing pain ripped through his abdomen. Blood seeped through his bandaging as he struggled. The orderly pressed the emergency button and two nurses came running in, followed by the doctor.

'We need to sedate him. Pin his arms,' ordered the doctor.

As the sedative flowed into Vincent's veins, he faded into a state of strange calmness. The thrashing tapered off and his body became still. His breathing slowed and he groggily looked up into the cop's eyes, the man's pupils huge and dark.

'I will come for her,' Vincent told him. 'You won't stop me.'

His eyes rolled back and he drifted into a tormented sleep.

ONE

Three years later...

IT was 3:30PM on a Tuesday afternoon in early August. A cool winter persisted. Jarrod sat at his desk and fired up his computer in readiness for his 4:00PM to midnight shift. As the computer whirred to life, he gazed out the window to the street below. His office was on the second floor of the Lockyer Police Station, directly above the front entrance to the building. The heritage-listed complex was built in the early 1930s. Its ornate brick façade had been restored thanks to council funding, but much of the interior had been gutted and refurbished with modern fittings.

The front of the police station was dwarfed by a Moreton Bay Fig. Its massive roots had cracked and lifted the concrete pavement at its base. The ancient tree's thick canopy of sprawling branches swallowed the front of the building in an enormous ring of late afternoon shade. However, its magnificence was lost on the procession of people coming in and out of the police station, their lives consumed by whatever crisis had befallen them.

Jarrod stared at his desk phone, the red message bank light flashing with menace. He sighed and dialled the access number to listen to the messages.

His pre-recorded greeting played. 'This is Detective Sergeant Jarrod O'Connor. You've reached the office of the Lockyer Police Child Protection Unit. Leave a message and either myself or

Detective Senior Constable Brad Harding will get back to you as soon as we can.'

The telephone beeped and the first of a stream of messages played. 'This is Natalie from the Crown Prosecutor's office. Just a message for Detective O'Connor to call me in relation to the trial of Stevens, which is starting in the next sittings of District Court. Please get back to me.'

Joel Stevens was a piece of shit Jarrod had charged almost a year earlier for bashing his girlfriend's ten-month-old baby girl's head against a coffee table, fracturing her skull. The baby had been placed in foster care, but the huge backlog of court cases meant Stevens had not yet gone to trial.

Jarrod pressed the hash key on the phone's keypad. 'The message has been deleted,' announced the message bank voice.

Jarrod recalled the next message. 'This is Mrs Shilling. Grant won't go to school again and he just won't do as he's told. I want somethin' done about him.' The phone clunked. The machine beeped.

Jarrod sighed. Dorris Shilling was a single mother with three children, each to a different father, and she had no control over any of them. According to her, it was everyone else's fault except her own. He pressed the hash key. 'The message has been deleted.'

The red light on the telephone continued flashing. Next message. 'Yeah G'day, Jarrod. Colin Day here, mate. We've had some local grubs hanging around the school threatening to assault teachers and students. Could you get back to me as soon as you can? Thanks mate.'

Colin was the deputy principal of the high school and was always happy to provide the local police with information to help with investigations. Jarrod always made an effort to help him out in return. He pressed the hash key.

'The message has been deleted.'

The red light still flashed. *Come on, seriously?*

'Hi, this is Sarah from Children's Services. Could someone get back to me? We need to do a joint child protection follow up case with you guys in relation to the Shearer family. Bye.'

'Argh shit, not that family again,' mumbled Jarrod. The last time he'd been to that squalor, they had to take the three little kids into care, carrying them out of the house kicking and screaming while restraining the mother. The hallway was littered with soiled nappies and rotten food. Cats roamed about the house and there was a stench Jarrod had never experienced before. All the windows and doors were sealed, and the children were found sitting at the cluttered kitchen table, taking turns at eating spoonfuls of margarine. A dead guinea pig was wrapped in a plastic bag tied to the clothesline. The children had recently been returned to the mother by the Department of Children's Services under supervision. He guessed the situation had deteriorated again.

He pressed the hash key. 'The message has been deleted. There are no more messages.'

He went back through his notes, trying to decide which call to make first. He was distracted by the disorganised piles of reports and half completed court briefs on his desk. He had only managed to reshuffle the pile, not making any headway with the ever-growing mountain of paperwork. Each time he sat down to start a report, the phone would ring, a new job beckoning meaning even more paperwork. He had resorted to coming in on his days off just to make some headway.

Brad Harding lumbered into the office in a pair of shorts with a backpack slung over his shoulders. His red cheeks puffed and the armpits of his t-shirt were drenched. Sweat beaded on his brow and scalp. He'd recently shaved his head after conceding defeat at the hands of his receding hairline. 'Hey mate, have we got much on this arvo?' He plonked his heavy frame on his chair and started pulling off his joggers.

11

Jarrod looked up from his phone messages notes. 'Same shit, different day.'

Brad shook his head and a ghost of a smile crossed his face. 'Sorry I asked.'

Jarrod shifted in his chair and studied his partner, tapping his bottom lip with his pen. 'Did you jog in to work?'

'Nah, I'm not that stupid. Rode my pushy in. Part of my new fitness regime. Bloody nearly killed me, though.'

'Better you than me,' Jarrod chuckled.

'I'll just grab a quick shower, won't be long.' Brad headed off in his socks towards the locker room across the hallway from their office.

Jarrod leaned his elbow on the desk, cupping his chin in his palm. He absently stared at a framed photo standing behind a pile of reports. The smiling faces of his gang beamed back at him, his wife Jayne, six-year-old Katie and two-year-old Matty.

He jumped with a start when his phone rang. 'Shit! Not a job already,' he grumbled, stalling while he decided if he should answer it.

'CPU, O'Connor speaking.'

Allan from Comco downstairs was on the other end. 'Hey Jarrod, sorry to ruin your day before it even starts. Got a job for ya. Ready for details? This one's a doozy.'

Jarrod gave an exasperated sigh. 'Yeah mate, what've you got?'

'Thomas Barton's full of grog and has barricaded himself inside a unit. He's carrying on like a dickhead, threatening to stab himself. We've sent a uniform crew around there and they've contained the scene, but he's now calling for you. He says if you don't come within ten minutes, he'll do himself in.'

'So, you're telling me not to rush over then, hey Al?'

Allan gave a hearty chuckle. 'It wouldn't be any loss, I know.'

'Yeah righto, I'll grab Brad and we'll head straight out. Is anyone else in the unit with him?'

'Don't know that much. His girlfriend was there, but she's been arrested.'

Jarrod took more details and then banged on the door to the locker room to give Brad a hurry-up. 'We've got a job.'

'Yeah righto, be there in a tick.'

A few minutes later, Brad re-emerged in shiny black shoes, crisply ironed trousers, white long-sleeve business shirt and a plain navy tie.

Jarrod glanced down at his crumpled Polo shirt, jeans and scuffed Colorado shoes. He looked back at Brad. 'You just have to show me up, don't you?'

Brad winked. 'You make it easy for me, Sarge.'

Jarrod sniffed the air. 'What's the name of that deodorant, "Eau de Toilette"?'

'Close,' said Brad. 'It's a Giorgio Armani, it's called...'

'Don't care,' Jarrod cut in. 'You ready to go?'

Brad shook his head and sighed. 'Yeah, what's the job?'

'Thomas Barton,' said Jarrod.

Brad just rolled his eyes. He didn't need to ask.

They threw on their jackets, kitted up and headed downstairs.

'I'll drive. We wanna get there in one piece,' said Jarrod as they headed across the car park towards their unmarked Holden Commodore.

'Turn it up. You drive like you're driving Miss Daisy. Just get us there before the end of the shift, old fella.'

'What? You're five months older than me.'

'Yeah, but you look ten years older.'

Jarrod raised his eyebrows. 'Yeah, well working with you has stripped years off my life. Let's see how chipper you are when you've been in the job as long as I have.' Jarrod suppressed a grin as they got in the car. 'Oh, and I can't wait until you have kids and have to function with two hours' sleep a night. Speaking of which, when are you going to give up the single life and settle down?'

Brad shrugged. 'That's not for me. Besides, I haven't found the right woman.'

'You're too fussy, you know that. Like Julie, for instance. What happened between you two? She's a great girl.'

'I don't really know. I guess we just didn't click,' said Brad with a note of regret.

'Well, there're not many fish in the sea in this bloody town, especially for someone with a rude melon like yours.'

Brad clicked his seatbelt and turned his face towards Jarrod. 'Nah, I'm not worried. If you were able to con a great girl like Jayne into marrying you, then I guess there's still hope for me.'

'You have a point there, my friend.' Jarrod pondered for a moment. 'I even wonder how she's put up with me for so long. I've stuffed up a lot of things over the years, but that's one thing I got right. That woman is my rock.'

For a moment, they sat in a pocket of silence, lost in their own thoughts.

Jarrod kicked over the engine and dropped the car into gear.

Brad turned the radio dial on and reached for the handset. 'VKR, this is Sierra 501. Booking on air station, O'Connor and Harding in the vehicle. Proceeding to job.'

The radio crackled to life. 'Thank you 501, show you proceeding job at sixteen hundred,' replied Allan, with a little too much exuberance for Jarrod's liking.

As the car leapt forward, Jarrod wondered what surprises Thomas Barton had installed for them.

Same shit, different day.

TWO

THOMAS Barton and Jarrod went way back. Jarrod first became acquainted with the Barton family just two days after transferring from the city to Lockyer eight years earlier. At the time, Thomas was twelve and his younger brother, James, was ten. They lived just out of town on a small pig farm and the boys often rode bicycles, usually stolen from neighbouring properties, into town while wagging school. They were picked up for shoplifting countless times and soon progressed to burglaries. Jarrod's first time inside the Barton home was when he'd gone there with a search warrant looking for stolen property. He was shocked by the family's squalid conditions.

Countless mangy dogs and cats had defecated on the floor of the old farmhouse and Jarrod gagged from the acrid odour. Fruit flies buzzed around stacked crates of over-ripe vegetables in the kitchen, picked from their own vegie patch. The boys' parents were both in their late fifties. The mother, Margaret, was a simple soul with an intellectual disability. She was an overweight woman with grey curly hair and always wore an old-fashioned style housedress and slippers. She wasn't equipped with the skills to raise two boys and manage a household. Her husband, John, was a short and rotund, nasty little man who waddled around like a penguin. Jarrod only ever saw him wearing the same navy-blue work singlet riddled with holes, an Akubra hat and gumboots. A piece of rope served as a belt to hold up his baggy shorts. In his mind he ruled the roost, however the boys ridiculed him and treated him with contempt,

15

though keeping their distance to avoid a backhand across the side of the head.

'Can't you just attach one of those electric shock tracking devices on their legs? Ya know, give em' a zap every time they're outta line,' John had asked Jarrod one day as they sat in the police station interview room.

Jarrod had scratched the back of his head and chuckled. When he made eye contact, John sat there staring back at him with a blank face. Evidently, he was serious.

Jarrod made a noise in his throat and tried to contain the laughter threatening to erupt. 'Um, no John, we can't actually do that,' he had said tactfully with a polite shake of the head. He couldn't help but let out a chuckle. John raised one eyebrow and shrugged. He didn't see the funny side.

As time went on, the situation seemed to deteriorate for the family. John and the boys were often seen scavenging discarded food from industrial bins at the back of Coles and there were reports of physical abuse. After James and Thomas had been hog-tied and whipped by their father, Jarrod was called in to assist the Department of Children's Services to remove them and place them into foster care. Jarrod arrested John, however he never lived to stand trial. He died from a heart attack and was found face down in the mud in his pig pen. It was a fitting end.

Tragedy struck a year later when James was killed after losing control of a stolen trail bike on a dirt road without a helmet. He was thrown into the air and cracked his skull against a solitary tree surrounded by acres of open field. The irony of that single tree was cruel.

James' death hit Thomas hard and he went off the rails, choosing a path of self-destruction. He ran with a nasty crowd of petty criminals who discovered a taste for joy riding and setting fire to stolen cars. Thomas saw the inside of juvenile detention for longer periods. His mother, suffering dementia, was moved into nursing care. The family home and farm fell into ruin, abandoned.

Over the years, Jarrod had developed a soft spot for Thomas, believing he had become another victim of "the system". The pair had crossed swords on a few occasions, but over the years they developed a good rapport. Thomas visited Jarrod in his office, usually wanting to bum money for fags. On the odd occasion, they had a decent chat about life in general. In his own way, Thomas opened up about his problems and there were times Jarrod believed he was trying to get himself back on track. Sadly, he'd always find a way to get himself into trouble. He had just turned twenty years old and had not long gotten out of Westgate Correctional Centre where he was on remand. He had become a one-man crime wave in town: petty theft, burglaries and graffiti. He had shacked up with his twenty-two-year-old girlfriend, a local girl and known drug supplier.

Arriving at the front of the well-known Housing Commission complex known as "The Hole", Jarrod and Brad pulled into the driveway. It was a cluster of dingy, two storey town houses with dislodged roof tiles, bleak and weathered from years of neglect. Rust stains from leaky guttering streaked the concrete walls. There were five separate buildings in the complex, each containing two adjoining townhouses. The buildings were positioned in a u-shape surrounding a grassed courtyard area which had been the stage for many a drunken brawl and bonfire. They drove down the driveway which led to the complex and parked behind the marked police vehicle. Secured in the back seat was a screaming Lisa Doolin, Thomas Barton's girlfriend. Her arms were handcuffed behind her back and she lay on her side, kicking out at the windows and cage with her bare feet. Many of the residents sat on their back stairs or peered out through their windows, beers in hand, watching the performance. Incidents like this were a common form of entertainment for the residents of "The Hole".

Jarrod and Brad got out of the car and vested up. A bogan's

voice echoed from somewhere within the complex. 'Shit, the Ds are here.'

'Hide the drugs,' someone else chuckled.

'Hey, Bazza, the coppers are here to lock ya up,' quipped another moron, impressed with his own wit. Jarrod scanned the faces, but there was no sign of Barry Carpenter, the resident dealer.

The two uniformed officers, Senior Constable Graham Savage and Constable John Prentagast, stood on either side of their vehicle taking cover behind the open doors. Both were wearing their vests, taking turns at trying to reason with Thomas. His shirtless, pale upper body leaned out through a window near the front landing, his arms waving erratically. His unmistakable carrot-top flopped in his eyes like a mop, his face freckled with an auburn smudge of hair above his top lip. Despite his boyish face, he was developing into a muscular young man.

With a nod, Jarrod gestured to a crack in the windscreen of the marked police car. 'What happened here?'

'Boxhead Barton let loose and tossed a beer bottle at us as we drove up,' explained Graham. 'The bloody thing hit the windscreen and smashed.'

Jarrod cupped an elbow with one hand and rubbed his jawline with the other. 'So what's the story? Has he asked for a briefcase full of unmarked hundred-dollar bills and a helicopter giving him safe passage out of town?'

Graham smirked. 'Nah, he just asked for a can of bourbon and coke and wanted his girlfriend to come up to the flat so he can talk to her. She started swinging punches at us when we arrived. She was the one who called us here, mind you. We tossed her in the back of the car. She and Thomas got on the piss together, had a blue and he started threatening to do himself in.'

'What's he armed with now?'

'From what we can see, he has a collection of carving knives. He threatened us with them and even hurled one at us – just missed Johno's foot.'

John held up the black-handled knife with a deadpan look on his face. 'It's a real bastard,' he said. 'He's barricaded the back entrance to the unit and the only way in is by the front door. We're perfect knife throwing targets if we try to get any closer. It's a stalemate at the moment, well at least until he runs out of knives or passes out.'

Jarrod kept his eye on Thomas who staggered around inside the unit, leaning in and out of various windows to yell slurred abuse at no one in particular. He then disappeared, turning up the already loud music. Marilyn Manson screamed about death and doom. Thomas came back to the front window holding a carving knife in each hand.

Thomas shot Jarrod a look of recognition, making eye contact. 'O'Connor, you dog, you're late.'

'Hey, Thomas,' Jarrod called with a friendly wave. 'Good to see you too, mate. I got here as soon as I could. What's goin' on, buddy? Can't you just come out so we can talk without all these other dickheads watching on?'

'No way, you coppers will just lock me up.'

'Come on mate, you'll only make it worse the longer this goes on.'

'No way, man. Bring Lisa back or I'll do it.'

He pressed the sharp edge of a knife against his throat. Jarrod expected to see blood, but Thomas was careful enough not to cut himself.

'Bring Lisa to me. I just wanna talk to her.'

'We can't do that, Thomas. Can I come up and talk to you?' called Jarrod, not sure if that was such a wise suggestion. 'Come on, why don't you put the knife down and come and talk to me?'

'I only wanted you here so that you could see me kill myself. It's your fault my life is so screwed.'

Jarrod sensed how potentially volatile Thomas was. He wasn't just after the attention. He was capable of anything in that frame of mind.

'Come on, mate, I'm just here to help.'

'What, by locking me up? Nah, screw you!' spat Thomas.

Jarrod backed off towards the other police and the stalemate continued for another fifteen minutes. Another uniform crew arrived and Lisa Doolin was taken back to the watchhouse. Her presence only seemed to inflame Thomas, who was getting more agitated by the minute.

'Where's my phone? I need my phone,' he demanded.

This gave Jarrod an idea. He turned to Graham. 'Where's the phone?'

Graham reached into the vehicle and handed it to Jarrod. 'Doolin had it on her when we arrested her.'

Jarrod tossed the phone in the air and caught it. 'This is our best chance to get close to him. If we can knock him down with capsicum spray, we'll have a chance to get inside.'

'Yeah, we'll be standing around like stale bottles of piss all night if we don't do something,' said Graham. 'He'll end up stabbing himself or someone else.'

Jarrod held up the phone and yelled to Thomas, 'Is this what you want, mate?'

Thomas smiled and for a moment his demeanour changed. Jarrod recognised a glimmer of the naïve little boy he once knew. 'Yeah, bring it over. I won't do nothin' man, I promise.'

'I'll bring it over to you, but first, you need to put the knives down and keep your hands there above the windowsill so I can see them,' Jarrod urged.

Thomas dropped the knives onto the floorboards with a clatter. He leaned out the window and displayed his empty hands. Jarrod cautiously moved closer. Thomas' eyes were a combination of confusion and mistrust. He seemed to drop his guard as Jarrod reached the base of the stairs that led to the front landing. He concealed the canister of capsicum spray in his left hand and held up the phone with his right.

'I'll have to walk up the first few steps to reach you.'

Thomas leaned further out the window, ushering Jarrod to come closer. 'Here, pass it up.'

He was half hanging out the window, reaching down with his left hand. Jarrod reached up and passed the phone to him. Thomas took hold of the phone but Jarrod maintained a firm grip. As Thomas tugged at the phone, a knowing look flashed across his face. He knew he'd been duped. He froze with wide eyes as Jarrod reached up with his left hand and depressed the canister button. The thin stream of foamy spray hit his target in the chest, splashing up into his face. In the same motion, Thomas snapped his head to one side and withdrew inside the window.

'Hah, you missed you dog,' he mocked.

Jarrod feared he'd blown it. This wasn't good.

There was an eerie moment of silence and then a scream. 'Oh Jesus, what the fuck have you done to me!'

Delayed reaction. They were back in the game.

Thomas came into view, pacing around the room in panic, rubbing his eyes with his knuckles. He gagged and gulped for air. His burning eyes were seared closed.

Realising the small window of opportunity, Graham, Brad and John stampeded past Jarrod up the stairs. Graham slammed his heavy frame against the door, but it refused to budge.

Jarrod was the first to see Thomas pounding the handle of the knife against the windowpane in the door. 'Get back!' he yelled.

Just as they cleared away from the door, the glass shattered with fragments flying outward and smashing on the landing. Thomas waved the blade wildly through the opening, just missing Graham's head. John reached up and gave Thomas another spray. Thomas recoiled, yelling in pain and anger. He lost his balance and stumbled to the floor with a heavy thud. Graham reached in through the smashed window, unlatched the door and stormed the unit, followed by Brad and John. Jarrod's shoes crunched over the glass as he stepped inside, where Graham was kneeling on Thomas' back as John and Brad placed him in handcuffs.

The knife had been kicked aside, freed from Thomas' grip after a well-aimed strike from Graham's extendable baton. They all started coughing from capsicum spray fumes lingering in the musty air of the confined unit. Thomas was led out of the unit and onto the grass downstairs, where John and Graham flushed his eyes with a water spray bottle.

'What have you bastards done to me?' he spluttered as water dripped down his face.

Jarrod kneeled on the grass beside him. 'You'll live, mate. So tell me, Thomas, do you still want your mobile phone?'

'Screw you, copper bastards.'

Yep, same shit different day.

THREE

AFTER the adrenaline rush of Thomas Barton's arrest, the routine of the afternoon shift dragged on. Despite the neglected stack of paperwork calling for Jarrod's attention, he was too hyped to concentrate on writing reports – he looked for any excuse to avoid the office. As daylight bled into evening, Brad and Jarrod patrolled the streets of Lockyer, propping local kids loitering in the shadows of the town square. Bored and disengaged, they wandered the streets in packs, waiting for trouble to find them.

It was around 8.00PM when they swung by the twenty-four-hour BP Roadhouse on the highway to pick up coffee and a bite to eat to get them through the rest of the shift. Jarrod's head thumped and he craved caffeine. They headed out of town, taking the highway turnoff and driving north. The dim glow from the green and yellow neon BP Roadhouse sign cut through the darkness ahead. A vast blanket of low hanging fog floated across the road. The town lights dipped beneath the horizon in Jarrod's rear vision mirror.

He parked next to a large gas tank off to the side of the roadhouse café.

'How you doin' tonight, gents?' said Carol with a chubby grin as they stepped inside. The automatic glass doors slid closed behind them with a whoosh.

Brad headed towards the hot box. 'You'll make our night a whole lot better if you have some of those chunky beef pies.'

'You're in luck, boys. Two coffees as usual?'

'You bet, darlin', nice and hot with two sugars in each,' flirted Brad.

Carol gave a bashful smile and opened the hot box. Jarrod savoured the enticing aroma as she handed the pastries over the counter. Carol fired up the coffee machine, the hissing steamer frothing the milk just right.

'You boys stay safe now,' said Carol as she passed the takeaway coffee cups through the security wires. She waved Jarrod away as he held up the twenty-dollar note. 'You know it's on the house, boys. It's nice to have the coppers drop in on me from time to time when I'm out here on my own at night. Your uniformed mates were here just earlier. Makes me feel safe, ya know, knowin' you boys are out patrolling the streets.'

'Well thanks, Carol. You have a nice night and we'll see you soon.' Jarrod discreetly tucked the money behind the chewing gum stand for her to find later. They sat at their usual booth in the corner. Just as they finished eating, the handheld radio crackled to life. 'Any unit, any unit that can respond to a breakers-on alarm at Kingsfords Rural Supplies,' called Allan from Communications.

'Shit, that's us. We're only five minutes away,' said Brad eagerly.

'Yeah righto, make the call.' Jarrod didn't share the same enthusiasm.

Brad raised the radio handset to his mouth. 'VKR, this is Sierra 501, Harding and O'Connor. Responding from the BP Roadhouse north.'

'Thank you 501, show you proceeding code 2. Any other units?'

The radio fell silent. As they made the dash out into the car park, Allan came back on air. 'No other units available. The other crew's still tied up at a DV job in town.'

'Looks like it's just us,' Jarrod said as they jumped in the car. Coffee in one hand, he steered in reverse with the other and then jammed the stick into drive. Carol gave a smiling wave through the front console window as they skidded out the driveway. The gearbox dropped a gear and the engine roared as they hurtled towards town along the empty highway.

Kingsfords Rural Supplies wasn't far from the highway exit leading back into the outskirts of town. They passed a plant hire business, tractor and farm machinery sale yard and various warehouses. Up ahead, the rural supplies building stood out, the largest in the entire industrial estate. It was no more than a monstrous navy-blue tin shed but a favourite of locals for purchasing stockfeed, irrigation supplies, fertiliser and horse-riding gear. A bright floodlight shone skywards from a garden, illuminating the bold white lettering of the front signage. Moths and bugs flitted in and out of the yellow beam. As Jarrod and Brad approached, their attention was drawn to the flickering of torch lights inside the glass doors of the reception area.

'Bastards are still inside,' Jarrod said, steering the car into the driveway. He skidded to a halt with the headlights illuminating the reception area.

Brad unclipped the radio handset and spoke into it with urgency. 'VKR, 501 off job. Confirmed breakers-on. We'll be on foot and on hand held.'

They grabbed their torches and jumped from the car. Jarrod was momentarily blinded by the reflection of the headlights in the windows. The high-pitched shriek of the alarm was deafening.

'They're still locked,' said Brad, pulling at the door handles. Inside, two hooded figures scurried away from the headlights, their torch lights swallowed by the darkness.

Jarrod pressed his face against the glass. 'Shit, they're heading for the back door.'

He turned on his heels towards the rear of the building. He flicked on his torch, the beam of light boring into the darkness to guide his path. His shoes slipped on the dewy grass. He regained his footing and turned the corner, Brad a few steps behind. The back door flung open and under the dim glow of the emergency exit sign two small figures, backpacks over shoulders, leapt outside. A child-like voice squealed, 'Come on, run!'

Jarrod couldn't tell if it was a boy or a girl.

'This is the police! Don't make me chase you, ya little pricks!' he yelled.

He shone his torch in their direction but could only make out their dark hoodies and baggy camo shorts. They took off, disappearing into a thicket of spindly grass. Jarrod honed in on the spot where the grass had been trampled and he followed into the dark unknown. His shoes slid out from under him and he fell, seemingly in slow motion. The torch dropped as he braced for the landing. He flopped onto his backside and rolled down the embankment of a small creek meandering behind the industrial buildings. Brad's torch light shone from behind and Jarrod saw the silhouette of the two miniature figures scampering across the creek and up the opposite slope. His torch rolled into the water and died. 'Bloody waterproof, my arse,' he muttered.

He dragged himself up and stepped into the cold trickling water, his shoes sinking into the muddy creek bed. Brad slid down the slope, staying upright. He arrived shoulder to shoulder with Jarrod and shone his light across the creek, but the kids were gone, slipping away into the darkness.

'Shit!' Jarrod spat in frustration. 'Little bastards were like gazelles.'

Brad bent over with his hands on his knees, panting to catch his breath. 'They're gone Jarrod, we'll never catch 'em.'

Jarrod prised his shoes from the boggy creek bed and shook the water and mud off.

'Come on mate, let's head back.'

'Hold on,' said Brad. 'I'm just trying to keep that meat pie down.'

'Times like this, I wish we had our own dog squad unit,' said Jarrod. 'They won't send a dog unit all the way out from the city for a shitty juvie break and enter.'

'Nope,' agreed Brad. 'Those boys got their hands full with all kinds of major shit going down in the city.'

They were on their own and the trail was cold, so they headed back to the warehouse to inspect the premises.

'I'd say this is how the little monkeys got in,' said Brad, shining his torch on a large panel of steel mesh used for reinforcing concrete slabs. It was leaning up against the side of the building and the grid pattern created a perfect climbing ladder.

'Yeah, look up there. Looks like that window up in the loft's been forced open,' Jarrod said, still catching his breath.

The steel back door creaked, left ajar as the little thieves made their escape.

Brad pushed the door open with his torch. 'They just had to push on this emergency release bar to open it from the inside. Might have left some good prints on it, though.'

'Yeah, we'll get Larry to come out first thing in the morning to run the print brush over.'

They stepped inside and shone their torches around, but the screeching alarm was unbearable. They went back out to the car and gave a sit-rep over the radio, asking for the key holder to be contacted.

It didn't take long for Gary Jansen, the store manager, to arrive and they were grateful when he deactivated the alarm. As the final wail of the alarm echoed off the tin walls, the residual silence was deafening. The only sound that could be heard was restless pigeons shuffling about in the roof cavity. The vast warehouse, lined with long rows of shelves of produce, was otherwise quiet. They turned on all the lights to inspect the premises. Apart from the forced window up in the storage loft, nothing else appeared disturbed or stolen. Gary went upstairs and secured the window. Brad followed and looked around the loft before they met Jarrod downstairs again.

Jarrod took details for the report and Gary reset the alarm as they exited.

As Jarrod was handing Gary his business card, they all jumped with a fright as the alarm shrieked.

'That's strange,' yelled Gary over the top of the racket. 'These alarms are activated by motion sensors. They're pretty reliable and only go off if there's a decent amount of movement detected, otherwise they'd be going off all the time from bloody rodents and possums.'

'We'd better check it out. Do you mind, Gary?' Jarrod asked apologetically.

'Yeah, no probs. I'm sure I reset it properly, but I better check. I'll need to get back inside.'

After finding the right key from a bunch on a steel ring, Gary pulled open the front sliding glass door and flicked on the light switch in the reception area. He keyed in the code and the alarm fell silent once again. They stood inside and listened. Jarrod heard movement up in the loft, a subtle shuffling of feet.

'Did you hear that?' he said.

Then a loud clang as something heavy crashed onto the floor up above.

'I heard that!' said Brad.

'Gary, get all the lights. Light this place up,' Jarrod instructed.

As the fluorescent light bulbs flickered to life, Brad and Jarrod made for the staircase.

Jarrod called back to Gary, 'Stay there.'

He bounded up the stairs in his wet shoes, Brad on his heels. As the loft lights came on, a tiny figure darted out from behind a stack of crates and raced to the window. They frantically pulled at the window, but it wouldn't budge. Gary had wedged the frame of the window slide with a strip of dowel. The hooded head whipped around in panic and a pair of squinting, intense eyes flashed back at them.

28

Jarrod recognised the startled face of the Aboriginal boy staring at him. He was cornered, his eyes darting from side to side, looking for an escape route. Jarrod crossed the room and grabbed a handful of the boy's hoody, lifting him so that his toes barely touched the floor.

'Gotch ya, you little bugger.'

'Let me go, copper!' squealed Billy Mason as he grappled to free himself from Jarrod's grip.

Jarrod turned to Brad. 'Didn't you check it out up here? Or did you look around with your eyes closed?'

'Look at the size of him. He's easy to miss.'

'Yeah, well you owe me a carton of beer, that's if you want me to keep my mouth shut about it back at the station.'

'Anyway, you should throw him back, Jarrod. He's an undersized hatchling,' said Brad, arms now folded.

By then Billy had settled down, having realised his struggling was futile. 'You got a smart mouth, copper!'

'Oh look, he's so cute,' said Brad with a pained expression.

Jarrod lowered Billy and spun his shoulders around so he was facing him. He stood not much taller than Jarrod's waist, so he dropped to one knee to make eye contact.

'Who were your two mates, Billy? They left you alone, they ran out on you.'

'I'm not tellin' you nothin', pig. You can suck on this bad boy,' he said, grabbing his crotch as he motioned a pelvic thrust.

'Nice dance moves for a twelve-year-old. You been watching Michael Jackson music videos?' Jarrod said.

'Michael who?'

'Never mind, Billy. Let's march.' Jarrod led him down the stairs with a firm grip on his arm. The slippery little mite would make a run for it as soon as he could.

It wouldn't be the first time he'd tried to give Jarrod the slip. Only two weeks earlier, he'd chased Billy through the town mall after he was caught shoplifting. Jarrod had been walking back to the station from court in his suit and sleek business shoes when the pharmacist came rushing out onto the footpath. 'Hey detective, that kid just stole a pair of sunglasses.'

'Hold this.' Jarrod had handed the pharmacist his case file. He took off after Billy and despite the protest of his sleek soled shoes he mowed him down, latching onto him by the scruff of his t-shirt. He'd just about run out of steam, another few metres and Billy would've left him for dust.

'You pretty fast for an old white guy,' he'd said to Jarrod with a cheeky grin.

Jarrod's tailbone now ached and his wet socks squelched in his shoes after his earlier mishap. He was in no mood for any more foot chases. He gripped Billy's hoodie tight until he was belted securely into the back of the car with the child locks on.

From the driver's seat, Jarrod twisted around and leaned back towards Billy who sat innocently with his hands between his knees. Butter wouldn't melt in his mouth.

'When was the last time you ate, Billy?'

'Dunno, yesterday maybe. Those Christian people who run that soup kitchen van gave me some tucker.'

'You like pies?'

His eyes lit up. 'Yeah, they're deadly!'

Jarrod made eye contact with Brad. 'Let's swing by Carol and see if she's got any left.'

Brad shot him a look in return. 'You're driving this bus,' he said with a sigh. 'If it was up to me, I'd toss his cheeky little arse in a cell for the night.' Brad turned and glared at Billy, who flipped him the bird in reply.

~

Back at the station, Billy sat in the interview room and finished off the last of his pie, wiping crumbs off his lips with the back of his hand. He washed it down with a chug of chocolate milk.

'Where's your mum tonight, Billy?' Jarrod asked.

'Dunno. She been out drinkin with that old white fella from the caravan park – Old Teddie. He turned up with his pension money and a goon of wine and they started chargin' up. They been drinkin' all day, eh.'

'Where's your sister, Sasha?'

'She gone off with her boyfriend. I haven't seen her for days.'

Jarrod figured it was just another typical day for Billy, left to his own devices to get up to no good. The kid's eyes drooped. He needed sleep. With the hoodie off his head, a mess of curly brown hair flopped down over his eyes. The bravado was gone, leaving just a neglected little boy who needed a solid home life and proper care.

Jarrod knew he had no father figure. In fact, no one seemed to know who his father was. His mother, Dorothy, did her best on her own, but the grog had taken hold of her. She had another older boy who was in custody on remand for a string of robberies in town. He and his gang had taken a liking to mugging people at knife-point, stealing their wallets and mobile phones.

Jerome Johnson, a tall, handsome Aboriginal man who worked for the Indigenous Legal Service, wasted no time in coming into the station. He was the on-call support worker and a good guy. He'd taken many street kids under his wing, giving them a warm bed and a meal in the group foster home he managed.

He shook Jarrod's hand with a firm grip. 'Thanks for giving him a feed, Jarrod. What now, you keeping Billy here in the lockup?'

'Well, mate, if you can give him a bed for the night and keep a close eye on him, we'll release him on bail curfew conditions in your care. He'll be charged with one count of break and enter and we'll set a date for the Children's Court in two weeks. He's not telling us who his mates were, so maybe you can bring him back down for a formal interview after he's had a good night's sleep. Do you have room at the group home?'

Jerome ruffled Billy's hair. 'Yeah, I think we can manage that, hey big fella? I'll try to contact your mum.'

Billy nodded with a sleepy look of indifference.

As Jerome and Billy headed out of the interview room, Billy stopped and looked up at Jarrod. He then did the strangest thing. He reached out his hand. Jarrod took his little hand into his own and the boy gave him an awkward handshake. His hand was clammy and thin. 'Thanks for the pie and chocolate milk, hey copper.'

'Yeah, well, you stay out of trouble, Billy. And stay away from those other boys. You and I are having a big chat real soon, you got that?'

Billy nodded and then reached his hand out to Brad. With a look of surprise, Brad reached down with an open hand, but Billy slipped his hand away and ran his fingers through his hair. 'Too slow, old man.' He coolly strutted from the interview room.

'So precious,' said Brad, wrinkling up his face with a strained smile. 'Stay out of trouble, kid.'

Billy gave Brad the bird without looking at him as he brushed past. Jerome shook his head and smiled as he wrapped his arm around the boy's shoulders. They all headed down to the watchhouse to take Billy's mug shot and fingerprints.

FOUR

JARROD arrived home just after midnight and discarded his wet shoes and socks on the front porch. As always, he first checked on the kids. He peered in through the open doorway into Matty's room. His little boy slept soundly, bathed in the dim glow of his night light. He snuggled against his teddy, his body entangled in the blankets. Jarrod ran his fingers through his son's fluffy hair. He kissed his chubby cheek and savoured his smell. He closed the door and crept down the hallway to Katie's room. Her lamp was still on and she lay almost sideways across her bed with the covers strewn about the place. She wore flannelette pyjamas and her Winnie-the-Pooh story book rested on her chest, rising and falling with each gentle breath. As he straightened her up in bed and tucked in her doona, she murmured in gibberish before drifting back into a deep slumber. He swept her brown hair from her face and kissed her on the forehead. She cuddled into her doona and rolled onto her side. Jarrod turned her lamp off and left her dreaming.

He grabbed a quick shower and climbed into bed. Jayne rolled over to face him as he turned on his bedside reading lamp. 'How was your night, sweetheart?' she said with heavy eyelids.

'Oh, same shit, different day.'

They kissed and she rolled over and went back to sleep. He lay there staring at the ceiling, a million thoughts racing through his mind. Getting through the grind of another long shift did nothing to quell the unsettled feeling in his gut. He questioned where his career was heading.

After fifteen years as a cop, he no longer clung to the naïve notion that he could really make a difference. He was treading water, worse than that, in fact. Each day was one step forward, three steps back. He made no progress with the continuous backlog of paperwork and his frustrations with the way the system dealt with young offenders were intensifying.

The constant exposure to child abuse cases was wearing him down. Not so much the abuse itself – he'd become hardened to that. It was more the emotional strain of dealing with the families and issues that went well beyond just criminal investigation. There was no such thing as a clear-cut child abuse investigation – there were always complications. It was impossible to avoid becoming emotionally involved. The burden of preparing for court cases was horrendous. He couldn't remember the last time he'd been able to take holidays with his family without being called back to prepare witnesses for a trial. He was worn out. Something was about to give and Jarrod feared it would be him.

As usual, jumbled thoughts churned in his mind, his most troubling cases tormenting him as he tried to sleep. The deaths of two teenagers six months earlier haunted him the most. Seventeen-year-old Jamal Lewis and his sixteen-year-old cousin Douglas Blair had gone on a crime bender through the western suburbs of Sydney. Armed with a sawn-off shotgun, they held up a service station and carjacked a Ford Mustang. As they tore up the streets, ramming cars off the road and running red lights, they hit the highway at speed with a posse of police cars pursuing in their wake. The police chopper tracked them as they headed south-west out of the suburban sprawl of the city towards open country, passing through small towns as their trajectory put them on a collision course with the town of Lockyer.

The pursuit continued out of the range of the chopper, which had to turn back for refuelling. Attempts to intercept the Mustang had failed. Meanwhile Lockyer Station received word the pursuit was heading their way, so they scrambled all available crews and headed out towards the highway. The uniform crews set up a roadblock, tossing stinger spikes across the bitumen. Jarrod and Brad waited further up the road behind the barricade in their unmarked vehicle. As the Mustang came into view, followed by a swarm of red and blue police lights, the sports car swerved at the sight of the awaiting blockade. The driver slowed before veering off the highway and gunning it again, fishtailing off-road to avoid the spikes. As the Mustang slid past Brad and Jarrod, the barrel of a shotgun pointed at them through the passenger window. The *boom boom* of the gunshots reverberated in Jarrod's ears. Senses sharpened with adrenaline, they ducked as the car was peppered with pellet holes.

Jarrod slammed the Commodore into drive, spinning its wheels in pursuit. The Mustang slid in a cloud of dust as it turned off into a forestry service road. Jarrod and Brad were now the lead vehicle and soon deep inside the pine forest. The trailing dust cloud was their only way of tracking the Mustang as it weaved in and out of service tracks, changing direction at various crossroads.

The forestry bordered a fenced-off private property owned by a mining company and the Mustang was heading straight for it. Jarrod eased off, allowing enough distance behind in case the Mustang stopped suddenly. As they pierced through the outer edge of the forest and into a clearing, the Mustang raced ahead along the dirt road. Up ahead, the road led to a closed steel gate with a bright red 'Keep Out' sign. The Mustang had nowhere else to go. The dirt track was too narrow for them to turn around.

The neon glow of red and blue lights flashed through a haze of dust in Jarrod's rear-view mirror and he braked, expecting the Mustang to do the same. Instead, it did the opposite and sped up, slamming through the gate. Strips of orange panelling flapped and broken glass from the shattered headlights flew into the air. The gates swung open and rebounded, scraping the side panels of the Mustang.

Jarrod and Brad followed through the gates and along a narrowing track slicing through thick scrub on either side. The Mustang had accelerated out of sight.

'Holy shit, you know what's up ahead, don't ya?' Brad pivoted his head towards Jarrod with eyes wide. Jarrod returned a nervous glance, his gut wrenching.

The dirt road led straight towards the abandoned limestone quarry lake, surrounded by sheer forty metre rocky cliffs. The lake was perilously deep and littered with car bodies and abandoned machinery. The boys in the Mustang had no idea of the danger ahead as they sped on.

Jarrod and Brad came upon another wooden gate splintered into shards. Fresh tyre tracks lined the sandy track. Just beyond the quarry cliffs, the earth fell away to a treacherous drop. Brad's eyes met Jarrod's as they pulled up at the gate. They jumped out and waved their arms towards the approaching police cars.

The line of vehicles slowed in single file and skidded to a halt, a mushroom cloud of dust drifting over them. Jarrod and Brad sprinted towards the quarry lake. As they came to the cliff, they shimmied closer, grabbing each other's arms to avoid toppling over the crumbling edge. The car tracks led right up to the edge. There were no skid marks. They wouldn't have seen it coming until it was too late.

Down below, a distorted orange shape was sinking in the eerie turquoise water, large air bubbles gurgling to the surface as the Mustang disappeared from view. Within seconds it was gone, swallowed by the murky water. The surface shimmered with ringlets that cascaded outwards forming larger circles. Small waves crashed against the foot of the cliffs.

The salvage operation, involving police divers and vessels using sonar equipment, lasted for two days. The incident was big news and a crowd of onlookers and frantic media crews gathered around the outer edge of the police cordon. The *thwap thwap* of media helicopters hovering overhead reverberated around the quarry. Jarrod and Brad endured hours of questioning by the Professional Standards Unit. The wreck of the Mustang was winched from the depths and dragged onto an embankment. The limp bodies of Jamal Lewis and Douglas Blair were trapped inside the vehicle.

The newspaper headlines read "Cops chase kids to their death". Civil libertarians were up in arms about the police pursuit policy and there were protests outside Police Headquarters in the city.

As the lead police vehicle at the time of the incident, Jarrod and Brad became the focus of public scrutiny and criticism. After months of stress and uncertainty, the coroner ruled the boys contributed to their own deaths due to their reckless and criminal conduct. This was no solace to the families who were still looking to lay blame.

Jarrod was still having trouble sleeping, often waking in a cold sweat after enduring the nightmare that played in his mind on a continual loop. The ghosts of the quarry lake were never far away.

Eventually, he dozed and his body relaxed.

FIVE

CLARE Kingston waited for *him*, sitting cross-legged on a blanket. Her bare feet caressed the damp grass as she meditated. She breathed slowly, her warm breath vaporising into a mist as it hit the night air. She didn't feel the cold, though. She had stopped feeling anything a long time ago. They had planned this final meeting. Soon her transcendence would begin, right there on that mountaintop.

She opened her eyes and savoured the pleasant view one last time. The full moon hung low among the stars and shimmered through a thick veil of fog, bathing the sleeping town below in its yellow glow.

Clare was startled as a colony of screeching fruit bats swooped low above her, flapping their wings with a loud whoosh. Extended bat wings were silhouetted against the face of the moon as it shone like a searchlight in the night sky. The flying foxes landed awkwardly in the canopies of nearby trees, shrieking as they prepared for their nocturnal feeding.

The streetlights below marked out the town grid, the headlights of the occasional moving vehicle the only sign of life. Most houses were in darkness. Who else would be sitting up at this late hour? She wondered if there were others out there who no longer slept, spending the long hours of the night alone with their fears?

The journey of Clare's miserable life had led her to this point. Before *he* came into her life, she had reached rock bottom, her soul tormented by an endless darkness. The emptiness in her heart, the wretched feeling of nothingness, had engulfed her. She was being consumed by madness. Insanity had stolen her mind, planting seeds of delusions and dangerous ideas.

When they met, he had been consumed by rage, his heart heavy with loss and bitterness. Yet born from this anger and despair came a sense of control, calm and purpose. His view of the world, his interpretation of the stars and the heavens, was an inspiration. He understood her path of self-destruction and taught her to channel her negative energy and emotions towards an ultimate inner peace. He became her salvation. He hurt when she hurt. They had walked together as one in this mad world, a world as foreign to her as an alien planet. They were kindred spirits. There were others who also followed his mantra who, like Clare, were born again as his disciples. She had met no one else with such passion, and power to influence others. There was a unique and charismatic aura about him; he had healed her emotionally and spiritually.

The turning point in the conversion process was the night of the ritual. Her time had come. Through the haze of burning incense and smoke from the open fire, *he* drifted into a hypnotic trance. He chanted in a guttural tone that vibrated from the back of his throat. His eyes snapped open and his sharp gaze locked onto hers, staring deep into her soul. He preached in a tongue foreign to her ears, as though all the languages of humanity had been blended in a melting pot of song and prayer. It was then that she had the vision, both beautiful and terrifying. A ghost-like, faceless woman with long grey hair and flowing white robe floated within a mist, circling around her. Inside her head, the woman's voice whispered, 'Go to them, take back what's yours. Set yourself free.'

The ghostly form dissolved into the mist, consumed by fire and smoke. Clare had slumped into *his* arms, drained of all energy and strength. She was suddenly at peace. In that moment, she vowed to give her full obedience to him, her angel.

She knew her life on earth would soon be over. This didn't

make her sad. She was now in a dream-like state and her mind was filled with joyful visions of the afterlife. No longer would she be lonely. Soon she would be reunited with her children. Not here on earth, but in a better place where she would be free of her earthly existence and all its evils.

With *his* help, she would no longer feel the pain. In the past, her depression had led to suicide attempts, but this night was different. She had a purpose in what she was about to do. He had taught her to believe in the powers of the angels and the notion that death is the doorway to eternal happiness.

He was the Angel of the Covenant, who had the power to bring her children to her in paradise. It was so long since she had seen her babies. How much had Olivia and Jamie grown? Would they still recognise her? Would they love her? She loved them so much and soon they would understand. Their father had stolen them from her, but soon he would pay. He had clouded their minds and turned them against her. Stewart didn't deserve to live and had to be punished. Soon she would be reunited with her children in a place where no one could ever take them from her again. Her angel would arrive soon to send her on that journey.

And so, Clare waited. She heard someone approaching. From the inky darkness stepped a cloaked figure. The silhouette of her angel appeared from the tree line. A robe was draped over his shoulders, its hood covering his head. His figure was haloed by the glow of the town lights below. He came to her and they entwined in a passionate embrace. She was mesmerised by his intense gaze that cut through the moonlight. Like so many times before, his presence and warmth consoled her. He was her strength. She had surrendered her life to him and now he would guide her to freedom.

'My sweet Clare, it's time. Do you still believe in me?'

'Yes, I believe in you. I remember everything you taught me. I trust you,' Clare whispered.

'Your faith will be your salvation. I am God's servant and he has brought us together. We share the same pain, but soon we'll all be together in the stars and the heavens.'

She looked up at him, tears streaming down her porcelain cheeks. 'Please promise me they won't feel any pain. Don't make the children suffer.' Her words hung in the air.

'I have entrusted this task to Sammael. It will be his rite of passage, a test of his loyalty. He won't fail us. He'll bring them to you. That's what you want, isn't it?' His voice was even and reassuring.

'Yes, with all my heart and soul. I know what I have to do. I'll be in paradise waiting for them.'

He cupped her face in his hands. 'Then you must give in to the power of the angels. You must not waver. Be strong, be brave. Soon we will be together in paradise, all of us. I promise.'

They had chosen this place for its peacefulness and isolation; it was their favourite place in the world. He had once told her they were closer to God up there, closer to the stars and the heavens. She stepped back from him and untied her hooded cloak. She let it drop to the ground to reveal her slender, naked body.

He was drawn to her like a magnet and wrapped his cloaked arms around her waist like the wings of the fruit bats spying from the trees above. Beneath his robe, he too was naked, their bodies pressed against each other. He was invigorated by her warmth. He caressed her soft skin as they embraced. In unison, they lowered their bodies to the blanket, becoming one. They knelt down together and kissed. He shifted and lay on his back, bringing her with him. She straddled her slender legs over him. His fingers followed the lines of her perfect curves, she responded to his touch. They savoured this last physical contact with each other. Soon they would meet again in a magical place. He had told her this. She was a believer. When it was all over, he would join her in paradise. He still had a score to settle with God.

As they shared their final moments, Clare remembered his promise.

'I will bring your babies to you and punish those who brought you so much pain.'

SIX

EARLIER that night, Stewart Kingston had been resting in his antique armchair, hand-carved from polished Tasmanian silky oak. *Is this happiness?* Contentment swept over him, relaxing his muscles and mind. Cradled by the old chair, the anxiety and pain of the past eased and his body melted into the cushions.

His empty mug, which had contained a rich brew of hot chocolate, nestled between his hands in his lap. As he sat in the lounge room, he was surrounded by fond memories he'd shared with his children and his new wife, Anne. A corkboard hung on the hallway wall. Pinned to it were precious works of crayon and water colour art drawn by his children, Olivia and Jamie. Olivia was now eleven years old and Jamie was eight. On the brick-cased wall surrounding the fireplace hung photos of the two little people who had captured his heart and soul. Stewart stared at a studio portrait of Jamie as a toddler with his big sister squeezing into an old wine barrel full of daffodils and teddy bears. Other candid photos – shots of Olivia wearing Stewart's gumboots as she helped wash the car and one of Jamie covered in mud.

A recent photo of Anne drew his gaze. The lens had captured her natural glow. She smiled with her eyes, a genuine smile so familiar. She had been staring at the camera so that her captivating gaze followed the onlooker from any point in the room. Her blonde hair was tied back by a simple red ribbon and she rested her chin on her hand. He'd taken the photo on their honeymoon – a week in a quaint log bungalow in the mountains.

Below this photo hung the framed image of a smiling little boy named Jake who had become a large part of Stewart's life. Jake was seven years old and Anne's son from her previous marriage. Her first husband had died from a sudden heart attack when Jake was only a baby. Anne's remaining family lived on the other side of the country in Broome. These people, Stewart's wife Anne, his children Jamie and Olivia and his stepson Jake, were his world. Everything in his life revolved around ensuring their happiness.

Yet hidden behind the happy images were the reminders of the emotional scars. His ex-wife, Clare, had been with them when the studio photos of Jamie and Olivia were taken. Stewart closed his eyes and forced his mind to break free of those bitter memories.

He turned his head and smiled as he watched his family. Anne sat at the end of the table, a gentle arm around Olivia's shoulders as she helped with her homework. Jamie and Jake squeezed onto a single chair, swiping their fingers through various levels of Angry Birds on an iPad. Anne glanced at Stewart and offered him a reassuring smile before turning her attention back to the children. Stewart knew she could read his mind, just as he could hers – they were soulmates.

Stewart's thoughts drifted back to his ex-wife. Stewart, Clare and the children had established their life in town in their modest workers' cottage. It seemed like yesterday, but it was a dark time in his life which he'd tried to put behind him. At first, Stewart and Clare were happy, but things changed. Clare changed. Losing Clare, his first real love, still weighed on his heart.

She was a beautiful woman with a slender figure, unblemished pale skin and ink black long hair. Stewart had loved to nuzzle the soft skin at the back of her neck with his lips as she brushed her hair, allowing it to fall to the front of one shoulder. She had once embraced him. She had once loved him. That was before she saw the world through hardened eyes. Before she lost her smile.

When the kids were little, Clare distanced herself from Stewart. She said she no longer loved him. She fell into severe bouts of depression but refused to see a doctor. She spent more time away from home, neglecting the day-to-day needs of Olivia and Jamie. She left home early in the morning and wouldn't return until late at night. Stewart had no choice but to take days off work so that he could be at home with the children. He tried to reason with her, but she refused to speak with him.

Bruises appeared on Olivia's back and upper arms. When he questioned her, she seemed terrified and cried. She refused to tell him how she got them. He didn't know what to do or who to turn to for help.

One night, Clare arrived home after Stewart had settled the children into bed. It was belting rain and she stood on the front porch, drenched to the bone, wet hair dangling over her face. He held the door open, but she stood motionless, distracted. She looked at him with vague recognition, mascara running down her cheeks, giving her a ghoulish appearance. She peered out towards the rain and then her eyes met Stewart's. He motioned for her to come inside and she pushed past him.

Stewart lingered in the open doorway, staring out at the rain. He wished it would wash away his sense of hopelessness. He closed his eyes and took a deep breath. He turned after her. 'Stop, Clare. Talk to me, please.'

He grabbed her by the arm and she swivelled, reeling from his touch. She pulled her arm free and stared at him, a vacant expression. Silence. Daring the other to speak first.

'What's happening to us?' he rasped.

She tilted her head to the side and opened her mouth to speak, but at the last moment seemed to change her mind. Silence. She stared past him towards the open front door.

'Where have you been all day?'

'I don't know,' she whispered.

45

'What do you mean, you don't know?'

'I'm lost. I don't know who I am anymore.'

'Let me help you.' He stepped closer.

As he reached for her hand, she looked in his eyes, but as his fingers touched hers, she snatched her hand away as though she had dipped her fingers in boiling water.

She spat, 'This is my house and my life. Who the hell are you to tell me what to do?'

'I'm your husband. Your kids need you for God's sake.'

Her eyes lowered. 'I don't know why I came here. I need to leave.'

She strode past him and stepped out through the threshold of the front door. She paused at the top of the stairs before disappearing into the rain.

Just like that. Gone.

He had no idea what to do. *Was she drinking or using drugs? Was she having an affair? What had occurred to transform the woman who once loved him?* She was having a mental breakdown and he blamed himself.

Clare continued to come and go at infrequent intervals. She never made phone calls and had no friends Stewart was aware of. She ignored the children when she was at home.

One Sunday morning, Stewart left Olivia at the house in Clare's care while he took Jamie with him to the Country Markets. He used it as an outlet to escape into the warm sunshine with his little boy. When he returned, the furniture in the living room was upturned. A terracotta pot from the porch had been smashed through the television screen. In the kitchen food had been thrown about the bench tops and at walls, bottles of milk and juice smashed on the floor. He found Olivia huddled in her bedroom. She was shaking, her shoulders heaving up and down with each silent sob.

She threw herself at him, hugging him tight. The three of them – Stewart, Olivia and Jamie – sat on the floor in a tight embrace. Stewart studied his little girl's face. The scratches on her cheeks from

46

Clare's nails had broken the skin and were streaked with blood. He examined her more closely, placing Jamie on the floor beside them. The welts on the back of Olivia's upper legs were red and raised. He lifted the back of her Bananas in Pyjamas t-shirt and the sight of bruising all over her back overwhelmed him. He could only hold her, blaming himself for allowing this to happen.

'Where's Mummy?' he whispered.

'I don't know. Please Daddy, don't let her hurt me again.'

'No baby, she will never hurt you again. I promise.'

She will never hurt you again.

~

That was three years ago. Stewart reported the abuse to the police and moved out with the children. Clare never came looking for them.

He found a rental house outside of town, hunched on the side of a hill surrounded by farms and native bushland. It was a four-bedroom log and mud brick cottage on a property called Glendale. An L-shaped veranda, shaded in the afternoon sun by bullnose corrugated iron, opened up to a rear deck. The veranda railings were painted a deep burgundy and the ironbark window frames were stained with lacquer. Inside, the exposed ceiling beams and interior brickwork added to the country feel.

A log fence stood as a reminder of the days when the land was first cleared as a citrus orchard. Access to the property was by an unnamed dirt road. A white structure, two vertical logs joined at their highest points by a horizontal beam, served as the archway entrance. Rows of lemon, lime, orange and mandarin trees in distinct rows lined the front yard. Two towering ancient maple trees with golden brown leaves guarded the entrance. An avenue of bougainvillea shrubs hugged the edges of the gravel driveway, their brilliant pink and red leaves concealing the fierce thorns on their branches.

The home overlooked a creek which meandered through lush

bushland. Cattle grazed on the neighbouring property on the other side of the creek. The only noise that could be heard was the wind rustling the branches of the eucalypt, grevillea and golden wattle trees shading the yard. A paved pathway bordered by logs and mossy rocks worked its way down the hill through the bush to the creek below. Every morning, they woke to the chorus of singing magpies heralding in the new day.

Stewart chose not to work and spent his time with his children, watching them thrive in the country environment. He had vowed to protect them. Their lives were so much more precious than his own, a concept he had never questioned. He had no other living immediate family. The children were his world.

When Jamie started preschool and Olivia was settling into grade three, Stewart resumed his engineering consultancy business for local tradesmen and farmers. He worked from his office at home, making his hours flexible enough to be with the children before and after school.

Stewart and Anne met when she started working in the Administration office of the Lockyer Primary School. They dated and Anne took an instant shine to Jamie and Olivia. Stewart and Anne fell in love and Jake entered Stewart's life. He grew to love the little boy as his own; and so formed this new family.

After his divorce with Clare had settled, he signed their old house over to her. He married Anne and together with the children, they rebuilt their lives at Glendale. New beginnings. The children were collected at the front gate by the rural bus and returned in the afternoon. Stewart and Anne found time to potter around the yard, planting trees and working in the garden while the children played in the clean air. It was remarkable how Jake had been accepted by Olivia and Jamie; the "Three Musketeers" were inseparable.

Now, Stewart lingered in his old chair, watching his family. At bedtime, the boys ran off to their room, which they had insisted on sharing, despite there being another bedroom. Olivia jumped off her seat and ran towards Stewart, leaping onto his lap. She cuddled him around his neck, kissing him on the cheek.

'Hey, where did that come from? Do you want something?' smiled Stewart.

'No, Daddy, just cuddle time.' She was growing so fast, yet she was still his little girl.

She leaned in and held her face against his so their foreheads touched.

'What's the matter? Why does your face look sad?'

'My face isn't sad, baby. I'm just tired. But I'm happy.'

'We're always going to be happy now, Daddy, aren't we? I mean you, me, Anne, Jakey and Jamie.'

'You bet, kid.'

Stewart meant it.

'You'll never leave us, will you, Daddy?' Olivia asked with a concerned frown.

Stewart stared into his daughter's dark eyes and stroked her brown, wavy hair. She seemed troubled and waited for his answer.

'My little angel. I will never, ever leave you. I promise.'

He kissed her forehead, and she ran off to get ready for bed.

I will never, ever leave you.

It was the last night they would share together.

The family was being watched, stalked.

SEVEN

HE believed he was the Venom of God, the Prince of Demons. His mission had led him to this place, the Kingston family's home. Lingering in the shadows, he watched and waited. He had been sent as God's executioner. He didn't understand why, but he was clear about one thing. They all had to die. He had to earn the right to stand by the side of his master, the King of Angels. He had been watching for hours and it was now time. The anticipation surged through his veins.

He pulled the balaclava over his face. A flush bristled the hairs on the back of his neck. The house was draped in a blanket of darkness – the only sound his thumping heart. He paid no attention to the voices in his head; they only confused him. He had to focus on his task. He couldn't fail. There was too much at stake.

He had never killed before. He hoped it would live up to his expectations, his fantasies. He had always wanted to kill; now his master had provided him with that chance and he knew what he had to do. He had visualised it many times while watching the family to learn their nightly routine. In his mind, he replayed his master's instructions. Follow the plan. They all had to die. He repeated this over again until he could no longer hear the voices, those incessant voices tormenting his sanity. He gripped the .38 calibre revolver in one hand – fully loaded it was heavier than he had expected. With the other hand, he held the sledgehammer, his forearm tensing from its weight.

He emerged from the shadows and willed his legs to move, one foot in front of the other, weaving through the orchard towards the house. He breached the tree line and crossed the front lawn, leaving behind a trail of shoe prints in the dew. As he approached the front veranda, he paused and inhaled through his nose, exhaling through his mouth to control his heart rate. He climbed the stairs, the wooden treads groaning under his weight. Without hesitation, he stepped up to the front door. The hinges creaked as he opened the unlocked security screen. A gecko scampering across the fly screen stopped in its tracks, perfectly still. It tilted its head and stared at him with bulging, accusing eyes before disappearing to safety. He took another deep breath and knocked on the door with the butt of the revolver. At first, there was nothing but silence. He knocked again. He waited, fighting to contain the surge of anticipation. A light came on in the hallway and then someone was coming to the door. His heart pounded. Through the opaque frosted window panel beside the door appeared the blurred outline of a man, Stewart Kingston. His dark hair and tall frame were unmistakable. Kingston's bare feet echoed in the hallway as he shuffled towards the door. The veranda light came on.

'Who is it?' Kingston called out from behind the closed door.

Now. Before he could escape.

The Prince of Demons raised the revolver and fired into the closed door, three shots in quick succession. He slid the gun into his belt and raised the sledgehammer. With one powerful blow he destroyed the lock, the frame splintering as the door swung open. Stepping inside the doorway, he found Stewart Kingston on the floor, blood gushing from his chest. Adrenaline surged through his body. He looked down at the dying man – his first kill. He moved on. There were others who must die. The woman appeared in the hallway. She screamed and he moved towards her. Sensing her fear, he became high with a feeling of unbridled power.

He wanted to toy with her, prolong the thrill of the hunt. He stepped closer and was taken by her beauty. He had watched her before but had never been this close. As he inhaled her fragrance, he was overcome with the desire to touch her.

The woman's eyes bulged in terror. She stared in a moment of appalled silence at her husband writhing on the floor, covered in blood. 'No, no!' she whispered, her lips trembling. 'Why have you done this? Who are you?'

'Surely you understand. You must be punished like your husband. And of course, the children must die.'

He dropped the sledgehammer and inched closer to her, the revolver at his side. She gulped, panic stricken. He stared out from the balaclava, indifferent to her cries. He would show no mercy. She flinched as he ran his gloved fingers through her hair. He circled behind her, sniffing at the back of her neck. Her body trembled against his.

He stroked her cheek with the back of his hand. She reached up, taking him by surprise by grabbing his arm and biting down hard on his wrist. She dug her fingernails into his forearm and clawed at his skin, drawing blood. He grimaced as she turned and slammed her knee into his groin. She pushed past him down the hallway as he reeled over in pain.

'Run kids, run and hide!' she screamed.

He raced after her and grabbed her ankle. She tumbled to the floor but kicked out at him, freeing herself from his grip. He raised the revolver as she got to her feet. She screamed, 'Run, my babies!'

Her legs crumpled after the first shot, the bullet striking her in the back below the shoulder. She dragged herself along the hallway floor, leaving a smeared trail of blood. He wanted her to suffer. He savoured her guttural moans as her lungs filled with curdled blood as she gasped for air. He watched and admired her courage. The children would be next.

'You're so beautiful, but you were foolish to try to stop this. This is all part of the master's plan. Nothing can stop this.'

She turned her head and looked at him one last time. Her eyes widened in horror. He fired, shooting her twice in the back. The life drained from her limp body as she exhaled a long and final breath. She lay silent, her eyes open.

He reloaded the revolver, remembering to collect the shell cases as he'd been instructed. His shaking hands fumbled and two shell casings fell onto the floor, spinning and rolling in various directions.

'Damn it!' He tried to find them, but they were gone. He had no time to search for them. He refocused on the task at hand. Six more shots, that's all it would take to finish off the children. He stepped over the woman's body and walked down the hallway to the girl's room. He entered and flicked on the light. The bed was empty. He ran to the boys' bedroom across the hallway, but they were also gone. Curtains fluttered with the cool breeze blowing through the black square of the open window. He rushed into the room and leaned out through the window. Nothing but darkness outside. He ran back through the house and searched the other rooms.

The children were gone.

'No! Come back here,' he yelled.

He shouldn't have wasted time with the woman. Now they had escaped. He ran out the front door, but he didn't know which way they had gone. It was pitch black outside as his eyes adjusted to the darkness. He had no idea where the little bastards had run off to.

He scurried up and down the fringe of bushland hugging the yard. It was a vast area to search.

The children had vanished.

He slid the pen torch from its belt holster and scanned it across the face of the tree line, the laser-like beam cutting through the darkness. The light threw flickering shadows across the tree trunks, playing tricks with his eyes as accusing faces stared back at him from the gnarled bark and woody knots.

'Come out kids, you'll be safe, I promise,' he called, trying to keep his voice even. He listened, crickets chirped and the croaks of cane toads echoed from the creek at the bottom of the gully. 'You need to come out now. I'll make sure no one hurts you,' he lied. Even the crickets and toads fell silent.

He was running out of time. The gunshots would have been heard for miles in the stillness of the night. It wasn't supposed to happen like this. The children had to die. That's what this was all about, he knew that much.

He ran back inside and paced around the lounge room, angry with himself. Panic set in and the voices in his head grew louder. He tugged at the balaclava that clung to his face and threatened to suffocate him. He pulled the woolly mask from his head and gasped in air as though he was drowning. He slammed the butt of the gun against his skull. Pulling at his hair, he screamed in anguish. He was overcome with a red mist of anxiety.

Then out of nowhere there he was, the little boy in pyjamas standing in the front doorway. He lunged at the boy, who reacted in a heartbeat and was gone as quickly as he appeared. He chased the boy outside and as he was vanishing into the darkness, he raised the revolver and fired. The loud crack echoed like an explosion in the bush's silence.

He pursued the boy, who disappeared into a curtain of fog, swallowed by the darkness.

The boy was gone.

He trudged through the dense scrub, desperate to find the children, shining the torch in frustration. There was only the sound of his own boots crunching on the dry undergrowth and his heavy breathing. He stopped and listened, but there was no movement. The bush fell silent. Circling around the house, he strained his eyes for any movement in the moonlight, but there was no trace of the children. They had gone to ground, concealing themselves in the shadows.

He couldn't stay any longer; he had to leave.

He had failed.

He slunk back inside the house and took another look at the dead woman. He stared at her pale face, intrigued by her deathly beauty, her body still. He didn't know what to do next, but had to get out of there.

He retrieved the sledgehammer and backed out of the house, taking one last look into the fog before disappearing into the darkness.

EIGHT

OLIVIA waited for what seemed like an eternity. She gave the boys the signal to rise from their bellies where they had lain prone, faces pressed in the dirt. The concealment provided by the undergrowth had saved their lives, for now at least. She held her index finger to her lips as they emerged from the safety of the shadows. The gunshots and screams that had shattered the tranquility of the night had fallen as silent as the fog. She took the gamble that he was gone, although she couldn't be certain. She had no choice. They had waited long enough. They needed to call for help. Anne and her father might need her. She couldn't abandon them.

Olivia led Jake and Jamie by the hand as they crept towards the house. She held her breath as the veranda stairs creaked, terrified the man with the gun would hear them and return. They tiptoed onto the veranda and paused when they reached the shattered front door. Olivia peered inside with the boys pressed against her, clutching her hands. She gasped when she saw her father lying on his back in a pool of blood just inside the door. Down the hallway lay Anne, slumped on the floor.

'Mummy!' Jake screamed and broke free of Olivia's grip. He ran to the far end of the hall where his mother lay covered in blood. He fell to his knees and shook her shoulders. 'Mummy, wake up, wake up.' He rested his forehead on hers and cupped her face with his hands. 'Mummy, wake up,' he cried. He lay next to her motionless body and sobbed.

Olivia knelt beside her father and took hold of his hand. Her heart thudded inside her chest when she realised he was still alive. He laboured through short muffled breaths, foamy blood coating his lips. His eyes drooped. She supported his head on her lap. She glanced up, tears welling in her eyes. Jamie stood frozen in the doorway, trembling in shock. Her eyes returned to her father and as his life force faded, she remembered his promise to her. 'I will never, ever leave you.'

'Don't leave us, Daddy,' she whispered, stroking his hair. 'You promised.'

He raised his hand and wiped a tear from her cheek with his thumb. His eyes sparkled as they welled with tears. His heartbroken smile gave way to a grimace as he gagged, blood trickling from the corners of his mouth. His eyes locked onto hers in a piercing stare. 'I'll always be with you.' He wheezed and coughed up more blood. His eyes flickered and then focused on an empty space in the air between them. His hand slid loosely by his side and his chest deflated, the air escaping from his lungs with a long, final sigh.

Olivia shook his shoulders, but his head fell to one side, his eyes lifeless. 'Daddy!' she cried. 'No, please don't go!'

His wheezing stopped and his body fell limp. She had never witnessed death before, but she knew he was gone. Pain rose from her throat and her sobs echoed through the house. Her eyes burned and her chest felt heavy, as if it were filled with lead. She could no longer see clearly. All she knew was that he was out of her life forever. They were all alone. She turned to Jamie and reached out to him. He took her hand and stared at her, and then at his father, with confusion and disbelief. He dropped to his knees, his bottom lip quivering. His shoulders shook with grief as tears slipped down his cheeks.

Olivia curled on her side and embraced her father, not wanting to ever let go. But she knew they needed help. They couldn't stay

there all alone. The man could return any minute. She willed herself
to her feet and headed for the telephone.

NINE

IT was 1AM and first-year Constable Kirsty Loudin looked at her watch for the fifth time in as many minutes. Her Field Training Officer, Senior Constable Mick Jones, was at the wheel of the patrol car.

'Looking at your watch won't make our shift go any faster, ya know,' he said.

'I wish. I still haven't gotten used to these 10PM to 6AM shifts yet. Five hours to go.'

They were back on patrol after attending a street disturbance outside The Phoenix nightclub. The term "nightclub" was a stretch; it was a dodgy dance floor at the back of the Imperial Hotel. A handful of drunken patrons staggered outside, arm in arm singing Cold Chisel's *Khe Sanh*. Kirsty had discovered this was a standard job for a late shift.

There was a chill in the air. Kirsty rubbed her hands together and zipped up her leather jacket. 'Let's hope the rest of the shift will be a quiet one.'

'Oh, now you've done it,' said Mick, rolling his eyes. 'You've just put the mocker on us. Things always turn to shit when someone uses the Q word. Didn't they teach you that at the academy?'

'No, I don't recall that lecture. Well, you never know. I might just break the omen then.'

Mick looked at her with a frown. 'I hope so.'

The police radio came alive. 'VKR, to any unit – any unit,'

crackled the voice of Maggie in the communications room. 'Triple zero call received re shots fired. More details to follow. Any unit to proceed to Johnsons Road, exact location yet to be verified.'

Mick turned and glared at Kirsty. He opened his mouth but decided against whatever he was about to say and shook his head instead.

Kirsty shrugged. 'What?'

'What did I tell you? Anyway, that's us. Let her know we're proceeding.'

'VKR, this is Lima 204, we're proceeding from town. What code is that?'

'Code 2, proceed Code 2,' Maggie instructed.

Mick reached down and activated the lights and siren. 'So much for a quiet night,' he muttered and planted his foot on the accelerator.

Kirsty spoke into the radio handset. 'VKR, do you have further details?'

'Standby, we have a child on the line. She says there have been gunshots. She's hysterical and can't tell us where she lives. She can only provide us with Johnsons Road as the location.' Maggie seemed unusually flustered.

'Receive that. We'll let you know when we get close.' Kirsty directed a glance towards Mick, whose attention was focused on the road ahead, his expression hard to read.

Mick handled the vehicle like a touring car driver, remaining calm but pushing the vehicle to its limit. He slowed at intersections, making sure no traffic was coming as he proceeded through red lights and stop signs.

As they drove out of town, Kirsty asked, 'Do you know where we're going?'

'I know Johnsons Road, but it's a bloody long road. There are heaps of dirt tracks that run off it into private properties. Let's just hope Maggie comes through for us.'

Five minutes later, they had left town and were approaching the T-intersection with Johnsons Road. Mick slowed until he came to a stop at the intersection. A cloud of dust from the tyres drifted into the headlight beams. Kirsty stared at her partner, hoping he would know what to do next. 'Where to from here?'

'I wish I knew. We have a choice of left or right,' said Mick as he swivelled his head in both directions.

The radio speaker vibrated. 'VKR, to Lima 204, we're still trying to ascertain the exact location. We've received other calls in relation to gun shots being heard in that area. The little girl is still on the line. There are other children crying in the background. She says their house is off a dirt road. Standby...'

Seconds passed. And then minutes. The police car idled, the blue and red lights swirled. They were a beacon in a sea of darkness. They could do nothing but wait.

Kirsty bit the inside of her lip. Her mouth was dry, hands clammy.

'VKR, to Lima 204, the child is now saying that her parents are hurt. She's there with her two younger brothers. Their surname is Kingston, parents are Stewart and Anne. The station Sergeant is still on the phone to her and is relaying the information. Standby...'

'Shit, what now?' said Kirsty.

'We'll have to wait until we know where they are. If we take a punt we could end up at the wrong end of Johnsons Road.'

'VKR to Lima 204. Child has confirmed that a male person has entered the house, shots fired. Unknown if offender is still on site. Standby...'

'Christ, where are they?' Mick hit the steering wheel with the palms of his hands. He snatched the radio handset from Kirsty. 'VKR, can you get a physical description of where they live? That might help us head in the right direction at least.'

An excruciatingly long pause, then Maggie replied. 'The girl says they live on a property on a hill. Their house backs onto a creek.

We're doing computer checks now on the name Kingston. We've got a few hits. Standby...'

Mick scratched his head. 'Shit. Let me think. I've been down this way before. There are some properties down here to our left which back onto Nundulla Creek. They're a few clicks away, but I think that's our best possibility. Our main problem is there're a heap of dirt roads and half of them aren't even signposted. It's time to take that punt, Kirsty.'

Mick muscled the car to the left and accelerated along Johnsons Road. They approached several dirt roads which turned off from both sides.

'It's got to be one of these turnoffs on the right here somewhere. The creek is over there to our right over these hills.' Mick drove past a few dirt tracks, each looking well used by local traffic. They all led to farmhouses, but which one was this little girl calling from?

Maggie was back on air. 'VKR to Lima 204, we've got it. Vehicle registration details confirm they live on a property called "Glendale". It's on the route the local school bus takes. Are you familiar with that?'

Mick's eyes lit up with optimism. 'Yeah, I know the general area. Can you direct us to the property?'

'The little girl has described a big white log structure at the front entrance to the property,' Maggie replied.

Mick sped up, driving with purpose. He approached a dirt road to his right and turned, passing a yellow school bus stop sign at the corner. He passed several properties, each having their own unique front fence and mailbox. Some mailboxes were converted plastic oil containers and others were hollow logs or old tin milk crates. The white log structure at the front of the Kingston's property appeared in the headlights. Mick slid the car to a halt on the loose gravel.

'Quick, get your vest on.' He popped open the boot and jumped out of the car before Kirsty had a chance to mentally prepare for the gravity of the situation. They stood at the rear of the car, helping each other with the vest straps. The word POLICE was marked in white lettering across the front of each vest. Once they had buckled the straps into place, Mick reached back into the car and grabbed the radio handset.

'VKR we're out the front of the property. We can just see the lights of the house from the road. Do we have any back up?'

'The crew in Lima 203 were off at a domestic dispute on the other side of town. They're on their way but will be about fifteen minutes behind you. An ambulance is on its way. We've lost contact with the girl. The phone's gone dead. Be careful,' urged Maggie.

'We intend to,' said Mick into the radio handset. 'We'll have to go in by foot, otherwise we'll be an open target if we just drive up to the house. Get the ambulance to remain out the front until we confirm what's going on. We'll be on hand-held.'

Mick walked over to Kirsty, who stood terrified behind the car. He put his large hands on her shoulders. 'You okay? You ready to do this?'

Kirsty nodded, but said nothing.

'I'm shittin' myself as well, but there are kids in there, so we just have to do this. Now, you take the radio and stick it on your belt, but make sure it's turned right down. We'll take a mag light each but don't use it unless you have to. We don't want to make ourselves stick out like dog's balls. We'll make our way to the house on foot until we can get close enough to see what's happening. You right to go?'

Kirsty looked up at Mick. 'I'll be right, mate. Let's do this.'

They walked beneath the white log archway and set off into the darkness towards the house. Mick walked on the left side of the driveway and Kirsty on the right, edging along a line of trees on each side. Mick stumbled. 'Ah, Jesus, be careful. These trees have spikes,' he whispered.

They quickened their pace, guns drawn. Kirsty held her Glock with confidence, her recent academy training still fresh in her mind. She planted one foot in front of the other with caution, heel then toes, heel then toes, just as she'd been trained.

Mick held his Ruger .357 revolver. He'd resisted the transition to the new Glock, one of the last of the old school generation of coppers. They shuffled forward until they came to a halt in the darkness, scanning for any movement near the house. Kirsty was relieved to see that a lot of the house lights were on. The house itself was engulfed by an eerie fog which had crept up the hill from the creek, swallowing everything in its path. A haze of moonlight glowed through the mist.

The front veranda lights pierced the thick fog. Mick turned to Kirsty and motioned towards the far side of the house. Kirsty understood he wanted her to take a position near the veranda. He pointed to the other side where he intended to go. She nodded and they ran in crouching positions, using the darkness for concealment.

Kirsty's mind raced. *What if the shooter is still here waiting for us? What if he can see us? What if there is a house full of dead people, dead children?*

She pushed her fears aside. She was a police officer and lives could depend on her ability to keep it together. She ran to a dark corner beside the veranda and leaned up against the wall. Mick positioned himself on the other side of the house, taking cover beside a small shrub. They peered around the corners, maintaining visual contact with each other from opposite ends.

Mick signalled for Kirsty to wait and he moved around onto the veranda, becoming a potential target as he entered the lit area. He glanced through the first window. He crouched low and shuffled across to the next window. He crept forward, making his way to the front door.

Kirsty peered in through a window, but there was no sign of movement. She made her way around to the front of the veranda and covered Mick with her Glock. She was terrified at the thought of something happening to him and leaving her alone. She feared she couldn't handle the situation by herself. She wiped her brow with her jacket sleeve. Despite the cold, she sweated.

Mick signalled and Kirsty hurried to his side, pressing herself against the wall. She took in every detail. The security screen door was open and creaked to and fro. The only sounds came from a wind chime hanging from a hook on a veranda post. The wooden door hung open, riddled with bullet holes. Shards of wood were splintered onto the veranda floor. The door had been kicked or smashed in with something heavy. The doorframe was shattered and the lock pulverised.

Mick gave a nod and peeled outwards, giving himself room to clear the doorway through the sights of his revolver. Kirsty followed suit, covering from her side. She remembered her academy training and the dangers of lingering in a doorway, known as the "fatal funnel". Following the aim of her Glock, she poked her head through the doorway to get a perspective of the layout inside the house. The first room off the hallway was the lounge room and she noted that a coffee table, lamp and chair had been knocked over. She then made out the grim sight of a body lying in the hallway.

Mick whispered, 'I'm going in. You cover my back.'

Kirsty knew they had to secure the house – they had to go in. There was no waiting for backup.

'On me. Moving,' whispered Mick as he pivoted from cover and entered the doorway.

'On you. Covering,' responded Kirsty as she rolled in behind him. They proceeded inside, their feet moving in unison.

Kirsty glanced at the poor soul laying on the floor, a barefoot man in his early thirties, dressed in flannelette pyjamas. He lay in a pool of blood and she knew straight away he was dead. They progressed down the hallway.

There was a noise in the kitchen and they jumped, swivelling their guns towards the sound. Kirsty had a clear view of the kitchen.

What she saw broke her heart. Three small children huddled together on the floor in a corner. They were all terrified and shaking. They clung their arms around each other for protection, two little boys and an older girl.

'It's okay now kids, you're safe. We're the police,' Kirsty whispered, her voice trembling.

She moved into the kitchen and crouched beside the children, who huddled even closer to each other as she drew near.

Kirsty whispered, 'Is there anyone still in the house?'

The girl shook her head. 'He's gone.'

'Which way did he go?'

'I don't know, he hurt our parents.' Tears streamed down the girl's face.

'Stay here, don't move. Do you understand?' said Kirsty.

The three children nodded, eyes wide.

Kirsty returned to Mick's rear and they moved down the hallway, turning light switches on as they went. They entered the first bedroom. Posters of teen pop bands plastered the walls. A collection of Barbie dolls and trinkets had been carefully positioned on top of a pink chest of drawers. A laptop computer covered in rainbow stickers sat on a homework desk. The bed had been slept in, but the doona had been pulled back.

'First room clear,' said Mick. He gave Kirsty a nod and they progressed to the next room on the right. Mick flicked on the light. The beds in the boys' room had also been slept in. Kirsty then noticed the smudged trail of blood on the floor. She made out hand marks and bare footprints in the blood.

'Second room clear,' Mick called.

They passed what appeared to be a spare bedroom and continued on. They came to the entrance of the laundry where a woman lay on her side, her eyes open but staring blankly towards the floor. Her blonde hair was soaked with blood. She wore a white lace nightgown soiled with blood from wounds in her back. It seemed she had crawled from the hallway, bleeding out on the tiled floor of the laundry. Her hands and bare feet were caked in blood.

The back door of the laundry was open and Kirsty could see out into the darkness. She turned on the lights of the bathroom to her right. 'Bathroom clear.' She followed Mick to the end of the hall to the main bedroom. He flicked on the light. Kirsty noted the unmade bed where the poor couple had been asleep before some monster had invaded their home in the middle of the night.

'House clear,' announced Mick.

They returned to the kitchen, where the children remained huddled together. Kirsty crouched and placed her arms around them. They felt tiny and frail. As Mick took the radio from her, she noticed his hands were shaking.

He cleared his throat, gathered his composure and made the radio call. 'VKR, the house is secure. We have two deceased persons, a man and a woman. Three children safe and well. Whereabouts of the offender is unknown. How far away is that back-up?'

'Yeah, Lima 203 we're just pulling up out the front now. The ambulance has just arrived ahead of us. We're coming straight in.'

Kirsty felt like they were being watched from somewhere out there in the darkness. They were still exposed to danger. Large windows and a sliding glass door led from the kitchen to the backyard and they were easy targets. Mick crouched behind the cupboards with Kirsty and the children, the safest position to wait while help arrived. As her adrenaline levels dropped and her heart rate slowed, Kirsty became overwhelmed by sadness. It was such a terrible waste of life.

Mick gave Kirsty a wink. 'You did good tonight, kid.'

The back-up crew and the ambulance vehicles rumbled down the driveway. Doors slammed and the other officers ran into the house, guns drawn.

The smallest boy looked up at Kirsty and whispered, 'I want my mummy.'

'I know, sweetheart. I know,' she said.

TEN

JARROD tried to scream but his vocal cords defied him. He tried to inhale but there was no air. He was suffocating in a vacuum. Again he opened his mouth to scream, but silence prevailed. His legs were heavy, as though weighted down with stones. As he dragged one foot in front of the other, he was propelled backwards, dragged by an invisible force. He was surrounded by darkness, a type of dark that occurs in a complete solar eclipse, blocking out light and sound. His perception of time was distorted, everything a blur. The world around him had been erased in the blackness.

He was drawn closer to something unknown, something terrifying. The ground crumbled under his feet. He teetered at the edge of a cliff. He couldn't step away, every muscle in his body frozen. He became dizzy with a feeling of vertigo. His body leaned backwards over the edge and for a moment, he was suspended in the air. He closed his eyes and surrendered to the inevitable. He fell, his body twirling and jerking as he plummeted from an infinite height towards an invisible floor.

Gravity pulled him so hard his insides nearly burst, the speed of the fall constricting his throat so that he couldn't draw breath. Impact came and his body shattered against the surface of water. His bones contorted in a way they shouldn't. Unable to move, he gulped for air and his lungs filled with water. He was suffocating, slowly sinking deeper into the emerald water, air bubbles dancing around him.

Something grabbed his foot, then his arm. He was pulled deeper into the abyss. Two corpses, raw flesh hanging from their faces, eyeballs dangling from their skulls, clung to him, dragging him down. He couldn't move his arms or legs. The light above the surface faded. The faces of the corpses pressed against his. He recognised them.

Jamal Lewis and Douglas Blair had come for their revenge.

The ghosts of the dead were coming for his soul.

He was terrified.

He knew he was about to die.

He was jolted from the recurring nightmare, soaked in a lather of sweat. His heart raced, pounding inside his chest. His mind caught somewhere between delusion and consciousness. The phone beside the bed bleated. Jayne sleepily turned on her reading lamp and reached over to answer it.

'Hello. Yeah, he's here. I'll put him on.' She handed Jarrod the phone. 'It's the station.'

He groaned and took the phone, giving himself a few seconds to wake up. 'Hello?'

'Jarrod, it's Sergeant Paul Richardson from the station. Sorry to wake you. There's been a double homicide.'

Jarrod's thoughts scrambled. 'Where?'

'Out of town on a property called Glendale. All detectives have been recalled to duty. This one's different, Jarrod. The C.I.B boss has requested you and Harding attend the scene as a priority.'

'Why?' Jarrod was now alert.

'There are three kids. They were there when it happened.'

Jarrod sighed and ran his fingers through his bed hair. 'Okay, give me the details and I'll get there ASAP.'

'What is it?' asked Jayne after the call.

He paused for a few seconds, processing the news.

'A couple has been murdered in front of their kids. I have to go,' he said in a half daze.

Jayne gave a knowing nod. 'Please, just be careful.' She leaned over and kissed him on the cheek.

Jarrod smiled. 'You know me, always.'

He threw on clothes and made for the door. He hesitated and then crept back into the kids' rooms, kissing them both before easing the front door closed behind him.

As he descended the front steps, he was hit with a chilly breeze, the early morning air activating his senses.

He accelerated along the deserted streets of Lockyer in his ten-year-old Toyota Forerunner. He pushed the cumbersome vehicle to speeds it wasn't designed for. He'd bought it to go four-wheel driving up in Queensland in the rainforest tracks and along the eastern beaches of Fraser Island, but he was yet to take it off-road. Each time he made holiday plans, they were derailed by some new work-related crisis. The truck whined and rattled as he skidded the chunky off-road tyres on the bitumen around each corner.

There were no cars in sight. He'd never seen the streets so deserted. The town of Lockyer was sound asleep, its residents reassured by the notion they were safe in their own homes. Jarrod wondered if the poor souls who had been murdered that night had felt safe in their home.

As he sped towards the police station, he raced through intersections, the traffic lights flashing amber. The wide suburban streets were dimly lit by the occasional streetlight. A thick mist sat over the town. The windscreen fogged up from the condensation of his breath hitting the cold glass. He rebuked himself for putting off getting the heater fixed. He wiped the inside of the windscreen in a circular motion with his fist to create a porthole to see through.

At that time of the morning, there were few house lights on. Architecture in Lockyer was mostly renovated workers' cottages huddled together and high set colonials with open verandas on quarter acre blocks, a legacy of its heritage as an industrial town. There were occasional reminders of the days of the early settlers – a red brick storage depot had been converted into a tourist information centre, while historic pubs still boasted the old-fashioned country charm of their heyday. In the pre-dawn hours the abandoned streets, gloomy and leached of colour, took on a sepia hue like an old photograph.

Jarrod passed through the main street of town, the only sign of life being the occasional cab or early morning newspaper delivery van. The front wheels of the truck screeched as he turned sharply into the entrance of the police station driveway. The few cars in the car park belonged to the skeleton crews working the night shift. He recognised Kirsty Loudin's two-door Hyundai coupe and Mick Jones' restored Kingswood ute.

He'd been told they were the first crew at the scene of the murder. He guessed they were still out there guarding the crime scene. Mick was a streetwise copper hardened by many years on the job. Kirsty was a rookie; he hoped she was holding up alright. Jarrod had been first responder to his share of murder and suicide scenes but still found it confronting having to enter a room where fresh death lingered.

He steered the truck into a parking space at the end of the car park. A stream of cars drove in behind him and screeched to a halt in unorthodox parking positions. As Jarrod jumped from his car, he recognised the detectives from the Criminal Investigation Branch who had also been recalled to duty. Detective Senior Constable Liam Dawes, a chubby red-head with freckles, sluggishly climbed from his rusty Landcruiser and shuffled towards the back door of the station. Unshaven and his curly hair a mess, he yawned and rubbed his eyes.

Brad had also just arrived and joined Jarrod as they crossed the car park. He looked as weary as Jarrod felt, his eyes puffy from lack of sleep.

Detective Sergeant Murray Long strode across the car park with a spring in his step. He was a seasoned detective who had high regard for himself, his hair slicked back with a subtle arrogance. He was a large man and could intimidate others. Jarrod had always felt that Long looked down on him as an inferior detective. There had always been an opinion by some old-school CIB detectives that the Child Protection Unit was a lower standard, that they weren't real detectives. Jarrod tried not to let that attitude get to him, but it wasn't easy.

They all approached the back door simultaneously, wearing matching crumpled shirts, jeans and jackets. Even Brad apparently had no time to iron his shirt.

'Ah, they even invited the kiddie cops along. You might learn something, lads. Try and stay out of our way,' Long directed the cheap shot at Jarrod and Brad.

Brad glared at Jarrod, his eyes telling him to ignore the smart-arse dig. Jarrod opened his mouth to respond but thought better of it. He clenched his jaw instead.

'Let's move it guys,' said Long. 'I know about as much as you do, so let's get our shit together and get out there.'

They filed inside and rushed past the communications room. Paul Richardson sung out, 'They're waiting out there for you boys. My uniform crews have contained the house and Scenes of Crime are on their way.'

'Yeah, mate, we're on our way,' Jarrod called back as he turned at the base of the stairs. He was pissed off already by Long's wise-crack but was determined to not let him get under his skin.

Jarrod and Brad hurried up to their office and grabbed their gear and firearms. They moved with purpose and within a few minutes were down the stairs again, dashing to their unmarked police vehicle. Long and Dawes raced out of their office a few paces behind. Both cars screeched out of the driveway with dash-mounted blue lights rotating. Brad was still fumbling with his seatbelt as Jarrod sped around the corner and down the main street.

In his rear vision mirror, Jarrod could see Dawes behind the wheel of the CIB car, his stern face illuminated by the glow of the strobing police lights. Long waved his hands around in an animated, one-way conversation with Dawes, whose head bobbled like one of those novelty dashboard figurines. As Jarrod sped out of town, he gathered his thoughts, concentrating on the job ahead. He prepared himself for the crime scene. His stomach became unsettled as nervous butterflies fluttered.

Nothing could prepare him for the rollercoaster ride ahead.

ELEVEN

IT was just after 2:30AM when Jarrod and Brad arrived at Glendale, the white log archway marking the entrance to the property where a police vehicle restricted access. They had relied on instructions over the radio to find the place. Jarrod and Brad were waved through and drove into the property, closely followed by Dawes and Long. Wild hedges of thorny bougainvillea shrubs lined the gravel driveway, their woody vines forming a natural tunnel. A halo of swirling blue and red lights glowed through the fog, shrouding the house in a whitened haze.

The Scenes of Crime van had been reversed close to the house and was parked with its sliding door open. Crates of forensic equipment were ready to be unloaded. Sergeant Larry Carson paced across the front of the house, marking out a perimeter with blue and white chequered police tape. He paused to hold up his camera, a photo flash ghosting the house. Larry was a first-rate scenes of crime officer. He was awkward interacting with people but had an impeccable eye for detail and an uncanny sixth sense for interpreting subtle clues at crime scenes.

Jarrod parked and killed the ignition. He and Brad hesitated, neither saying a word. Jarrod was coming off the adrenaline rush that had surged through his veins and he was now on edge. Now that they had arrived, things were very real.

Brad turned to Jarrod and drew in a deep breath. 'Let's do this.'

Jarrod sighed. 'Remind me. Why do we do this job again?'

Dawes and Long were out of their car and already heading towards the house with stern looks. Jarrod wondered if the others shared his feeling of anxiety, or maybe he was the only one who self-doubted whether he still had the stomach for what lay ahead.

They reluctantly got out of the car. Brad followed Dawes and Long towards the front door. Jarrod hesitated, taking in as much detail as he could, capturing mental snapshots of the scene. Mick Jones leant against the veranda railing. He looked weary and pale, his eyes staring at nothing in particular. As the other detectives climbed the stairs to the veranda, Mick startled. He seemed not to have noticed them approaching. They all shook hands and Mick regathered his composure. He gave his account of what had happened. Jarrod walked over to them and Mick gave him a nod as he continued with his briefing. He explained how they had found the dead couple lying on the floor inside and the three children in the kitchen. The offender had fled the scene.

Jarrod's attention was then drawn to the ambulance. The rear door was open and the interior light inside the van silhouetted three small figures. Jarrod left the others and walked around to the back of the ambulance where he saw two boys and an older girl huddled together, sharing a grey blanket. Their little heads poked out, like three peas in a pod.

The paramedics, a middle-aged male officer and a younger female officer, had just finished examining the children. Sitting alongside them was Constable Kirsty Loudin. She looked up at Jarrod with a vacant expression. She offered a faint smile, her features softening.

Jarrod surveyed the children. The young girl had dark hair, alert brown eyes and olive skin. Her eyes met Jarrod's and she regarded him with suspicion. With the back of her hand, she brushed away a tear as it ran down her cheek.

He was hit with a sudden realisation. He knew this girl. He hadn't connected the relevance of the surname. A few years earlier, he was called to investigate a physical abuse case. He would never forget those brown eyes and the bruises inflicted by her mother.

'Olivia, is that you?' he asked.

She nodded, her eyebrows squishing together, head tilted.

'My word, you've grown so much,' said Jarrod.

One of the boys, who he assumed was her little brother, had the same olive complexion, brown hair and bold brown eyes. His eyes welled with tears and he whimpered as he snuggled against his big sister. *What was his name?* Jarrod remembered. Jamie.

He didn't expect them to remember him. A few years was an eternity for kids that age and he hoped they had blocked out those painful memories.

The other little boy was the smallest of the three and he had fair skin and sandy coloured hair. He sat still, staring at the floor. Jarrod could only imagine the fear and grief the children were dealing with. *What horrors had they seen?* They were still in shock.

Jarrod was overcome with sadness for these kids and for their parents lying dead inside their family home. He was also saddened to learn that Stewart Kingston was one of the victims. He had only known him briefly, but he remembered him as a genuine, decent man who fiercely protected his children.

Jarrod gave Kirsty a subtle gesture to come for a chat.

'I'll be back in a second. You guys will be safe here,' she told the children.

Jamie gave a pained stare, his body restless. 'Don't leave us, please.'

'It's okay. I'll be just over there and I'll come straight back.'

Jamie nodded and hugged his knees. Olivia placed her arm around his shoulders.

Kirsty climbed out from the back of the ambulance and followed Jarrod a short distance out of ear shot.

'How are you holding up, Kirsty?'

'I'll be okay. It's the kids I'm worried about. The brave little buggers found their dead parents. God only knows how they escaped. There's blood everywhere inside the house, it's even on the kids' clothes and feet. Have you been inside yet?'

'No, not yet. I'll go in and have a look soon.' Jarrod paused and looked back over to the children waiting in the back of the ambulance.

He turned to Kirsty. 'I'll have to interview them as soon as they're up to it. I'll see what I can find out from the others, but at this stage we don't want to underestimate what they might be able to tell us. There's no rush, but we'll have to do this properly so we can record their evidence without any risk of it being tossed out in court down the track.'

'I understand,' said Kirsty.

'As far as I know, we've got nothing else to go on at this stage. I need to check out the scene so I'm not going in cold when I interview the kids. Would you mind staying with them for a bit longer?'

'You didn't have to ask, Sarge. These kids are not leaving my sight. I think they trust me now and I want to stay with them. Come on over, I'll introduce you properly.'

'Sure,' said Jarrod.

'How do you know these people?' she asked as they walked back over to the ambulance.

'From an old case.'

Kirsty nodded knowingly.

Jamie and Olivia's eyes followed them, the smallest boy continuing to gaze at the floor.

Kirsty did the introductions with a warm smile. 'Now kids, this scruffy looking man is a police officer as well. His name is Detective Jarrod. Is it okay if he talks to you?'

Jamie and Olivia nodded and seemed less afraid. Jarrod gave them his most reassuring smile, a hollow gesture, he thought. He looked down at his crumpled shirt, jacket and blue jeans. He ran his fingers through his messy hair. What a sight he must have been.

'Thanks Kirsty, although I try not to look this scruffy all the time,' he said lightly.

Kirsty placed her hand on the back of the smallest boy's head. 'This little bloke here is Jake.'

'Nice to meet you, Jake,' said Jarrod.

The boy continued to stare at the floor.

'This young lady here is Olivia and this is her little brother Jamie. I think you've already met Detective Jarrod.'

'You might not remember me. It was a few years ago,' he said.

Olivia and Jamie stared at him.

He continued, keeping his tone light and friendly. 'As Kirsty said, my name is Jarrod. I'm a special policeman because it's my job to talk to kids to make sure they are safe. I don't wear a police uniform like Kirsty because I'm what's called a detective. So, if you guys don't mind waiting here for a bit longer, I'll come back and have a bit more of a chat with you then, alright? Kirsty and these nice ambulance officers will stay here with you.'

Olivia and Jamie nodded in agreement. Jake stared at the floor. Jarrod left them and walked back over to the house, its perimeter segregated by crime scene tape. Jarrod ducked under the tape and climbed the stairs onto the veranda. It was there that he saw the first real physical sign of this nightmare. The wooden front door was splintered with bullet holes.

Long asked Mick to stay at the front of the house to preserve the crime scene and to keep an activity log of who came and went. The backup uniform crew was called over and directed to assist with guarding the front entrance to the property, as it wouldn't be long before the media got hold of the story. They knew the local media monitored police radio channels using scanners and could only assume they knew what was going on and would swarm all over the place in minutes.

They each gloved up and covered their shoes with disposable

crime scene booties from Larry's kit box. Jarrod followed the other detectives into the house through the front doorway, mindful not to disturb any physical evidence. The lock on the door had been smashed inwards as if the killer had slammed it open with great force. The first blood splatter patterns were on the wall to the left of the doorway, about a metre inside. The patterns of reddish-brown drops were in two distinct groupings, one just below head height and the other slightly lower. Small droplets had tumbled and spread across the white wall, making arcs of scarlet.

There were neat holes in the door from the barrage of bullets. Just to the right, a lamp and sideboard had been knocked over and there were blood smears on the carpet. It was there in the hallway that the body of Stewart Kingston lay. It appeared that before he had a chance to open the front door, the killer had sprayed several rounds through the closed door from the outside. The victim had no chance, caught by surprise. He had fallen backwards, knocking over the furniture, before slumping to the floor where he died.

Jarrod stepped closer to the dead man who was lying on his back in a pool of blood around his upper body, soaking his pyjama shirt. His face was turned side on and his eyes were still open, staring down at the floor. He had familiar brown eyes, olive skin and dark hair. The resemblance to Olivia and Jamie was unmistakable.

The other detectives had moved into the kitchen and down the hallway. Jarrod followed, but continued to stare at the dead man. He scanned the lounge room and took in as much information as he could. Happy photos of the three children with Stewart and a blonde woman hung on the walls. There were toys and children's slippers on the carpet beside the television.

He imagined the children playing happily while watching cartoons on TV, being watched over by their father. He imagined a house full of love and warmth, a secure environment for children, a place of safety. It unsettled him knowing the home of a young family could be violated in such a horrific way. Only a short time ago, some vile creature had, in a single instant, destroyed this family.

He walked down the hallway to where the other detectives stood near the body of Anne Kingston, the woman in the photographs. Her blonde hair soaked up the blood from her back wounds. She lay cold and still near the laundry. It appeared she had tried to escape from the killer who had entered the house after shooting her husband. A small set of bloody footprints had been walked from the pool of blood near the woman's upper body towards the kitchen.

Jarrod tried to piece together in his mind the sequence of events. He wondered where the children had been when it played out. Had they seen the killer and witnessed the murder of their parents? The time of night and the slept-in beds suggested they had been woken from their sleep. Like an old film the replay of events ran through his mind. Stewart Kingston had gone to the front door to see who their late and unexpected visitor was. He was shot through the door before he had a chance to open it. Anne must have jumped up and started coming down the hallway, by which time the killer had forced his way into the house and shot her as she tried to flee. She had crawled a short distance before dying where she now lay.

The other detectives spoke in low voices, piecing together the crime scene. 'Righto guys, let's back out and let Carson start forensics on this place. We'll have a better look after he's done,' said Long.

They eased out of the house, careful to avoid walking on any blood or disturbing potential physical evidence. They had touched nothing in the hope that Carson would find some forensic evidence to point to the killer.

They regrouped on the veranda and Long turned to Mick. 'I need you to stop anyone else from going inside.'

Mick nodded indifferently.

'We'll have to call a lot more blokes in on overtime and as soon as possible we'll get someone to relieve you,' said Long.

Jarrod noticed Mick's hands shaking. 'Are you alright, mate?'

'Yeah, I'll be fine, don't worry about me.' Mick looked down at his hands and slid them into his trouser pockets. His eyes met Jarrod's, fixed in an intense gaze. 'But we need to keep an eye on Kirsty. It's hit her pretty hard, ya know, with the kids being involved and all.'

Jarrod nodded and glanced over at the ambulance. The children remained inside, vulnerable and alone.

Mick stared at the shattered front door and the dead man lying on the floor inside the doorway. He turned his face towards Jarrod, his eyes narrowing, expression grim. 'That mongrel has to pay for what he did here. We have to catch him.'

Jarrod felt a heavy weight in his stomach. 'I know mate. This son of a bitch will pay.'

TWELVE

AN unmarked police sedan was waved through by uniform officers manning the roadblock. It made its way down the tunnel of bougainvillea shrubs. The crunch of gravel under its tyres broke the solemn hush that had descended on the homestead. It parked alongside the row of police and ambulance vehicles – eyes squinted and heads turned away from its headlights. The door flung open and the headlights died, the driver's features illuminated by the interior lights. Jarrod recognised the sharp edges of the man's military style flat-top haircut. He barked instructions into the mobile phone pressed against his ear as he swung his long legs out of the car, groaning mid-sentence. The man's wiry frame stood towering and upright as he surveyed the scene, the moonlight catching the silver streaks in his hair. The boss, Detective Senior Sergeant Ross Benfield, had arrived to take over as commander of the investigation.

Benfield hung up his phone. 'Nice morning for it, boys and girls,' he announced, deadpan. His breath appeared as a mist in the chilly air. 'I've only got the basics, so what are we dealing with people?' He directed his question at Murray Long, who fell in alongside him.

They walked towards the house. 'It's a real shit show, boss. The victims are a man and a woman, both in their thirties. Multiple gun shots. Looks like the offender took out the male first at the front door and then the female in the hallway. The three kids are okay. No obvious motive at this stage. The couple didn't stand a chance, poor bastards.'

Benfield turned to Jarrod. 'Righto, O'Connor. The kids are your responsibility. You and Harding keep them safe and see if they can tell you what happened.'

'Yes, boss, we'll take them back to our office for interviews and will pass on any new information. We'll advise Children's Services to organise a safe house.'

'Righto, good. And find out as much as you can about the family history and anything that might establish a motive or identify our man,' ordered Benfield.

Jarrod opened his mouth to speak, but Benfield had already turned his attention back to Long. 'For your info, Murray, I've just gotten off the phone with Crime Operations Branch in Sydney. The Homicide Squad and their Scientific Unit will provide support as soon as they can get here.'

Long shook his head and shot Benfield a look. 'We're the lead on this, Boss. The city boys better not come out here thinking they can railroad us off the case. They've done it before.'

'This isn't a pissing contest, Murray. I have every faith in our ability to manage this case, but we need all the manpower we can get.'

'Yeah I know, Boss but...' Long was cut off by Benfield's raised hand.

'But nothing. It's a done deal.' Benfield's sentence was a full stop. 'I've recalled to duty more of our local guys, both uniform and plain clothes. The city guys will set up a major incident room in the upstairs conference room back at the station. We'll establish the forward command post right here. Have you secured the crime scene?'

'Yes, boss,' said Long. 'Larry's all over it.'

'Position what uniforms we have around the external perimeter to lock down this place as best we can,' said Benfield as he scanned the surrounding shadows. 'I want a media assembly point set up out on the road. I'll liaise with our Media Unit. Media are not to get anywhere near the crime scene. I want another briefing in an hour. Okay?' It wasn't a question.

Long nodded.

'Let's get to it then,' said Benfield.

Jarrod and Brad headed back over to the ambulance where Kirsty and the children sat patiently. The ambulance officers stood at the front of their vehicle, puffing on cigarettes. Fog clung to the air and it seemed to get colder as the morning stretched on, the ground already moist as fresh dew formed. The air was filled with the murmurs of the country. The calls from nearby swallows in their treetop perches echoed down into the creek gully as they prepared for the approaching dawn.

Jarrod was about to talk to the children when something in the corner of his eye caught his attention. It was a subtle movement, a disturbance in the shadows. He sensed a presence about thirty metres away. Behind a line of shrubs a figure skulked closer, hiding in the darkness. Jarrod squinted to adjust his eyes until he made out the silhouette of a man. The man raised an object and pointed it in their direction. *Jesus Christ, a gun?* thought Jarrod. He pivoted and moved towards the man, drawing his Glock from its holster. In that instant, Jarrod was blinded by a series of bright flashes. The camera the man was holding clicked and flashed three or four more times. Brad had also reacted and scampered behind him, his gun drawn. In the back of the ambulance, Kirsty drew the children close to her to shield them from any threat of harm.

Jarrod's vision was blurred from the bright flashes, but he blindly ran towards the man. His initial fears surged into anger. He sprinted into the darkness, hurdling a log fence and bounding towards the man who had turned and run towards the road. A camera dangled from the man's shoulder strap.

'You better not make me chase you any further, arsehole!' Jarrod screamed.

The man kept running.

'Police officer,' Jarrod yelled. He sprinted after the man, making good ground. 'One more warning!' he hollered and at that moment, the man turned and looked back over his shoulder. He didn't see the stack of old fence posts lying on the ground just in front of him and down he crashed, arms and legs flailing about as he fell face first into the dirt. Jarrod was standing over him by the time he rolled over and sat up, his face grimacing in pain, clutching his ankle. The moonlight shone through the fog and there was enough light for Jarrod to recognise the man's face.

'Jim Caxton, I should have bloody well known,' he said, his breathing ragged.

Caxton was a freelance journalist who wrote tacky editorials and inaccurate news reports for the major city newspapers. He had set up an office in Lockyer, which he used as a base when he wasn't chasing stories. He had never let the truth stand in the way of a good story. He was as unscrupulous as they came and Jarrod didn't trust him as far as he could throw him. He had misquoted him in articles and written biased reports on criminal court proceedings, making scathing comments about alleged police harassment or suggestions that police had fabricated evidence.

'I should have known you'd be lurking in the shadows, you piece of shit.'

'Back off, O'Connor. I mean it. What are ya gonna do, shoot me?' Caxton sat in the dirt looking up with an indignant expression.

Jarrod realised he still had his firearm pointed at him. He scanned the immediate surroundings until his eyes fell back onto Caxton.

'Not a bad idea, Jim,' Jarrod whispered. 'It's dark. No one for miles. I'm sure the other coppers will back up my story. Don't tempt me.' He holstered his Glock. 'You're lucky I didn't put a few slugs in your stupid mug back there. What the hell are you doing sneaking around like that?'

'Hey, this is big news. The uniform coppers wouldn't let me through, so I used my initiative. I'm just doing my job, O'Connor,' he said, smug. He stood, brushing the dirt and grass from his cargo trousers and army green photography vest.

Caxton was a life size Ken Doll, with unmoving hair neatly parted to the side and bleached blonde tips, square jaw and fake tan. Aged in his late thirties, he considered himself a local celebrity and ladies' man. He'd now regained his composure and stood upright with defiance.

Brad ran up behind Jarrod, puffing and limping.

'Thanks for the back-up partner. Where did you get to?' Jarrod said.

'I hit the deck like a bag of shit trying to jump over that fence.'

Brad looked at Caxton with disdain. 'What's he doing here?'

'I was just asking Mr Caxton to leave.'

'Hey, as a member of the media, I have a right to cover this story,' Caxton whined. 'Is it true, two people murdered? What about the kids, what are their names and ages and what did they see? Come on, give me something.'

'Follow the correct protocols like the rest of the media and we might throw you a bone, but I'm sure you'll make up what you want, anyway. Piss off before we lock you up for obstruct police and trespassing.'

Caxton folded his arms. 'I'll find out what's going on. I have my ways to…'

'Go!' said Jarrod, pointing to the road.

Caxton backed off towards the road like a spoiled brat who hadn't gotten his own way.

The station had worked hard to develop a mutually beneficial working relationship with the local media. They knew the police relied on them for relaying information to the public. In return, the police gave them as much detail as they could to run their stories. Most of the journalists could be trusted to write balanced pieces. In a small town like Lockyer, the media and coppers sometimes mixed in social circles. The good journos knew the difference between what was for print and what wasn't. They also knew that if they breached the trust of the police, they were cutting off their information supply. Jim Caxton was an exception to the rule. He was an outcast even within the media fraternity.

Jarrod assumed that was the reason he was a freelance operator. He'd burnt too many bridges. No one else would work with him and the networks and major newspapers wouldn't employ him, but they were willing to pay him for trashy photos and beefed-up yarns. How and why he had ended up in Lockyer was a mystery, but they were stuck with him and had no choice but to tolerate him. He was also very dangerous – not physically. He was a wimp and a coward. No, he used his camera, voice recorder and "informants" to dig up dirt against anyone, and Jarrod suspected he wasn't above the occasional blackmail. He was to be treated with caution. He had given them hell after the two boys drowned in the quarry.

Jarrod then remembered the photos Caxton had taken of him and the kids. He shuddered at the thought of their innocent faces becoming front page fodder, but there was nothing he could do. He was tempted to run after Caxton and rip the data card from his camera, but he was gone – disappeared into the darkness. They had no more time to waste. Caxton was just a distraction. They had a job to do. Jarrod and Brad headed back to the ambulance.

It was time to find out what the children had seen.

THIRTEEN

JARROD ushered Kirsty away from the children, who sat silent and stunned in the back of the ambulance. 'Benfield gave the okay for you to be released from the crime scene. You already have a rapport with the kids so you're far more valuable helping Brad and I than hanging around here.'

Her eyes met his and she nodded.

Kirsty enticed the children from the ambulance, leaving the blanket behind. Jarrod noticed their clothes. Jamie and Jake wore winter flannelette pyjamas and Olivia wore a pink nightie, the front smeared with dry blood. They were all barefoot. Jarrod made a mental note to arrange the collection of shoes and fresh clothes from the house once forensics had finished up. They led the children to the car and they huddled together in the back seat with Kirsty.

Jarrod tossed the keys to Brad and slumped into the front passenger's seat. Brad reversed from the house and steered towards the driveway. Bougainvillea formed a floral guard of honour, thorns scraping the car like fingernails. Olivia peered out through the back window, tears running down her cheeks as she gazed back at her family home. The veranda lights became a blur through the cloud of dust that trailed behind. *What was she thinking?* Jarrod sensed she was saying goodbye to her loving parents and to her home. As the house disappeared, she turned away and sunk into the seat.

The uniform police guarding the property allowed them through and they veered onto the dirt road. On the other side of the roadblock, a Channel 8 van was parked off to the side of the road, its bright red paintwork unmistakable. The satellite dish mounted on the roof pointed skywards. Beside it, a cameraman operated a sophisticated camera mounted on a tripod. Upon seeing their approaching vehicle, he flicked on the camera spotlight, blinding them like the sun. The camera fixed onto their position, swivelling and keeping them in frame as they drove by. This would have been the local on-call cameraman. Jarrod guessed the rest of the media from Sydney would not be far. By daylight, the place would be crawling with news crews.

Not much was said on the way back to the police station. Jarrod glanced into the rear vision mirror. Olivia and Jamie huddled together, and Jake snuggled into Kirsty. The children were dozing, and Kirsty gazed out the window. It must have been a draining night for her, the adrenaline of being the first response crew, the discovery of the bodies and then having to protect the children. Jarrod guessed these things were going through her mind now she had time to absorb the gravity of the night's events. He left her to her thoughts as they drove back into town.

Kirsty gently woke the children as they arrived at the police station. Jamie and Olivia climbed out of the car themselves, but Jake clung onto Kirsty. She lifted him from the car and slid him up onto her hip, nursing him with his legs dangling. Olivia took hold of Jamie's hand, assuming the protective big sister role.

Jarrod crouched down beside them. 'Now guys, we're just going to go into the police station and up to our office where we have a special kids' room. We'd like to have a talk with you about what happened tonight. Is that okay?'

Jamie nodded. Olivia's eyes met Jarrod's, her eyes shining. 'Do you want us to tell you about the man who hurt our parents?' Her direct response surprised Jarrod. She was clearly an astute child.

'That's right, Olivia. We'd like to talk to you about what happened at your house tonight.'

'That's alright, I want you to catch him. And Mr O'Connor, you can call me Liv. That's what my friends call me.'

'Thank you, Liv, and you can call me Jarrod.'

Kirsty nursed Jake who had nuzzled his head into her neck. It then occurred to Jarrod the children were not crying anymore and he was amazed by their resilience and courage. He sensed they wanted to tell what had happened, to do their part in catching the person responsible for killing their parents. Jarrod recognised a look of determination in Olivia's face and realised she was trying to be strong for the sake of the boys.

Jamie reached his hand up to Jarrod and he took hold of it. Olivia still had hold of his other hand as they walked towards the back door of the police station. Brad followed behind, scanning the immediate area for any unexpected threats or the reappearance of Jim Caxton.

When they arrived upstairs, they led the children into the Child Protection Unit office and showed them the interview room. About six months prior, Jarrod and Brad had turned a windowless interrogation room into a child friendly interview suite. They had come into the office on their days off and painted the walls a light pastel orange colour with cream trimmings. They lobbied local community groups who donated furniture, toys, DVDs and colour-in books and pens. There were bean bags and lounge chairs, teddy bears and toy fire trucks and police cars along with other donated toys in a large wooden crate. Framed pictures of country scenes and teddy bears hung on the walls.

The police department came to the party and funded the recording equipment, and a video camera was covertly installed into an old stereo unit that sat on top of a wooden cabinet. Inside the cabinet was the recording equipment. A microphone lead ran under the carpet and up the leg of a coffee table in the middle of the room.

It was best to interview the children separately to avoid any later suggestion they were influenced by each other in describing what had happened. Interviewing child victims and witnesses was at the core of what they did as detectives in this specialised field. Despite their training, Jarrod knew it wouldn't be easy. The investigation could hinge on what information the children could provide and they had to be careful not to taint it in any way. Admissibility of evidence was crucial if they were to get justice for the children's parents. They also had to be mindful they were dealing with fragile little people who had just experienced the most horrific loss of their lives.

They sat Jamie and Jake on the floor in their main office with colouring books and crayons. The boys welcomed the distraction from the horror of the past few hours. Brad crouched down to their level and sat on the floor with them. He picked out a Walt Disney colouring book and chatted with Jamie and Jake as he coloured pictures with crayons. Brad was a big kid at heart and seemed to enjoy Jamie and Jake's company.

Jarrod led Olivia into the interview room. He placed the DVDs into the triple deck and pressed the record button. The equipment buzzed for a few seconds and then started recording. Olivia had taken a seat on the lounge chair and was cuddling a white teddy bear she had chosen from the pile of stuffed toys. Jarrod started the interview. The time was 3:46AM.

It was difficult to ease into any structured questioning. He was about to ask a child to describe the murder of her parents. It was his job to get information from her which would be vital to the investigation. He couldn't push too hard. This child had suffered enough, and he was about to ask her to relive the nightmare all over again.

No two interviews were ever the same; there was no script or template to follow. The child dictated the pace and direction of the interview, and it was Jarrod's role, through subtle but deliberate questioning, to assist the child to talk about events without use of leading or suggestive questions. It was a difficult thing to do, to entice a child to disclose details of a traumatic experience.

A year earlier, Jarrod had to interview two little boys who had watched their father stab their mother to death during a drunken domestic dispute. Their distraught faces were seared into his memory. He had hoped he would never have to interview a child under those circumstances again.

Yet here he was, about to meddle with a child's fragile emotions once again, or at least, that's how it felt. A hollow in his stomach grew and he paused, searching for the right words.

'Tell me all about the monster who killed your parents.'

FOURTEEN

THE interview commenced. 'Now, Liv, do you remember what my name is?'

Olivia gave a decisive nod, her eye contact unwavering. 'Yeah, you're Jarrod. You're a policeman and it's your job to talk to kids.'

'That's right. It's quite early in the morning now, isn't it? Are you feeling okay to talk to me right now? Not too tired?'

'Yeah, I'm okay. I had a bit of a sleep before.'

Jarrod leaned forward and spoke in an even tone. 'Okay, well I'd like to have a talk with you about some things that happened tonight. Do you think you could tell me about what happened at your house?'

Olivia stared at him, deep in thought, then nodded.

Jarrod admired her strength.

'A man was in our house,' she began. 'I was woken up by loud noises, like a bomb had gone off. Then I heard more loud bangs. I heard Mummy screaming. She's not my real mum, but we call her that. I ran into the boys' room and Jakey and Jamie were sitting on the floor. They were so scared.' Olivia looked at the floor, tears dripping.

Jarrod gave her a moment. 'And what happened then, Liv?'

'I heard Mummy, um Anne, yell out to us "run and hide, run". She was screaming and crying. There were more bangs, and then it was quiet. I couldn't hear Anne or Daddy anymore. Someone was coming down the hallway. I could hear the footsteps. I opened the window and we climbed out. We just ran into the dark and hid in the bush. Jamie was crying and I told him to be quiet. We left Anne and Daddy in the house. We were scared. We should have stayed and looked after them.'

Olivia sobbed and hugged the teddy bear. Jarrod moved over next to her on the lounge chair. He put his arm around her shoulder and her little body shook as she cried.

'It's okay Liv, we can stop now if you want,' he said. He'd never been so moved by a child during an interview.

Olivia sat up straight and wiped her tears and her strength rose again.

'No, Jarrod, I want to tell you.' She took a breath and continued. 'I told Jamie to stop crying. Jakey never made a sound. I looked back at the house and I could see a man. He was looking out the window. He came out the front door and I was scared he would find us. I could see a gun in his hand.'

'Did you see what he looked like?'

'No, he was too far away. He was big and had something over his head. I don't know what it was.'

'Have you ever seen this man before?'

'No, never.'

'What happened then?'

'Jakey, the little idiot, just ran off. He said that he had to help his mummy. Anne is his real mum. I tried to stop him, but he was too quick. He ran back up to the house and the man saw him and started chasing him. He chased Jake around to the front of the house and I couldn't see them. I don't know why Jake did that. He just ran off.'

'He's a very brave little boy. What happened then?'

'I don't know. It went quiet for a bit. There was another big bang, a gunshot. We were so scared. Jamie was crying and we just hid there in the dark. Jake came running back and he hid with us. The man was looking for us, but he didn't find us.'

'What did the man do then, Liv?'

'I don't know where he went. We waited for a long time and

then we went back up to the house. We needed to see if Anne and Daddy were alright. We walked in and I saw Daddy just lying there. He had blood all over him. He was still breathing but then he stopped. He was so still.' Olivia started shaking and she tightened her fists.

'Where was Anne?'

'In the hallway. She wasn't moving either and there was more blood. They both were just so still.' Her teary eyes met his. 'Why did the man hurt them? Why did he kill our mummy and daddy?' Olivia broke down and cried. She'd had enough. Jarrod wouldn't push her anymore. He turned the recording device off and led her back outside where Kirsty and Brad were chatting with the boys.

Kirsty took Olivia under her arm, and they moved over to the corner of the room and sat on the floor together. Olivia hung her head, shoulders dragging low.

They had to push on. The information the children could provide was vital to the investigation. Jarrod asked Kirsty to contact the Department of Children's Services. They needed to arrange a safe placement and proper supports for the children. Brad volunteered to interview Jamie and they padded off into the interview room and closed the door behind them. Jarrod sat on the floor beside Jake who lay on the carpet colouring in. Jarrod hadn't yet heard him speak.

'And how are you travelling, little buddy?' Jarrod asked.

Jake gave no response and kept on colouring.

'It's okay if you don't want to talk right now. We'll be here to listen when you're ready to talk.'

The little boy's tongue poked out from the corner of his mouth as he concentrated on colouring inside the lines. Jarrod lay down next to Jake, who didn't seem to mind him being there. Jarrod lay on his side with a bent elbow, supporting the weight of his head in the palm of his hand. He could only imagine what Jake was going through, and he wanted to offer him as much reassurance and security as he could. Olivia had stopped crying, and she and Kirsty were sitting quietly together.

There was not much more he could do for the time being. Jamie was being interviewed by Brad, and Jarrod had obtained as much information from Olivia as she could give for now. As he lay on the floor beside the little sandy-haired boy, he wondered what had happened after he had been chased by the killer. In his own way, he had tried to protect his parents. He'd been chased and shot at and somehow escaped. *Did he see the killer? Did he know him? Was he too terrified to say?*

Jarrod drifted off. Lack of sleep was catching up with him. His chin dropped onto the colouring book and he fought against the temptation to sleep. Losing the fight, his head became heavy and his eyelids betrayed him. He was falling, faster and faster, from a great height. His stomach churned from the gravitational pull. Walls closed in around him. He was unable to make out any features around him. He was engulfed by the blackest of black, total nothingness. His hands moved until his fingers scraped against the rough texture of panels of timber. The rich smell of pine wood was familiar. He was suffocating in a box, trapped. Then a sudden crash sent a violent jolt through his body. The collision with the surface of water sent shockwaves through every bone, tendon and muscle. His spine snapped and the pain was excruciating. The box flooded with water. Frigid fluid filled his lungs with every gasp for breath. The box continued to spin and tumble; his senses thrown into confusion. His chest cavity was crushed by the weight of the water. Death was taking hold of him. A ghostly face appeared in the darkness. The facial features melted and distorted, mangled by scars and rotten flesh that fell away, exposing the skull. The grotesque demon hissed and opened its jaw wide, leaning in to bite into his throat. He clenched his eyes shut, bracing himself for the searing pain of the demon's sharp teeth piercing his skin.

He was startled to life from the nightmare, bathed in a lather of sweat. His arm was numb from lying awkwardly on the floor. He had no idea how long he'd been asleep. It seemed like hours, but his watch defied this. Only ten minutes had passed. The interview room door swung open and out came Brad and Jamie.

Jarrod groggily lifted himself to his feet.

Brad looked at him with a concerned expression. 'What's the matter with you? You look like you saw a ghost.'

'That's not the half of it. I'm okay.'

Brad and Jarrod stepped out into the corridor to compare what the children had said in their interviews. It turned out that Jamie couldn't tell Brad much at all. He didn't understand what happened and seemed to be in a state of shock.

'The poor little bugger can't tell me much,' said Brad. 'He heard the gunshots and screaming and said that all he can remember is climbing out through the window with Olivia and Jake. He says he didn't see the killer. He just clammed up. That's as far as I got with him.'

'That's alright mate, we shouldn't expect too much from them at this stage. Hey, can you go and find out what's happening, see if the others have got any more information for us. They'll want to know what the kids have told us. Also, we need the intel guys here to run background checks on the family, find out if there are any other relatives we can contact.'

'Righto, I'm on it.' Brad headed off downstairs towards the communications room.

Jarrod went back into the office where Jake was still colouring in. Jamie and Olivia were flicking through the pages of an animal book. Kirsty sat staring into space.

Jarrod noticed something on Jake's bare feet. Dried blood was caked in between his toes. He guessed he must have walked in his mother's blood as she lay on the floor. Jake made eye contact with him for the first time. He cast a glance at his feet and then stared back into Jarrod's eyes. *Those blue eyes. What had they seen?*

'Hey little man, how about I take you for a bit of a clean-up, would that be okay?' Jarrod asked, not knowing how he would respond, if at all.

Jake nodded and jumped to his feet. Jarrod held out his hand and Jake reached up and held on tight. They headed down the hallway holding hands and Jarrod led him to the bathroom, where he sat him up at the basin bench. Jarrod placed Jake's feet into the sink and soaped up his hands. With warm water, he washed the blood from his toes. The water turned a rich burgundy colour and swirled around the sink before disappearing down the drain. Jarrod scrubbed in between his toes with his fingers until his feet were clean.

Jake reached up and pulled out a few sheets of paper towel and handed them to Jarrod.

As Jarrod wiped the blood of this little boy's dead parents from his feet, a wave of anger tore through him.

Strangely, Jarrod sensed the warmth of the dead couple around him. Stewart and Anne Kingston somehow seemed more familiar to him now. He pictured their faces, not the pale skin and hollow eyes of their dead bodies, but their smiling, living faces. He had a connection to these people through their children.

Jarrod knew he had to find the killer and bring them to justice. Not just because it was his job, but because of the feeling stirring inside him. He had been charged with this responsibility by Stewart and Anne Kingston. The couple were not just the victims of a murder he was investigating, but the loving parents of the three children he now vowed to protect. As their ghostly presence faded, Jarrod imagined the despair the children were experiencing.

Jake was looking up at him and for the first time, he spoke. 'I'm scared. Will that man come back after us?'

'No buddy, you're safe. The man won't find you. We won't let anything happen to you.'

Jarrod spoke in his most reassuring tone, but he wasn't sure how convincing he was. *Was this madman going to come back after the children?*

They had to bring the bastard down before he ever got the chance.

FIFTEEN

AS they made their way along the corridor towards the CPU office, Jake reached up and squeezed Jarrod's hand. They returned to find Olivia and Jamie curled up alongside each other on the carpet, resting their heads on cushions. They appeared drained of all energy, succumbing to their heavy eyelids. Kirsty sat in an office chair in a half daze, watching over them.

Jarrod led Jake into the interview room. Jake plonked cross-legged on the carpet and selected a Banana in Pyjamas colour-in book. Jarrod lowered himself to the floor and sat beside him and they armed themselves with crayons.

Jake coloured in silence, focusing on his artwork with his tongue poking out as B1 came to life with a mix of yellows and greens.

Jarrod began his makeover of B2 on the opposite page with reds and blues.

A few minutes later, Jake stopped colouring and turned his eyes towards Jarrod, wrinkling his nose. 'I don't like snakes. Do you?'

His question came out of the blue. Jarrod pondered for a moment. 'You know Jake, I've never really thought about it, but I guess I don't like snakes very much either. I much prefer frogs. My little girl Katie loves frogs. Even though they have clammy skin and sticky feet, she loves to handle them. She sometimes even gives them a kiss before putting them back where she found them. I like frogs, but I don't think I could bring myself to kiss one.'

Jake giggled. 'Yuck, I wouldn't kiss one. But frogs are nice. We have them under our water tank stand. They croak and sing all night.'

They continued colouring in. Jarrod could tell Jake was deep in thought. Jarrod waited until Jake broke the silence.

'Do you think frogs are scared of snakes?' said Jake.

Jarrod scratched the bristles on his chin. 'I'm not sure, Jake. I suppose they are. Snakes can be pretty nasty. Frogs are harmless little creatures, but I'm sure they are clever enough to hide from the snakes.'

Jake thought some more. 'I hate snakes. That man had a snake.'

'What man, Jake?' Jarrod's ears pricked.

'The man in our house tonight. He had a snake drawn on his neck.'

'What did the snake look like? Can you describe it?'

'It had a scary head and a long, thin tail. The snake was wiggled around a cross.'

'Would you be able to draw it for me, Jake?'

'I think so.' He selected a black crayon and closed his eyes for a moment, concentrating to retrieve the memory. With remarkable precision for a seven-year-old, he directed the crayon on the white space on the page beside B1's waving four-fingered hand. First, he drew the cross with a tall vertical post and shorter horizontal beam. The pointed tail began as a squiggle at the base, spiralling upwards around the vertical post. The large head, with evil slits for eyes and a forked tongue, hooked around the beam and pointed downwards. He coloured in the cross so that it contrasted with the white snake.

'There,' he said, quite proud of himself. 'That's what it looked like.' He rotated the page so Jarrod could see the drawing.

'Where on the man's neck was the snake?'

Tilting his head to the left, Jake drew a line with his index finger from behind his right ear down to his collarbone. 'It was long, from here, all the way down to here.'

'What colour was the drawing on his neck?'

'Black.'

'Did he have any other drawings?'

'That's all I saw.'

'What did the man look like, Jake?' Jarrod pressed, careful not to push too hard.

'I can't remember. I didn't really see his face.'

'Have you ever seen this man before?'

He shook his head. 'Nope.'

'What was he wearing?'

'Um, at first he had a black beanie on his head, pulled down over his face. There were holes for his eyes. He pulled the beanie off his head later. That's when I saw the snake on his neck.'

'What clothes was he wearing?'

'It was all black. He had black gloves on his hands too.'

'Where were you when you saw him?'

'After we heard the first loud bangs, we ran and hid, but I wanted to help Mummy and Stewart. I snuck back up to the house.'

'What happened when you got to the house?'

'I went to the front door and looked in. The man was still in our house. Stewart was lying on the floor and the man was standing next to him. The man saw me and he chased me. He chased me outside and I ran down the side of the house. He had a gun in his hand. I was scared. He shot the gun and it made a big loud bang. I just kept running. I ran back to the trees in the dark where Olivia and Jamie were hiding.'

'What did the man do then, Jake?'

'He ran around, but he couldn't find us. After a while he left. I didn't see him after that.'

Jake had told his story, dry eyed and resolute. 'I don't know why he did that to Mummy and Daddy. Why did he hurt them?' He looked up at Jarrod with big, sad eyes. His bottom lip quivered.

'I don't know, Jake, but we're doing our best to find out. Did you hear any sounds, like a car driving away?'

'No, I didn't hear a car.'

'Was there anyone with the man?'

'No.'

'Did you hear him say anything?'

'No. That's all I know. I can't remember anything else.' Jake buried his face in the crook of his elbow and cried. Jarrod took him in his arms. No more questions. The snake tattoo was a vital piece of information.

Jake continued to cry until his little body slumped fast asleep in Jarrod's arms. Jarrod laid him down on the carpet and propped his head on a cushion. He murmured but fell into a deep sleep. Jarrod closed the interview room door and stepped back out into the office where Olivia and Jamie lay on the floor asleep. Kirsty was typing up her witness statement on the computer. 'I figured it was best to get this done now,' she said.

'Good idea. Well, we may just have gotten our first break. Little Jake has given us a tattoo.' Jarrod held up the drawing.

Kirsty's jaw dropped as she let out a gasp.

'I need to pass this info onto the guys in the MIR.' Jarrod hurried out of the office.

The Major Incident Room hummed with activity. Phones rang and police radios chattered non-stop in the background. The intelligence officer had arrived and Jarrod gave him the new information about the tattoo. He photocopied the drawing and searched the criminal history data on the system. A persons of interest description search was initiated and suspects with matching or similar neck tattoos were flagged. The complete search would take some time as the data had to be cross-referenced with other systems and interstate data. It would become a process of elimination to identify possible suspects. It was a hit and miss process and depended on the accuracy of information entered into the system. But for the first time Jarrod was optimistic, it was their first genuine lead.

He passed on the additional information they'd been able to

glean from the interviews with the children. In particular, he provided a rundown of his previous dealings with the family.

Jarrod returned to his office to check on Kirsty and the children. Olivia and Jamie slept soundly.

'Poor little buggers. Do you think they understand what has happened tonight?' said Kirsty. 'I mean, it's just so much for anyone to go through, especially little kids.'

'It's hard to say,' said Jarrod. 'I'm sure it'll hit them pretty hard once they've absorbed everything. But you know, I think kids are more resilient than we give them credit for. They have their own way of coping.'

'I don't know how I should be feeling. I keep asking myself if there was anything else we could have done out there, could we have stopped this?'

'Kirsty, you did a great job out there. There was nothing else you could have done. What you're doing now is more important than you might think. These kids will remember you and everything you did. You're human. That blue uniform doesn't change who you are. And the kids have seen that you are more than just a blue uniform.'

Kirsty stared at him for a while. 'Jarrod, when you first spoke to Olivia and Jamie, you said you knew them. How do you know them?'

'I arrested their mother for assaulting Olivia. Poor woman had lost the plot. From all accounts, she'd been showing signs of depression or some kind of mental illness for a while leading up to it.' He paused, remembering the details of the case.

'What happened?' Kirsty asked.

'I remember the interview with Olivia. She described her mother throwing her about the room, punching her in the back, pulling her hair and scratching her face with her fingernails. The thing is, it was all over a drink that Olivia spilt on the floor. That's all it took to trigger the violent outburst.'

'What happened to the mother?'

'Well, she went to court and pleaded guilty to serious assault.

She was sentenced to two years' probation because of her clean record. She was ordered by the court to have her mental health assessed. I don't know if that ever happened and I lost track of her. I've had no dealings with the family since. I'll never forget the interview I had with the woman; Clare Kingston was her name. Her mood swings were all over the place. At first, she denied assaulting Olivia and seemed confused as to why she was even being interviewed. She then had sudden outbursts of aggression saying that Olivia deserved it, followed by remorse and tears. She was on another planet.'

'What about Olivia? How badly was she hurt?'

'She had no fractures, but she was pretty messed up. She was covered in bruises and scratches. She was a tough little kid. I hadn't seen her again until tonight. Stewart Kingston got custody of the kids. I heard they later divorced.'

They sat in silence for a while. 'I couldn't do your job, Jarrod. Doesn't it get you down? I mean, all this, seeing kids abused all the time?'

'I'd be a liar to say it doesn't get to me. I don't know why I've been doing it for so long, I just keep coming back to work each day.'

'But surely you could transfer to another division, like CIB or traffic?'

'Yeah, I've thought of that, but I guess I'm a creature of habit. I suppose I feel some ownership of my job. We don't have too many happy endings but when we do it's all worth it. We've pulled kids out of some pretty shitty situations. It's sad though because we can't save them all. We can only just keep doing one job at a time. Sometimes that's not enough, but it's still worth trying.'

The truth was, he was bound to the job after all those years. He couldn't just walk away.

'Anyway, I need you to stay here while I check in with the boss out at the crime scene. Can I get you anything? Coffee?' he said.

'No thanks. And Sarge, thanks for the chat, it was good to talk to someone.'

'Don't mention it, these jobs can be pretty tough, but you'll be alright.'

Before long, daybreak came. Rays of sunlight pierced the window blinds in bright shards, bathing the carpet in a crisscross of iridescent colours. The rising sun banished the gloom of that horrible night.

The start of a brand new day filled Jarrod with renewed optimism.

SIXTEEN

THE one who called himself the Venom of God, stood alone draped in darkness, surrounded by the eerie silence of the abandoned chapel. The rotting floorboards creaked under his weight. A damp chill hung in the air. Paint crumbled from the walls. The gloomy building was a ghostly shell of an era long gone. Floating dust particles sparkled in the air, energised by rays of the dawn sunlight beaming through holes in the roof. The sagging ceiling beams, covered in spider webs, served as perches for pigeons nesting in the decaying house of God. Decrepit wooden pews were all that remained of the internal furnishings. The ghosts of those who once worshipped and sang hymns there still lingered.

The place of worship was dying, falling victim to vandalism, theft and decay. Most of the once ornate stained-glass windows had been smashed or boarded over, however one remained intact. At the centre of the windowpane at the highest point of the A-framed roof glowed the image of a serpent curled around a cross. The sunlight shone through the window, illuminating the image that personified who he had become. He believed he was the Angel Sammael, who for centuries the Jews had referred to as the Prince of Demons. The tattoo on his neck represented the angel who had disguised himself as a serpent to tempt Eve in paradise. He believed his master was the supreme angel, The Angel of Death, to whom God gave orders as to which souls were to be taken. These orders were transmitted to Sammael to be carried out.

Before meeting his master he was a pitiful soul, dabbling in petty crime and substance abuse. All his life he'd been ridiculed, belittled and told he was "not right in the head". They said he was a sick son of a bitch when he tortured animals. They said he was insane. Maybe he was insane, but he embraced who he was. His body was a vessel sheltering the true spirit inside, desperate to be unleashed. His desire to inflict pain on others intensified, driven by a growing sense of anger at the world and unrelenting defiance. Torturing animals was just the beginning. Something inside his heart told him it shouldn't feel so good, but in the end, he gave in to his inner temptations and allowed his killer instincts to flourish. It was pointless to resist his natural urges.

He remembered an old parable he learned in primary school called "The Wolf I Feed". Once upon a time, there was a Cherokee grandfather who told his grandson, 'There are two wolves inside me. One wolf is white, good, generous and kind. The other is black, mean and greedy, violent and angry. The two wolves are in a constant fight within me.'

The grandson, with wide eyes, asked, 'But which one will win, Grandpa?'

The grandfather said, 'The one I feed.'

He had chosen to feed the black wolf.

It was his master who taught him to discover his true self, to unleash the inner black wolf. Hunched up in a pathetic ball in the dirt of the prison exercise yard, he had endured a beating that would prove to be his salvation. They kicked his ribs and head without mercy; it was the closest he ever came to believing he would die. No one came to his aid. At the time, he didn't understand why they had focused their attention on him. He later realised that in prison, no one needed a reason. It was about power and asserting dominance. Every chance they got, they humiliated and beat him. They broke him.

But on this occasion the beating had stopped. He heard the

blood curdling sound of snapping bones, cries of pain, fists striking skulls and cracking jaws. The confrontation ceased and the battlefield fell silent. He opened his eyes, squinting from the bright sunlight. It was as though the hand of God itself had emerged. As his vision cleared, the outstretched hand of the stranger reached down, helping him to his feet.

He was captivated by the man's eyes and in that moment, he knew his salvation had come. The stranger's first words were the most powerful he'd ever heard. 'Take my hand, my brother, and no longer will you be the prey. Join me and become the hunter. Or lie there and be a victim for the rest of your life. Choose now.'

He reached up his hand and the man's powerful grip lifted him to his feet. Strewn around the prison exercise yard like discarded rubbish were the thugs who had beaten him. They squirmed in the dirt in agony – broken limbs, blood gushing from their noses. He turned to the stranger. 'Teach me to be the hunter.'

As he was led away by his new master, he spat on the gang leader and kicked him in the ribs. As another gang member clambered to his knees, he kicked him in the face. The crack of the man's nose breaking gave him a surge of energy he'd never experienced before. An insatiable hunger for revenge burned.

His master turned and smiled.

From that point, his master nurtured and mentored him, convincing him he had an exceptional role to play in a grand plan.

He abandoned his fears and doubts and followed his destiny. He followed the teachings of his master, who gave him guidance, wisdom, empowerment and protection. His master was an intermediary between the divine and the human; between Earth and the heavens.

Together they studied the bible, focusing on scriptures describing the power of the angels. This became their doctrine, a code they swore to live by. After their release from prison, they maintained their friendship and his master continued to mentor him, promising him eternal power and glory if he swore allegiance to him.

They discovered the abandoned chapel and it became their secret meeting place. They sacrificed animals and performed blood rituals and it was there that his conversion to a higher being occurred. He was reborn as the Prince of Demons. He brought *her* to their secret place and her relationship with the master flourished. They shared their secrets with her and she embraced their vision for vengeance and eternal peace. She performed the fire ritual and gave herself to the master. So too did other disciples who swore to live by their secret code.

It was there in the old chapel that the three kindred spirits swore a secret blood oath, a death pact to help each other fulfil their destinies. The plans had been made and they each knew the part they had to play. They were three broken souls, but together they would become whole and find eternal peace.

But now their plans were unravelling, spiralling out of control. He had failed and soon he would face his master's wrath.

He was terrified.

The pigeons became unsettled and with the flapping of wings, feathers and straw fluttered into the air as the birds scuttled out through broken windows.

Someone was coming.

Sammael waited in silence where an altar once stood.

It had to be him.

Boots stomped up the stone steps. His master appeared.

Soon his master would learn of his failure.

'Good morning, brother,' his master said in a soft but commanding tone. 'We don't have much time. Her journey has begun. Where are the children? Where are their bodies?'

Sammael dropped to his knees, legs weakened. He was at his master's mercy now. He bowed his head, too fearful to look into his eyes.

'Look at me! Where are the children?'

111

'The man and woman are dead. I killed them,' whimpered Sammael. 'The children escaped. I couldn't find them. I'm sorry.'

'What do you mean they escaped? How is that possible? We had planned this. You knew what had to be done.' The rage in his master's voice intensified

'Give me another chance. I'll find them and I'll bring them to you. Let me do this. I won't fail again.'

His master placed a hand on Sammael's shoulder. 'Stand up.' He helped him to his feet and embraced him like a loving father.

'Did anyone see you?' he whispered in Sammael's ear.

'I don't know, one of the children might have, but I don't think he saw my face,' Sammael said. Like a feeble child, he muttered, 'I'm sorry, I won't fail you again.'

'I know you won't fail me again,' the master whispered. He plunged a dagger blade into Sammael's abdomen with deathly speed.

Burning pain ripped through Sammael's body as the blade twisted inside him.

A second blade strike ripped his chest.

The Angel of Death cradled Sammael's weight in his arms as his knees buckled from underneath him. Sammael gasped for air, choking on blood.

As his life force drained from him, his master whispered into his ear. 'You failed your mission, but you have proven your loyalty, my brother. You have earned the honour of the ritual of fire. Your remains will be turned to ash and your soul committed to the angels. Soon I will join you in paradise.'

SEVENTEEN

OLIVIA and Jamie were moved into the interview room with Jake. With the lights turned off, they slept for a few hours, nestled on blankets and sofa cushions on the floor. Kirsty sat on the floor, leaning upright against the wall. Jake lay fast asleep with his head resting on her lap. She was pinned, but made the most of the opportunity to rest her eyes.

Jarrod and Brad leaned back on their office chairs, feet up on desks. Jarrod jostled about but couldn't get comfortable. There was no use trying to sleep. His eyes burned and his exhausted body ached. His mind raced with flashbacks of the events of the past twenty-four hours, replaying over in jumbled sequences.

His thoughts returned to Clare Kingston. *Could she have been involved?* They needed to track her down as a priority; she was their only other lead so far. The dead couple had no criminal history and he doubted they had any enemies. He was baffled as to the motive. Stewart and Anne Kingston led simple lives that revolved around their children. Stewart had worked from home as a civil engineering consultant and Anne worked at the local primary school. *Who could possibly want these people dead?* Nothing made sense. The murders were planned. It was no botched robbery. Nothing appeared to have been stolen from the house. *What were the killer's intentions for the children? Was he trying to kill or abduct them?*

By 8AM the police station was abuzz and the children stirred. For the most part, they had kept the children isolated from the frantic activity unfolding around them. Jarrod rummaged through the downstairs meal room cupboards and refrigerator, finding the essentials to fix the kids an improvised breakfast: strawberry jam and peanut butter toast and glasses of milk.

He clumsily balanced the plastic plates and cups back up the stairs to the CPU office.

'Breakfast is served. What do you think, kids?' he said, peering into the interview room.

The kids' eyes lit up at the sight of their police room-service breakfast delivery. The toast and milk were a real hit. 'Yum,' said Jake, with peanut butter smeared across his cheeky grin. They all laughed. It was a momentary but welcome distraction.

Brad made instant coffees for himself, Kirsty and Jarrod, which they savoured while watching the children finish the last of their toast and milk. Although Kirsty had finished her shift at 6AM, she wanted to stay on. Word was received that the Department of Children's Services had found a temporary foster safe house for the children until more permanent arrangements could be made. Kirsty offered to remain with the children until they arrived.

On call support officers from the Homicide Squad in Sydney had arrived and were setting up in the MIR. Jarrod wandered down to see if he could get an update. The forensic officers were still at the crime scene and the on-site detectives were conducting a grid search. Inquiries were being made with residents of neighbouring properties. Gunshots had been heard, but no information regarding vehicles had come to light. It was likely the killer had entered the property on foot. A forward command post with radio communication was now well established at the scene. Local intelligence officers had teamed up with the Homicide Squad officers and were conducting background checks on the deceased couple. It was important to find any link that would provide a motive for the killings.

Sarah Morgan, a relatively green Children's Services Officer, arrived after some delays and spoke with the kids. Olivia, Jamie and

Jake, still dressed in their pyjamas, prepared to leave. They all held hands to be led out of the interview room by Sarah. In that short time, a bond had been formed and it was time to say goodbye, for now anyway.

Jarrod knelt so that he was at eye level with Jake. 'Well, guys, it's time for you to go now with Sarah. She'll take you somewhere safe. You'll get to have a wash and put on some clean clothes. I'll arrange for someone to go to your house and collect some of your own clothes and we'll drop it off to you later. Is there anything special you each want from your house?'

He knew the house would be secured by the crime scene officers for hours yet and they didn't want the children to be taken back there. Olivia was the first to reply. 'I have a gold heart-shaped locket on a chain. Dad gave it to me for my birthday. It's got a photo of me and him in it. It's on my dressing table.'

'Sure thing, we'll get that to you, I promise. What about you, Jamie? Anything special you'd like?'

'My skateboard, it's under my bed. Oh yeah, my Nintendo Switch, it's in my school bag,' he said after great consideration.

'Done,' Jarrod replied. 'And my little mate, Jake. What would you like, buddy?'

He stared at Jarrod thoughtfully. 'My Paddington Bear teddy, he's on my bed. My mummy kisses me and my Paddington every night.' His eyes lowered and tears welled. 'I want my mummy now. Why has she gone?'

To Jarrod's surprise, Jake leaned forward and placed his arms around his neck and squeezed. The little boy held tight and cried. Jarrod held him until he let go. Jake brushed away the tears with his pyjama's shirt sleeve.

'Now this isn't goodbye,' said Jarrod. 'We'll come and see you as soon as we can. It's just while we sort some stuff out, okay? You've all been so brave. We're here for you, don't forget that.'

Kirsty said her goodbyes and they led the kids down the stairs.

Brad met them at the bottom of the staircase. Jake stopped and turned to Jarrod. 'That man who hurt our mummy and daddy, where is he now? Is he going to come back?'

I don't know, thought Jarrod, but he kept that to himself. He paused and looked at Brad and then back at Jake. He knelt to Jake's level. 'Jake, Brad will go with you guys and Sarah to a safe place. Brad will stay there with you until another officer is available to relieve him. We'll have a police officer with you at all times. We're doing our best to find this man, and when we do, you will be the first ones to know. Does that sound okay?'

Jake nodded. Sarah gave Jarrod a business card with the contact number and address of the safe house.

'How about another ride in a police car?' Brad said to the kids.

Jamie shrugged. 'Sounds okay,' he said with indifference.

They walked out the back door of the station and Brad led Sarah and the kids into the car park. The three children held hands, Olivia in the middle with the boys on either side. Olivia looked back over her shoulder. It was the same look she had when she stared back at her house as they drove from the murder scene. Those sad eyes remained fixed on Jarrod until she rounded the corner of the building. It was a tough moment. Kirsty stared out into the car park long after the children were out of sight. An emptiness lingered in the air.

It was a beautiful but strange morning, the air crisp and cool. The cloudless sky was an infinite deep blue up above and, through bleary eyes, it seemed brighter than usual. The warmth of the sun made Jarrod's skin tingle, giving him a sense of hope. However, the morning daylight highlighted the weariness in Kirsty's face. The darkened areas under her bloodshot eyes were prominent. She looked exhausted.

'They'll be okay,' said Jarrod. 'It'll take time, but they'll be okay.'

'I hope so, Jarrod. I really hope so.' Kirsty turned and headed back inside. She tried to conceal the tears, wiping them away with her fingertips.

Jake's question replayed in Jarrod's mind.

'That man who hurt our mummy and daddy, where is he now? Is he going to come back?'

I don't know.

EIGHTEEN

THE intelligence officers had made some progress with suspect profile searches. The database identified three potential persons of interest who were recorded as having similar snake tattoos. Gino Vincent Lancetti, forty-three years of age, was the first suspect. Along with several other tattoos, he was recorded as having a serpent and cross on the left side of his neck. He had an extensive criminal record dating back three decades. He started his illustrious life of crime as a juvenile committing break and enter offences, with a talent for stealing motor vehicles. This progressed to drug offences, serious assaults and armed robbery.

He had been in and out of prison for most of his adult life. More recently, he had been identified as having links with outlaw motorcycle gangs and was suspected of being involved in drug trafficking and the sale of restricted semi-automatic weapons. His most recent conviction was for his involvement in a stolen motor vehicle re-birthing racket. There were no hits on the database relating to any activity in the last eighteen months.

He had either gotten smarter and was avoiding detection or he had moved interstate. Jarrod's bet was that he had left the state. A criminal with that much history and links to organised crime doesn't just stop coming to the attention of police. Intel officers liaised with interstate police departments to track down his last known whereabouts.

The second suspect was Alfred Norman McPherson, fifty-three

years of age. He was also recorded as having a tattoo of a snake on his neck, but the description did not include a cross. It was soon established that McPherson had been in prison for the last two years for a rape conviction. Confirmation was received that he had been sitting in a prison cell at the time of the murders. They could safely rule him out as a suspect.

The third suspect was Edward Marcus Ryan, twenty-one years of age. He was recorded on the Corrective Services database as having a snake tattoo on his neck. Records indicated he had spent the last five years in and out of juvenile detention institutions and remand centres in Sydney. His criminal history included sexual assaults on young girls, attempted abduction of a boy, arson and unlawful killing of animals.

He had been charged with torturing and killing puppies, kittens and birds after breaking into a pet shop. He had warnings on the system as being violent and mentally unstable. One particular court recommendation referred to him receiving drug counselling for his addiction to sniffing inhalants, known on the street as "chroming". He appeared to have no connection with the town of Lockyer, but his profile was a red flag. Since being released from Westgate Correctional Centre earlier in the year, he had flown under the radar.

It was all they had to go on, their only real leads.

Clare Kingston needed to be located. Ross Benfield had called a briefing to be held at the MIR at 10AM. The detectives at the crime scene were returning to the station while forensic officers continued their meticulous examination of the house. The bodies of Anne and Stewart Kingston had been transported by the undertakers to the morgue.

Before the briefing started, Jarrod had time to pay someone a visit, someone who might know Edward Ryan.

Jarrod unlocked the steel door and heaved it open. Curled up asleep on a vinyl mattress beneath a watchhouse blanket laid Thomas Barton. The mattress rested on a concrete slab which formed the base of the bed. As Jarrod entered the cell, Thomas sat up. He gazed around the cell, rubbing his bug-eyes with his fists. Jarrod looked around at the familiar sight of the grey walls scratched with initials of previous inmates, the stainless-steel toilet bowl and drinking fountain. An empty plastic bowl, spoon and cup were neatly stacked on the floor inside the doorway.

'Good morning, my old friend. How have you been enjoying our five-star accommodation and room service?' Jarrod said with a forced smile.

'What do you want?'

'Well, I'm glad to see you've slept off the grog. Woken up on the grumpy side, have we?'

'What do you reckon? Getting locked up isn't my idea of a good night out.'

'Hey, at least you've had a cup of coffee and some breakfast. I reckon you've had about ten hours more sleep than I have.'

Thomas just stared back with a miserable scowl on his face. He didn't seem in the mood for chit chat.

'How's your eyes this morning? That shit is pretty potent, hey?' Jarrod said, referring to his recent dose of capsicum spray.

'Yeah, you got that right. I don't wanna go through that again.'

'Well, that's up to you, mate. About yesterday, what was that all about, anyway?'

'I dunno. It was just the bourbon. The stupid thing is, I can't even remember what Lisa and I were arguing about.'

Jarrod sat down beside Thomas and their eyes met. He saw the naïve and confused look of the boy he had come to know over the years. 'Thomas, you and I go way back. We haven't always seen eye to eye, have we?'

'No, we've had our blues over the years,' Thomas said with an emerging smile.

'Have I ever bullshitted to you?'

Thomas folded his arms and shook his head. 'No, you've always been straight with me, Mr O'Connor. Although tricking me with the mobile phone yesterday was a bit of a dog act,' he smirked.

Jarrod was glad he saw the humorous side. 'Well, drastic times call for drastic measures.'

They shared a smile.

'So, why the visit? Haven't you got more important things to do than shoot the breeze with me?'

'Well, Thomas, at the moment you might be one of the most important people I know, depending on how you might be able to help me.'

'Help you? What's the catch?'

'Let's not get ahead of ourselves, Thomas. You got out of Westgate Correctional Centre not long ago, yeah? When did you get out?'

'Three months ago, and I've kept out of trouble since. Oh, except for yesterday. Why? What's going on?' His eyes narrowed and his lips tightened with a look of suspicion.

'Did you ever come across a guy named Edward Ryan? He's about your age.'

Thomas deliberated the question. 'Edward Ryan. Oh yeah, Eddie. I know him. He's mad as a cut snake, that guy. I once saw him bite the head off a Blue Tongue lizard for no reason at all.'

'I need to know a bit about him.'

'Hey, wait a minute! I'm not gonna dog on anyone. Do you know what it's like in the joint for dogs? No chance, Mr O'Connor. I'm not saying nothin'.'

'I'm glad you mentioned the joint. You're what, twenty years old now? Happy birthday, by the way. I forgot to send a card.'

'Yeah, right,' scoffed Thomas.

'My point is, until now you've only done time in the remand section. If you do a stretch for these fresh offences, you'll be with mainstream prisoners. A good-looking, fresh lad like yourself would be popular among some of those bad bastards serving long sentences. Do you know what they might do to a nice boy like you?'

Thomas lowered his eyes. 'Yeah, I get your point.'

'The thing is, mate, you'll go before the magistrate tomorrow because of yesterday's little incident. I don't like your chances of getting bail. To make things worse, you'll probably end up with some dipshit Legal Aid solicitor who will care more about what he's having for lunch than whether or not you get bail. But I can speak to the Prosecutor. With a good word, we should be able to make application to the court for conditional bail. Lisa got bail last night. You'll get to see her. How does that sound? That's my offer.'

'You reckon you'll put in a good word, hey? Will that count for much? How do I know I won't still get sent away?'

'There's no guarantee, but you need as many people in your corner as possible and with my personal recommendation to the magistrate, with reporting conditions, you stand a good chance of getting bail.'

Thomas rubbed his chin. 'Okay, what do you want to know?'

'Good man. Tell me about Eddie.'

'Well, I don't know much about him. He was a weirdo. I didn't hang around him. He was always getting beaten up. Them other fellas said he was a rock spider, ya know, a kiddy fiddler. He was fucked in the head, too much chroming. He kept saying that soon everyone would see how powerful he was, that he would start killing people. They reckon he heard voices in his head. He should have been in the looney bin.'

'When were you and Eddie in the lockup together?'

'Earlier this year. He got out a few months before me.'

'Have you seen him around here in Lockyer since you got out?'

Thomas rubbed the auburn bristle on his throat. 'No, I haven't seen him. He's got no reason to come to this shithole town.'

'Do you know where we might find him?'

'Nah. I hardly ever spoke to him. I had my own problems with some of those arseholes in there. If I made friends with him, I'd have got bashed as well.'

'Did he have *any* friends?'

Thomas considered his answer. 'There was this one bloke, real scary bastard. Eddie had been getting bashed by this gang who called themselves "The Brotherhood". They bashed Eddie every chance they got. It went on for weeks. The screws knew what was going on, but they did nothin' to stop it. Turned a blind eye. The leader of the gang was Jimmy Nguyen, a Vietnamese guy on remand for armed robbery. This one day in the exercise yard, the gang were laying into Eddie, more violent than usual. I reckon they were deadset trying to kill him. This bloke came out of nowhere and stood up for Eddie. Well, Jimmy didn't like that one bit, so the gang came after him as well. Bad decision. By the end of it, Jimmy had a broken jaw, two of his gang boys were pretty smashed up and the others ran off like chicken shit. From then on Jimmy and his gang left Eddie alone.'

'What was this guy's name?'

'Can't remember,' said Thomas.

Jarrod raised his eyebrows, sceptical.

'Mr O'Connor, honest. I met a lot of blokes in remand and I can't remember a lot of names. He was a real scary fucker though. Had evil eyes. They hung around each other a lot after that. This guy gave Eddie a home-made tattoo, some weird symbol. It was on his forearm. Eddie reckoned this was the sign that he was the "demon of death" or some crap like that. I reckon this bloke wanted Eddie to be his bitch in the lockup. You see that a fair bit inside. People protecting other people, but nothin' is for nothin'. You know what I mean, Mr O'Connor?'

'Yeah, I know what you mean, Thomas. Nothin' for nothin'.'

Jarrod stared into Thomas' eyes. 'I want you to think hard. Are you sure you can't remember his name?'

'Nah, buggered if I can remember.' Thomas shook his head, his eyes shifting to the ceiling as the cogs in his neocortex worked overtime.

'Did Eddie have any other tatts?'

Thomas pursed his bottom lip and nodded. 'Yeah, he got a few prison tatts.'

'Any on his neck of a snake?'

'Yeah, he did,' his eyes lit up. 'A snake wrapped around a cross. His crazy mate did it for him.'

Jarrod produced a sheet of folded paper from his shirt pocket. He pressed out the creases and showed Thomas the photocopy of Jake's drawing of the killer's tattoo.

'Did it look like this?'

Thomas took hold of the paper and considered it thoughtfully. He nodded. 'Yep, that's what it looked like, just like this.'

Thomas looked up at Jarrod and his inquisitive expression changed to a look of suspicion. 'Who drew this?'

'I can't say, but it's serious. Some people died last night.'

'No way! Who? What happened? I haven't heard shit being locked up in here.'

'A man and a woman were shot in front of their kids. A real sick bastard did it, Thomas.'

'And you think Eddie was involved?'

'I don't know, Thomas. That's what I'm trying to find out. If you can remember that other guy's name, you'll be doing me a huge favour.' Jarrod hesitated and then placed a hand on Thomas' wrist. 'This is important, mate. I need your help.'

'I'll do what I can, Mr O'Connor. If I remember his name I'll tell the watchhouse sarge.'

'Thanks, Thomas. I've got to get to a briefing right now, but we'll chat again. I'll do what I can about your bail, I promise.'

Jarrod got up and was about to leave the cell when Thomas called out. 'Oh, one more thing, Mr. O'Connor. Where's my mobile phone?'

Jarrod smiled. 'It's in with your property. You'll get it back, don't worry. I'll see ya around, mate.'

NINETEEN

DETECTIVE Senior Sergeant Ross Benfield shuffled documents on the lectern at the front of the conference room. A large contingent of uniforms, intelligence officers and homicide squad detectives were seated around tables in a 'U' formation. Local detectives stood at the back of the room, wearily leaning against the wall. Most were showing the first signs of fatigue and frustration. The aroma of instant coffee wafted throughout the room. Brad had been relieved at the safe house and had just returned to the station. Jarrod raced back up from the watchhouse and made it to the briefing just in time.

Benfield assumed control, as always. 'Righto, listen up!'

The rowdy chattering and murmuring fell silent.

'The investigation into the murders of Anne and Stewart Kingston will be known as "Operation Bravo Paradox" for future operational reference,' began Benfield. 'I'd like to welcome our colleagues from the Homicide Squad as well as scientific and intel officers from Sydney. I expect to see nothing less than full cooperation utilising all our combined resources.' He paused. 'Ladies and gentlemen, let's not lose sight of what we're dealing with. Stewart and Anne Kingston were executed in front of their children in their own home. We have a moral and professional obligation to get closure on this one as soon as possible, not to mention the pressure from the media. On that note, no one, I repeat no one, is to make comment to the media. Media inquiries are to be directed to the Police Media Unit. All investigators will remain on duty until otherwise advised, overtime has been approved.'

There was a collective groan. Although the offer of overtime pay was attractive, most officers in the room knew how these investigations played out. Working long days on end, no sleep, no fresh clothes, take-away meals on the run, and little contact with family.

Katie would be at school and Matty was probably watching Play School. Jarrod had missed the morning chaos, children's chatter during breakfast and of course, those precious hugs and kisses. He was scared he was missing too many of those magical moments. Sometimes the line between responsibilities for the job and family was blurred. He knew Jayne would understand. He would call her the first chance he had.

Benfield continued. 'I'd like to call on Detective Murray Long of the local CIB to provide a briefing as to what we've been able to establish at the crime scene.'

Long stood and made his way to the lectern. He looked weary, but Jarrod knew he relished his moment in the spotlight. Long gave Benfield a nod and then scanned his eyes around the room. 'First, to brief you on what we do know. Anne and Stewart Kingston were both shot with a .38 calibre handgun in their home sometime between midnight and 1AM. Subject to post-mortem results, it appears the deceased male was shot three times in the torso and the female was shot three times in the back. Assuming that a revolver was used, the killer would have had to reload. Two shells have been located in the house. The emergency telephone call from the little girl was received at 1:05AM. Witnesses on neighbouring properties heard the gunshots, but at this stage we have no information about any vehicle the offender may have used. He most likely approached the Kingston property on foot. Robbery does not appear to be the motive. As you all know, the three children escaped. We can safely assume this was a planned hit on the family and that the children were also likely targets.'

Benfield interjected. 'Thanks, Murray. Detective O'Connor, I understand you have obtained some crucial information from the children. You also had some dealings with this family in the past. Your briefing, please.'

Long glared at Jarrod, his mouth gaping. He rolled his eyes and stepped away from the lectern.

Jarrod rose to his feet and crossed the room to the front, all eyes following. He scanned the room full of exhausted police officers. Jarrod realised he must have been a comical sight, hair ruffled, unshaven, shirt hanging out. He straightened himself up as much as he could and stood at the lectern. He felt ill prepared.

'Thanks Senior.' His words caught in his dry throat. He gave an awkward cough and tried again. 'Um, yeah thanks, Boss. From the interviews with the children, we've been able to ascertain that a sole male offender, face covered with a black balaclava or similar disguise, entered the house having first shot Stewart Kingston. His wife was the next victim. She warned the children before she died and they managed to escape. One of the children ran back to the house and saw the offender. He recalls seeing a tattoo on his neck of a snake wrapped around a cross. The intel guys have identified three suspects from the database with similar tattoos. The first, Alfred Norman McPherson, is in prison and can be safely ruled out. The whereabouts of the second suspect, Gino Vincent Lancetti, is still unknown.'

Long piped up again. 'Hang on. How do we even know this isn't just a red herring? How did the kid see the tattoo if the guy was wearing a balaclava? How reliable is this info?'

All eyes in the room bounced to Long and then back to Jarrod.

'Well,' he paused. 'Jake – that's the boy's name by the way – says he went back into the house to help his mum. The bloke had taken off his balaclava. He chased Jake outside and fired a shot at him. He's pretty shaken up. He can only describe the tattoo, but he did a pretty good drawing of it.' Jarrod held up the colouring book and all eyes locked onto the seven-year-old's drawing. Eyebrows raised and there were impressed nods.

Long folded his arms and pursed his lips, dismissive.

A senior constable, who Jarrod recognised as an intelligence officer from Sydney, hung up a phone and raised his hand.

'Yes, what is it? Speak up,' said Benfield.

'I've just gotten word from detectives in Melbourne. Lancetti did surface about six months ago, but disappeared under suspicious circumstances. He was under surveillance as part of an undercover drug operation. He had connections to bikie gangs and they think one of his deals went bad. His car was found on the side of the freeway three months ago and fresh blood was found in the boot. He hasn't been seen since. They expect to find him floating in a river or in a barrel somewhere.'

'Suck shit, Gino,' someone muttered under their breath. There were murmurs and chuckles around the briefing room.

Jarrod continued. 'Well, bad news for Mr Lancetti, but that now reduces our known suspects down to just one, Edward Marcus Ryan, twenty-one years of age. He's recorded as having a similar tattoo and has a history of mental illness. There's plenty of red flags, but we haven't yet established if there's a link between Ryan and the Kingstons.'

Benfield had been reading through job logs while Jarrod was speaking. He looked up over his bifocal glasses as though he'd just remembered something. 'And your previous dealings with the family, Jarrod?'

Jarrod nodded. 'Oh yeah, Boss. About three years ago, I arrested Clare Kingston, the mother of Olivia and Jamie, for a serious assault on the girl. I had brief dealings with the father and the children at that time. Clare Kingston presented as being mentally unstable. She could be a major player in these murders. She may have motive against her ex-husband and his new wife, but I don't understand why she would want the children dead. I believe the kids would also be dead if Anne Kingston hadn't warned them.'

'No shit, Sherlock.'

Jarrod recognised Murray Long's voice from the rabble. No one laughed this time, frowning eyes from all over the room locked onto Long. His Cheshire grin dissolved. Jarrod ignored him.

'What about the kids? What's happening with them?' one detective from Sydney asked, breaking the awkward silence.

'As you can appreciate, they're pretty shaken up. They've been taken to a safe house with a rotating twenty-four hour police guard.'

Benfield replaced Jarrod at the lectern. 'Thanks Jarrod. Now, listen up everyone. You will work in teams to canvas background information regarding Clare Kingston and this Edward Ryan. I want them located and brought in.'

The conference room door flung open and a fresh-faced constable walked in. 'Sorry to interrupt, Senior, but I think you'll want to hear this,' said the young officer with an air of self-confidence. Benfield called him over with a wave. The officer approached Benfield and covered his mouth with his hand as he whispered in his ear, just out of earshot of the rest of the room. A restless rowdiness spread from person to person like a Mexican wave. Benfield gave a nod and dismissed the junior officer. He turned to address the room with a stern frown. He waited for everyone's full attention. The room fell silent.

'Ladies and gentlemen, Clare Kingston has been found deceased. Apparent suicide. Her body is up on Outlook Ridge.' Benfield considered his next move for a moment but was decisive. 'Jarrod, I want you and Detective Harding to head up there now. Take up with the uniformed officers who've secured the scene.'

Jarrod was shell-shocked. His brain was still processing the news.

'With respect, Senior,' interrupted Long. 'Wouldn't it be wiser to send a detective from the CIB?'

'And why would that be, Detective?' asked Benfield, knowing full well what Long was implying.

'Well, the CIB is more qualified to be attending a suspicious death. No offence, O'Connor, but I think the CPU should stick to dealing with kids and let the CIB deal with the serious stuff. We need someone with a bit of investigative nous going to a scene like that.' Long avoided eye contact with Jarrod.

'No offence taken,' Jarrod said with a sarcastic smile.

Benfield cut in. 'The competence of my Child Protection Unit officers has never been questioned. Jarrod has a greater insight into this family than anyone here. He's dealt with Clare Kingston and knows her background. Do you have a problem with that, Murray?' Benfield said with a sharp edge to his voice. It was a rhetorical question.

'No, Senior. No problems,' Long said under his breath.

Benfield continued. 'The CIB officers are to continue with witness statements, background checks, door knocks, all the usual. All investigation logs are to be completed at the end of each inquiry and lodged here in the MIR for collation. Locating Edward Ryan is now our priority. Next briefing here at midday. Briefing terminated.'

Benfield stepped away from the lectern and bulldozed his way out of the room. The crowd dispersed and everyone went about their business. Long gave Jarrod a hard stare. Jarrod found Brad and said loud enough for Long to hear, 'Come on mate, let's get out of here and let the real detectives do their job.'

In minutes, they were on their way to Outlook Ridge.

TWENTY

THE face of the slate rock cliffs stood as the backdrop to the town of Lockyer. Brad negotiated the winding road, cable guardrails offering the only protection from skidding off the edge of the mountain. They wound their way up the spiralling road until they reached the picnic area at the summit, parking beside a marked police car. It was a popular picnic spot during the day for tourists and families who came to experience the scenic view over the hinterland and beyond towards the coastline. A pathway led to a lookout platform perched at the very edge of the highest ridge. Any other time, it would have been a lovely place to come. Jarrod had brought his own family to the nearby playground for kids' birthday parties. Katie and Matty loved standing on the lookout platform, watching the flow of cars cutting through the valley like a line of ants, travelling along the highway between town and the coast. But on that morning, a sinister stillness hung in the air.

Clare Kingston's body couldn't be seen from the lookout. She had been found by a woman taking her dog for a morning stroll along the walking tracks. Jarrod and Brad were met by the uniform officer guarding the scene. He led them down to the area cordoned off with chequered police tape. In a thicket of bush, just below the lookout, a woman's naked body dangled by her neck from a rope tied to a tree limb.

The lonely, silent figure of Clare Kingston was an eerie sight. She had been strangled by a well-crafted noose. Her legs were slightly bent and the tops of her bare feet rested on the grass, as though she had simply lowered herself until the rope supported her body weight. She would have slowly lost consciousness before dying of restricted blood flow to the brain. This was not a violent suicide, unlike others Jarrod had seen, where irrational minds had flung themselves from a great height, snapping and stretching their necks in the process. From a distance, her body resembled a department store mannequin that had been hung from the tree in some sick prank. Her lifeless body was pale in contrast with her long, jet-black hair.

Her eyes and mouth were closed and there was no sign of blood or external injury. In death, she seemed at peace. Jarrod circled around the body and recognised the pretty face of the erratic woman he had once interviewed. Her belongings, comprising a set of keys, a purse, a black cloak and sandals, were neatly bundled at the foot of the tree. Her locked car had been parked in the car park near the picnic area. It wasn't the act of a deranged mind. She knew what she was doing. It seemed well planned. There was a sense of purpose, something deliberate about the location.

Jarrod's attention was drawn towards a sparkling object hanging around her neck from a leather strap. As he leaned in for a closer inspection, he made out the shape of a glass cube. It had been cut and polished with the craftsmanship of a diamond. Encapsulated within the cube was another cube. Internal geometric shapes emerged depending on the angle he viewed the cube. He could make out three-dimensional images of pyramids, pentagons and octahedrons. The beautiful pendant was mesmerising.

He tried to make sense of it all. *What had led her to commit suicide in this place and in this way? Her death surely had to be connected to the Kingston murders, but how?* The black cloak, the strange token around her neck and the remote mountain location created a sense of a pagan-like ritual. Her death had a ceremonial feel to it.

Clare Kingston could no longer provide those answers. Her

silence was eternal.

They remained at the scene until the scientific officer, on loan from the double homicide crime scene, completed his examination. The evidence pointed to a simple suicide, but something troubled Jarrod. There was something they were missing, a hidden message they were yet to interpret. They found nothing in her car that gave any insight as to what motivated Clare Kingston or drove her to suicide. A crowd of onlookers had gathered beyond the cordoned area. The government undertakers cut Clare's corpse down and zipped her inside a black body bag. They lifted her onto a trolley and wheeled her over to their van.

Jarrod's thoughts were with Olivia and Jamie. Within twelve hours, both their biological parents were dead in separate incidents, one a violent execution murder, the other suicide. Their father died before their eyes and soon they were to find out about their mother's death. He hated the thought but it was only right that he be the one to tell them. *God damn it! How would he break such news after what they had just gone through?* She was still their mother; they were still bound by a maternal bond. The kids would take the news hard.

As he and Brad snaked their way down the winding mountain road, Jarrod imagined Clare Kingston driving up there alone, knowing she would never make the trip back down. As though thinking out loud, Brad said, 'What was her connection to the murders? I mean, the timing of her suicide and the murder of her ex-husband and his wife are just too coincidental.'

'I've been thinking the same thing,' Jarrod replied. 'What really troubles me, is the idea she might have wanted them all dead – the children as well. Maybe she somehow orchestrated the whole thing?'

Jarrod mentally grasped about to put the pieces together. 'I know it's a long stretch, but if Edward Ryan is our trigger man, how is he connected to Clare Kingston?'

They continued to drive in silence, pondering over the strange sequence of events of the last day. They soon pulled into the driveway of Clare Kingston's house, nestled in a quiet, leafy street. Old ladies with hair rollers and slippers chatted over the fence as they watered their gardens. Dogs barked at the postman buzzing along the footpath on his scooter. The remaining houses were locked up and lifeless, their occupants at work for the day. As they entered Clare's front yard, Jarrod wondered if the neighbours had ever taken any interest in her or noticed her erratic behaviours. Maybe she concealed it well, keeping up normal appearances on the outside. He guessed she suffered in isolation, the world going about its business all around her. He made a mental note to canvass the neighbours.

The house was a neglected, unassuming weatherboard cottage. The sun-bleached picket fence had palings missing and the front gate, with broken hinges, lay on the ground just inside the fence line. The gardens were overgrown with weeds and knee-high grass grew wildly on either side of the pathway leading to the front landing. All the windows were closed, and the hinges covered in cobwebs. The curtains were drawn.

Jarrod jingled the keys they had found among Clare's possessions and after some trial and error, he found the front door key. He turned the ornate doorknob and the door opened with a creak. As the stale air entered his nostrils, he brought a hand up to cover his mouth.

As Jarrod pushed the door wide open, Brad stood back and watched on, one arm clasping the other at the elbow. 'There better be no more God damn dead bodies in here.'

Jarrod just gave him a glare in return.

'What? Nothing would surprise me today. Who knows what skeletons this crazy woman has in her closets.'

'Crazy is a relative term,' said Jarrod. 'Don't be too quick to judge.' The truth be told, Jarrod was also anxious about what they might find. He stepped inside the gloomy house. Boxes were stacked high along the walls. Nothing happened when he flicked the first light switch. Either there was no power or the bulb had blown. It took a few seconds for his eyes to adjust to the dimly lit room. The lounge room was like a small maze. Boxes, newspapers, clothing, rubbish and various household items were stacked into huge piles that almost touched the ceiling. A thin walkway of worn carpet wound itself around the pillars of stacked junk. The room represented years of hoarding and a deeply disturbed mind. The hallway was the same. The walls were lined with more boxes, books and toys.

Brad remained in the doorway, reluctant to come inside. 'My God, how did she live like this?'

'She was a very unwell woman. God only knows what demons she was living with.' Jarrod's words floated through the empty house. 'Go and get the torches from the car, will ya.'

'Yeah righto, don't go anywhere,' said Brad as he scurried out the front door.

As Jarrod waited for Brad to return, he stood inside the doorway, alone in the disturbing house. He imagined another time when the house was bright and alive with the echoes of Olivia and Jamie's voices. He could only imagine the tormented existence this woman had since endured.

Jarrod, lost in his own thoughts, was startled when Brad returned and placed a hand on his shoulder. 'And then there was light.' Brad shone a Mag Light torch around the living room. He handed Jarrod the other torch and scanned the room in a slow arc of light. They ventured further inside. Jarrod flicked another light switch in the hallway, but still nothing. 'Check out down the hallway. I'll look over here.'

Brad disappeared down the narrow hallway, the light from his torch flickering on the ceiling. Jarrod squeezed his way through the clutter, particles of dust dancing in the torchlight. The first bedroom leading off to the right was impossible to enter. It was cluttered with mattresses, cupboards and stacked chairs. More boxes were stacked on the furniture and on the floor right up to the doorway. It was as if everything had just been thrown into the room over the years until there was simply no more space left. He stepped back out into the hallway. The dark maze then led him out onto a side sunroom.

He wondered how long it had been since any sunlight had shone through the barricaded windows. He stumbled over a child's tricycle and in the darkness he reached out to regain balance. He fell against a pile of stacked books and clothes, knocking everything onto the floor with a loud thud.

'Are you alright?' called Brad from the far side of the house.

'Yeah, I'm fine,' Jarrod yelled, brushing cobwebs off his clothes. He sniffled from the dust and musty air. He climbed over the pile on the floor and found a closed door. He was hit by the stench of mould as he opened the bathroom door. Piles of damp clothes and towels covered the floor, the plugs were in the basin and the tub which were both full of stagnant water. Cockroaches scampered along the floor and up the walls when the torchlight entered the room. The toilet was beside the bathroom. Jarrod decided to leave it for now, he didn't have the stomach for it. He ventured back along the path through the lounge room and into the kitchen. He pressed the switch and the fluorescent light bulb flickered to life in a dull glow with a *tink-tink-tink*.

He scanned the room. The sink tap was rusted and appeared to have not been in use for a long time. Rubbish bags were piled on the floor and benches. Empty milk cartons, food tins and cereal boxes were everywhere. The fridge door hung open. It was empty and covered in mildew. Dirty dinner plates were stacked in the sink.

'Brad, where are you?' Jarrod called out, but there was no answer. 'Hey, where are ya?'

Silence.

Then from another bedroom, 'Holy shit! I'm in here. You gotta come and see this.'

Jarrod negotiated the piles of clutter in the gloomy hallway and followed the dim glow of Brad's torchlight dancing on the walls from within another bedroom. He found Brad standing with his back to the doorway, shining his torch around the room. The carpet had been rolled up, exposing the timber floorboards. The room was strangely free from clutter, in complete contrast to the rest of the chaotic house. Jarrod stood beside Brad and studied the floor. A blanket and a pillow indicated a person had been sleeping there. On the floor beside the makeshift bed, stood a shrine of candles and framed photos of the Kingston children. The hardened candle wax had dripped onto the floor, the flames long since extinguished.

Crucifixes, a wine goblet and porcelain angel figurines were set out on the floor in a semi-circle. Jarrod shone the light on the photos and knelt for a closer look. The photos were of a much younger Olivia and Jamie. The portrait of a once happy family had the faces of Stewart and Clare scratched off, leaving only the images of the smiling children.

Jarrod shone his torch around the room and made out images scrawled across the walls, crudely painted in black and red. He recognised an image prominent on all the walls among other cryptic inscriptions and three-dimensional geometric shapes. A hexagon was the focal point of each series of drawings. Each corner formed the centre of small circles. Lines were drawn from the corners through the centres of other circles within the diagram. More lines were drawn between the centres of these circles, forming a complex matrix of shapes within the hexagon. Jarrod then remembered the glass prism that hung from its axis around Clare Kingston's neck. That prism was a three-dimensional version of the same image. He didn't yet understand the significance of the image, but it seemed to represent a significant part of her life, and possibly her death.

Brad moved over to the window and pulled open the thick curtains. Sunlight penetrated the dusty windows and an image on the ceiling emerged through particles of dust catching the sunlight.

'Whoa, take a look at that,' whispered Brad, his head tilting uncomfortably and eyes drawn upwards.

Etched in charcoal and sprawled across the entire ceiling, a horned creature spread its bat-like wings so that it hovered in mid-flight, looking down through all-seeing, slitted eyes. A female with flowing hair, her stare filling the room with a dark emptiness. Just what it was, Jarrod was not entirely certain, though he guessed it represented a fallen angel or demon of some kind. It was an image from his blackest nightmares, a thing too hideous for this world, sprung from the flaming pits of hell. Her gaze burned into his eyes, looking into his soul.

A cold shiver shuddered through his body. He felt like he needed to get out of that house before she claimed his soul and haunted him forever.

TWENTY-ONE

JARROD called Benfield from his mobile to give an update on Clare Kingston's suicide and the search of her house. The CIB detectives were still having no luck locating Edward Ryan. He had not come to the attention of police in Sydney since his release from the remand centre. Inquiries were being made with previous associates and at old haunts he used to frequent, but there was no trace of him. If he had come to Lockyer recently, he had kept a very low profile and they had no idea where to start looking for him. Most resources were now being deployed to locate Ryan. Benfield directed Jarrod and Brad to continue with all leads relating to Clare Kingston.

They drove into the Lockyer Base Hospital and followed the signs to the Mental Health Unit, which was some distance away from the main hospital complex. The MHU building was a weathered, dreary looking red brick structure with colonial timber verandas and railings in need of fresh paint. The building was partitioned off from the car park by a high, thick hedge. More dense shrubs formed a screen down the sides of the building, which created a sense of privacy and isolation from the general public.

As Jarrod and Brad entered the main reception area, they were greeted by Dr Alex Wright, the head psychiatrist. He was a distinguished looking man who reminded Jarrod of George Clooney. Jarrod had phoned ahead to arrange the meeting. Alex had helped them out in the past by conducting mental health assessments on witnesses. He often assisted police who had taken suspected mentally ill people to MHU for assessment and regulation for their own safety and that of the community.

'Jarrod, Brad, good to see you both again,' he said, extending his hand.

'Thanks for seeing us at such short notice. We really appreciate it,' said Jarrod.

'Don't mention it. Come into my office.' Alex led them down a long corridor to his office and closed the door behind them. He joined Jarrod and Brad on the comfortable leather chairs centred by a coffee table, rather than sitting behind his desk.

'I've had the files on Clare Kingston pulled as you requested. Her suicide is sad news indeed,' he began, shaking his head in frustration. 'I thought we were making progress with her. Sadly, Clare wasn't my first patient to take their own life and she won't be the last, but that's the grim reality of my line of work. It's always terribly upsetting, as there's a feeling of failure on our part.'

'I understand,' said Jarrod. 'What can you tell us about her?'

Alex retrieved a thick file from his desk. As he opened the folder, Jarrod recognised Clare Kingston in the black and white photo pinned inside the cover. Alex flicked through the reports. 'Well, it's all here, her complete history with our unit. It depends on what you need to know.'

Jarrod leaned forward. 'Clare Kingston's ex-husband and his new wife were murdered last night. We believe there might be a link between this incident and her suicide.'

'My God, that's terrible. I saw the news reports but there were no names mentioned so I didn't realise the connection.'

'We need to know what her state of mind has been like over recent times and if she revealed any information to your staff that might shed some light on all this.'

Alex examined the file, flicking through the documents. 'Well, we haven't seen her for some time. According to the file, she was first referred to us nearly three years ago by the Magistrates Court as part of her sentencing order and she was diagnosed as suffering from clinical depression. I remember she was a very troubled woman when she came to us. She demonstrated symptoms of bipolar disorder, in particular, cycling mood swings, that sort of thing. The initial case assessment was to regulate her and conduct a full evaluation. She spent six months here as a voluntary in-patient.'

'What was the treatment?' Jarrod pressed.

'Well… a series of psychological evaluations. A diagnostic was conducted to determine if her cognitive functions or memory were affected because there was certainly some confusion in her thought patterns. Clare responded well to antidepressant medications as well as psychotherapy. But unfortunately, she discharged herself. Our community case workers attempted further intervention with Clare at her home, but she refused. Without further medication and therapy, her condition may have deteriorated.'

'So, in general, how would you describe her mental state when you last saw her?' Jarrod asked.

'The depression Clare suffered from was manifested by a combination of symptoms affecting her ability to live a normal life. She experienced mood swings ranging from mania to feelings of hopelessness. At times, she was confused and suicidal. When she wasn't responding to treatment, she had symptoms of grandiose notions.'

'Meaning what, delusions?'

'I suppose you could call them delusions. Clare started having fixations on what I'd describe as fantasies. I suspected she had other underlying mental health problems, however we weren't able to make an accurate diagnosis.'

'What sort of fixations did she have?' Brad asked.

Alex adjusted his sitting position to face Brad. He seemed to struggle to find the right words. 'How can I say this? She believed she had a guardian angel.' He paused, allowing Jarrod and Brad time to process this.

141

'A guardian angel?' said Brad, raising one eyebrow.

'Yes, that's right. But she was also focused on things such as the afterlife and being reunited with loved ones. She studied the bible and spent hours drawing pictures of angels and symbols. She became quite obsessed with angels, to the point that she was convinced this guardian angel of hers was real. She often referred to him as having taken the shape of a man who walked among us and that one day he would free her. This troubled me because of her suicidal history and perhaps this was her way of glorifying suicide.'

'Did her suicidal tendencies progress to actual suicide attempts?' Jarrod pressed.

'She did demonstrate self-harming behaviour. She cut her arms and legs. This disorder is quite common and is often a result of self-loathing. We tried to address this by restricting access to sharp objects, around the clock supervision and by providing counselling.'

'This guardian angel,' Jarrod said, searching for the best way to put it. 'Did they exist? I mean, was there a real person who Clare referred to as her guardian angel?'

'Quite possibly, she may have modelled this belief around some person she admired or was fixated on, but I don't know who. The whole idea was formed while she was an inpatient. It could have been a fantasy that resulted from her relative seclusion, her way of creating some kind of make believe companion.'

'Did she have contact with other patients?' Brad asked.

'The patients who were in the low security wing spent time in the communal lounge room or gardens. Some patients made friends and we encouraged that as they often support each other. I seem to recall that Clare pretty much kept to herself.'

'Did she have any visitors?'

'Not that I recall. She seemed isolated from the rest of the world. I knew she had two children who lived with the father, but she had no contact with them during her stay here. In fact, I don't remember anyone contacting her at all.'

Jarrod held up his mobile phone and showed him a photograph of the drawings on the wall in her house. 'What do you make of this, Alex? It seemed to have some significance in her life and she wore a similar pendant. She had other symbols painted on the walls and religious items.'

Alex studied the photo. 'It could mean something or it could mean nothing. I don't know what to make of it. Her delusions may have manifested into something that, in Clare's mind, became quite real.'

'Can we have a list of patients who were admitted when Clare was here? I'd like to know who she may have been having contact with,' Jarrod asked, half expecting the answer that came.

'Jarrod, you know I'll help you where I can, but confidentiality is a real issue here for us. Besides, we have many patients and most of them have long files as they often come and go over time. It would be very time consuming to identify what patients may have been here during that six-month period, unfortunately our data base has limited search facilities. The whole system is very out-dated. We've been trying to get funding for a tech upgrade but you know as well as I do the Government budget is tighter than ever before.'

He studied Jarrod's face, maybe reading his mind. He was a psychiatrist, after all. He sighed. 'Okay look, if you can provide me with more specific information, I might be able to pull out the relevant files, but no promises.'

'Thanks Alex, but our problem is that we don't really know what we're looking for, any connection between the murders and Clare Kingston's suicide. We have a suspect, Edward Marcus Ryan, twenty-one years of age. He could have mental health history. Are you able to run his name through?'

Alex made some notes. 'Sure, I'll do what I can. It might take time though. We'll have to search databases from other mental health institutions.' He stopped, remembering something. 'Actually, I do seem to recall that sometime after she left here she was admitted into hospital in the city following an overdose of antidepressant pills. She would have had follow-up mental health treatment in Sydney, but I'm not sure where and when. Leave it with me. I'll see if I can pull some strings. I probably won't have any information for you until tomorrow.'

'We appreciate your help, Alex,' said Jarrod, shaking his hand.

As Jarrod and Brad walked out into the car park, the sun was already setting. Time had gotten away from them. It had been a long day. Jarrod climbed into the car and leaned back against the headrest, his head pounding. He looked over at Brad, whose facial expression was cadaver-like, not just sagged but lacking its usual liveliness completely. Jarrod's head felt heavy, as though he was struggling against far more gravity than usual.

Exhaustion had become their constant companion.

TWENTY-TWO

WHEN Jarrod and Brad arrived back at the MIR, a handful of Homicide Squad detectives were still making phone calls and entering investigation logs into computer terminals. The intelligence officers were collating the information, separating probable leads from red herrings. Despite a huge allocation of manpower and resources to the operation, no real leads had emerged regarding the whereabouts of Edward Ryan. No other suspects or motives for the murders had yet been uncovered. Scientific samples had been conveyed back to Sydney for analysis. Overall, they still had little to go on.

Benfield called Jarrod over for a summary of the background information they had obtained about Clare Kingston. There wasn't a lot more they could do for the time being and they were authorised to finish for the day. Jarrod and Brad completed their investigation logs and tidied things up in their office. They switched off the lights and as Jarrod closed their office door, they were met by Murray Long at the top of the stairs. Jarrod had no intention of making small talk and wasn't in the mood for Long's bullshit. Long had different ideas.

'Ah, it's the legendary kiddie cops. Solved the murder yet?' he started.

'No, Murray, we thought we'd leave that to you real detectives,' Jarrod said in a controlled tone. He didn't want Long to think he could bait him.

'Don't worry, boys. Tomorrow you can go back to bum smacking or whatever the hell it is you blokes do in your little warm and fuzzy office. We'll sort out the real police work.'

Brad stepped up to Long, right up in his face. 'Oh, you mean like finding Edward Ryan? How's that coming along? I take it you haven't found him yet. How about we let you know once we've tracked him down and you can take the credit for it. That's what you real detectives do, isn't it?'

'Watch your mouth Harding, at least we lock up real bloody criminals. I don't have time for dealing with the shit you do, chasing after kids and all that crap. I can't believe Benfield is giving you blokes so much input into this investigation. You're both out of your league.'

Brad's face ignited red with anger, a bad sign. 'So, if a kid gets abused, we have the expertise to interview the child as well as interviewing and arresting the adult offender. Last time I checked, you still rely on us for this because you're not trained or competent at interviewing children. And you call us the inferior detectives. I could do your job blindfolded, you arse-wipe!'

Long exploded and grabbed Brad by his shirt with both hands. 'Right, that's it you little smartarse.'

Brad retaliated by holding onto Long's jacket collar, pulling him off balance. Long's height advantage meant nothing to Brad as they bounced off walls in the corridor, grappling with each other, locked in an embrace. They were as determined as each other, neither willing to back down.

'If something happened to a kid of mine, there's no way in hell I'd want the likes of you investigating it, you arrogant son of a bitch,' said Brad as they wrestled.

Jarrod stepped in like a boxing referee, separating them with his body, prising them apart. 'For Christ's sake, settle down,' he said, standing in between them.

They both let go and Long finished with a shove to Brad's chest.

Brad stumbled back and moved to pounce at Long again, but Jarrod cut him off with his body, restraining him by the shoulders.

'Brad, it's not worth it, mate, leave it.'

Brad focused on Jarrod and then glared back at Long, who was straightening up his jacket collar.

'I'll be seeing you around, mate,' spat Long with a sarcastic smile. He gave a sadistic wink and strutted off down the corridor towards the MIR. The confrontation seemed to do little to affect his arrogant swagger and he disappeared around the corner.

'That bloke's an arsehole, Jarrod.' Brad's eyes glared down the hallway after Long. Breathing heavily and all fired up, he was ready to go round two.

'I know, mate, some things never change. I don't worry about blokes like that anymore. Don't let him get to you. I'm way past justifying myself to the likes of him.'

'Easier said than done. I should just go down there and…'

'No mate, he's not worth it. Come on, let's get the hell out of here before the boss changes his mind and gives us another inquiry to chase up.'

Brad took in a deep breath and let out a long sigh. The fire in his eyes faded. 'Yeah, righto. Let's get the hell out of here.'

It soon occurred to Jarrod that he hadn't eaten all day and that he'd forgotten to call Jayne. On the way out, he fished out his mobile and dialled home. 'Hello, sweetheart. I'm so sorry I didn't call. There's been a lot going on.'

'Yeah, I know, Jarrod. The kids are asking for you and I didn't know what to tell them. Is everything okay?' she asked with concern in her voice.

'Yeah, I'm fine. How are the kids doing?'

'They've had a good day. They're just in the bath.'

'I'll be home soon. I'm heading out the door now.'

'I'm glad to hear it. See you at home.'

Home. He couldn't wait.

'Daddy!' cried Katie as Jarrod walked in the door. She ran to him in her pyjamas and slippers and hugged him around his neck as he knelt down to her. He heard the pitter-patter of little feet and Matty came running down the hallway. He nearly knocked Jarrod over and they rolled in a play wrestle on the carpet. Katie jumped on him as well until they both had him pinned on his back.

'Hey, dudes. How's Daddy's favourite little people?'

'Good,' they chimed in unison. More hugs and kisses all round and Jarrod sat up. Jayne stood in the kitchen doorway with a stern look on her face. He thought he was in for it for not calling her. He was ready to make more apologies, but her frown became a soft smile. He stood up, a kid hanging onto each leg. He dragged them with him as he walked over to Jayne. They embraced in a loving hug. The scent of her familiar perfume and her warm body against his was comforting. After a long sensual kiss, they discovered two little people looking up at them grinning. Jarrod met Jayne's eyes. 'Hey girlfriend, how you doin?' he said with his best Joey Tribbiani impersonation.

'Just fine, lover boy.' She kissed him again.

'After all these years, we've still got it, baby,' he said, now switching to an Austin Powers English accent. The kids laughed and Jayne's beautiful smile shone. It was a corny scene, but God it was great.

After the last two days, this was the best remedy. They goofed around for the rest of the night. After dinner, Jarrod and Jayne enjoyed a glass of white wine and then it was time for bedtime stories. Katie, Matty and Jarrod lay in Katie's bed cuddling until they dozed off together. Jarrod savoured the distraction.

However, as he drifted into a deep sleep, he was lured back to that horrible, yet familiar place where his dreams shifted to dark nightmares. The ghosts of the quarry lake came for him once again.

He fell from a great height, sickened by that all too familiar, gut-wrenching sensation of losing his stomach as gravity pulled him towards the murky water. He struck the water with a violent impact and cold water flooded into his throat and nose filling his lungs. The sensation of drowning was suffocating. Deep in the water, just below his feet, two ghostly figures leered up at him, their eyes begging as they reached up desperately for help. Stewart and Anne Kingston, their faces deathly pale and covered in blood, stared at him with terror in their eyes. Their screams, muffled by the water and bubbles, were heartbreaking. He reached for them with outstretched hands, but they were just out of reach. Skeletal arms wrapped around their bodies and limbs from the depths beneath, pulling them deeper into the abyss. Several sets of cruel blood red eyes appeared from the darkness. One of the grotesque demons swam towards him and hissed with venom and hatred. It reached up and grabbed his arms, pulling him deeper. Stewart and Anne were gone.

Jarrod awoke from the terrifying nightmare, startled by his own cries. In a momentary state of confusion, he looked around the dimly lit room trying to get his bearings. The glow of Katie's nightlight reminded him of where he was. Katie and Matty slept soundly beside him, snuggled together under the warm doona in the small bed. He was thankful he hadn't woken and scared the hell out of them. The remnants of the nightmare clung to his mind, haunting. He was lathered in sweat and his heart raced, his mouth dry. He pulled himself from the bed and made his way through the darkness to the kitchen. Leaning against the open fridge door, he guzzled cold water.

He took a hot shower and then climbed into bed beside Jayne. He was still haunted by the nightmare and his mind raced.

She rolled over sleepily. 'I was wondering if you were coming to bed. I didn't have the heart to wake you. You and the kids looked so cute sleeping together.'

He didn't answer and stared at the ceiling.

'What's the matter?' she asked.

'I had another nightmare. It was so real this time. They're getting worse, more vivid, more terrifying. I can't remember the last time I had a good night's sleep. This time the murdered couple were screaming for my help, but I couldn't help them.'

'You know none of this is your fault, stop torturing yourself. There was nothing you could have done to save those boys and that poor murdered couple.'

'Yeah, I know, but try telling my subconscious that. I don't know what's wrong with me. Sometimes I feel like I'm losing my grip on things. Everything's so screwed up. This case is making things worse.'

'You'll get through this, you always do. Stop being so hard on yourself,' she whispered, running her fingers through his damp hair.

She nuzzled her head into his neck and he savoured the smell of her shampoo. Her heart beat against his. It was the comfort he needed. He drifted back to sleep and the ghosts left him in peace, a brief reprieve.

They had tormented him enough for one night.

TWENTY-THREE

THE next morning, Jarrod shuffled barefoot down the front stairs in his pyjamas to collect the newspaper lying in the dew on the front lawn. He padded back inside but was jolted to attention when he opened the newspaper. Plastered on the front page was a photograph of him standing beside the Kingston children as they sat in the back of the ambulance at the murder scene. Their bewildered faces had been exploited by that bastard Jim Caxton for the sake of a headline.

Their faces were blurred as a token effort to conceal their identities. The headline read 'Children Survive Bloodshed'. Jarrod halted in his tracks and read the article. *Last night, three young children eluded the brutal killer of their parents in a courageous struggle for survival. Sources confirm there were long and unnecessary delays in police arriving at the scene, allowing the killer to elude capture. Poor police response times, placing the community at risk, is yet again under scrutiny. Sources confirm that...* Jarrod folded the newspaper in disgust.

'Arsehole. Sources, my arse,' he said out loud. He wondered how much the smug bastard got paid by the newspaper for the photo.

He went back inside to re-join the organised chaos. The ritual of breakfast and preparing for the day had begun. The house was filled with the comforting hum of chatter. Katie jabbered on about school and her friends while Matty sat in his highchair giggling with his breakfast smeared all over his face. Jayne and Jarrod crossed paths on occasion as they got themselves ready and shared household chores. By 7:45AM it was time for Jarrod to head off. His precious time with his family seemed to be allocated in rations. The department was always banging on about finding a work-life balance. What a joke.

'Daddy,' said Katie as he knelt down to give her a cuddle. She stared into his eyes.

'What is it, little girl?'

She wrapped her arms around him and squeezed. He held her body tight, her heart beating against his chest. 'Have a good day at work,' she whispered into his ear.

She pulled away and smiled. Her little face had changed little since she was a toddler, not to him anyway. She was growing up though. His baby girl was now in a school uniform and wearing her hair in pigtails.

'I'll try my best, my little angel. You have a wonderful day at school today. I want to hear all about your day when I get home, okay?'

'Okay, Daddy,' she said and ran off into her room.

Jarrod kissed Matty on the head and he waved both hands.

'Bye bye, Daddy.'

Jayne kissed him on the cheek, her breath warm and familiar. 'Ring me when you know what time you'll be coming home, just so I know you're okay.'

'I will, I promise.' He started heading out, but something struck him. He paused at the doorway and then turned to face her. 'Wait, I'm so sorry I haven't been around much lately. The only time we seem to see each other is when I'm rushing off to work. I haven't even asked how things are with you. I've been so caught up with, well, all the shit going on at the station.'

She came over to him and they hugged in the doorway. 'It's fine, really. I know this case is awful for you. Besides, I knew this was the deal I signed up for when I married you.'

'How's things been at work for you? You settled back into the A and E ward?'

'Yeah, it's crazy there, as usual. I was so out of touch after working in the admin office since coming back from maternity leave. I'm starting to get back into the old groove. What's that line you always say? Same shit different day.' Her lips formed a playful smile. 'That pretty well sums things up for me, too.'

'Well, you're the best nurse in that hospital, and the most experienced. They're lucky to have you back in the trenches.'

'Yeah, well, we need to pay the bills somehow.' She smacked him on the backside. 'You better scoot.'

He kissed her. 'Have a good day.'

'You too, and Jarrod…' she hesitated.

Jarrod smiled. 'Don't worry, I'll be safe.' He spread his hands in an open gesture. 'You know me. I'm always careful. What could possibly go wrong?'

'Yeah, right. Off you go or you'll be late.'

'You all good with the kids?' he asked.

'Yeah, I'll drop them both off and head straight into the hospital. I'll finish in time to pick them up this arvo.'

'I'm sorry, sweetheart, that you've been picking up the slack with the kids.'

'You don't have to explain,' she cut in. 'Go on, off you go.'

~

As Jarrod drove to work, his mind drifted back to the Kingston kids. He decided to run by the safe house and check on them. He was dreading having to tell them about their mother, but it was his responsibility. He pulled into the driveway of the safe house, an average looking lowset brick home with a neat cottage garden and pine wood paling fences.

At the front door, he was met by Mrs Wilson, a rotund woman with a warm heart and welcoming smile. She was wearing a floral apron over her house dress and she wiped her hands with a tea towel. She must have been in her sixties, but she was one of the sprightliest women he had met. She reminded him of Mrs Doubtfire from the movie. Jarrod heard she had no children of her own and with her husband Mervyn, who died a few years ago, she had committed her life to fostering children.

'Good morning, detective. Come to visit my new arrivals, have you?' she said with a beaming smile.

'Good morning, Mrs Wilson. I'm sorry to bother you this early. I need to speak with the kids. Do you think they're up to it?'

'They've settled in quite well. They're remarkable children, you know.'

'Yes, I know.'

'Come on in. They're in the kitchen with one of your officers.' She ushered him inside, locking the door behind them. Constable Kirsty Loudin sat at the kitchen table eating toast and drinking milk with Olivia, Jamie and Jake.

'Good morning, gang. How are we all today?' he said.

They all looked up at him and smiled. Jake jumped off his chair and ran up to him, hugging his leg. Jarrod was surprised by the gesture, but it warmed his heart. He knelt down, just as he did with his own kids, and they shared a little hug. 'How's my little buddy?'

'I'm okay. Mrs Wilson is nice and she has frogs in her back garden. Do you want to come and see?' he said with excitement.

'I'd love to.' Jake held Jarrod's hand and led him towards the back door. As Jarrod passed Kirsty, she gave him a smile.

'I requested to be put on security duty here with the kids,' she said. 'Ross Benfield approved it.'

'Good for you, Kirsty.' He stopped and glanced at Kirsty and Mrs Wilson. 'I need to talk with the kids. There's something I have to tell them.' They understood.

'What is it?' asked Olivia.

'Come outside and we'll sit with the frogs and we'll talk.'

He walked outside with Jake, hand in hand. Olivia and Jamie

followed. Out near the lush tropical garden in the corner of the backyard stood a weather-beaten log stool. The kids sat down on the stool and he knelt in front of them.

'What's wrong?' asked Olivia.

'I know you guys have been through a lot and I don't want to upset you any further, but Olivia and Jamie, I need to talk to you about your mum.'

'What about her? We haven't seen her for ages,' said Jamie.

'I'm sorry, guys. I have some bad news.' He swallowed. 'Your mum has died.' The words were like broken glass, jagged in his throat. He couldn't believe he was dropping this bombshell on them, but they had to know.

'What happened?' asked Olivia bluntly. 'How did she die?'

'She took her own life. We're trying to find out why. We don't really understand yet.'

'I'm glad. I'm glad she's dead. I hate her,' said Olivia in a steely tone. Tears welled in her eyes and she wiped the first one away as it fell. She was determined to be strong. Jarrod admired her courage. Jamie seemed distant as he tried to come to grips with the news. Jake looked up and said, 'Has she gone to Heaven?'

'I hope she rots in Hell,' said Olivia, controlled anger in her voice.

They sat there in the backyard in silence. Olivia and Jamie cried. The chirping sound of a green frog rose from the moist undergrowth of the tropical garden.

Jake's face lit up. 'See Jarrod, frogs. Mrs Wilson has frogs.'

They listened to the frog and something wonderful happened. Through their tears emerged a smile on Olivia's and Jamie's face. The children held hands and Jarrod reached out his. Jake held onto his left hand and Olivia held onto his right. Jamie was in the middle and together they formed a little circle. With their small hands in his, he experienced a gentle surge of strength. The kids were survivors; together, he knew they would prevail.

TWENTY-FOUR

WHEN Jarrod arrived at the station, he made his way straight up to the MIR. Liam Dawes was talking on the phone and he gave a nod as Jarrod walked in. Homicide detectives, who Jarrod didn't know by name, were tapping away on their keyboards in front of computer terminals. Others studied investigation logs and answered ringing phones. One whiteboard displayed photos and sketch plans of the Kingston murder crime scene.

Another whiteboard displayed a list of names, some circled, with arrows indicating their relationship or link to other names. The initial theory was that the murders related to a custody dispute, but this lost momentum after Clare Kingston's suicide. However, one thing remained clear. It was a hit on the whole family and no one could come up with a motive for that.

A third whiteboard focused on Edward Ryan. A colour photo of him and a suspect profile were stuck to the middle of the board, with arrows pointing to a list of associates.

There was nothing on the whiteboard that revealed the answers they needed.

Jarrod studied Edward Ryan's photo. It was a standard prison mugshot Polaroid, taken just before his release. Wearing his brown prison t-shirt, he held a photo board against his chest displaying his name, date of birth, date of photograph and prisoner number. He had a boyish face, yet one that had been hardened by a life on the street. The photo depicted a tormented young man whose blue eyes seemed dazed and confused. He had short cropped brown hair, a pale complexion and acne scars. His eyes stared beyond the camera lens, transfixed by something in the distance. A simple mug shot told a lot about a person. It was the eyes that seemed to reveal a person's character. Yet Edward Ryan was a mystery. Hidden in those confused eyes lay dark secrets.

And there it was, the tattoo on his neck. Jarrod studied the crude prison design of a serpent winding itself around a cross. There was no mistaking the symbol. Was this the same tattoo little Jake had seen? Was he staring into the eyes of a killer? Ryan was still their only suspect and locating him was the primary focus of the investigation.

Dawes hung up the phone and stood alongside Jarrod with his hands in his pockets, rocking back and forth on his heels as he studied the whiteboards.

'Welcome to the circus. Do you think this guy is our man?' He gestured with his chin to the photo of Edward Ryan.

'I don't know, Dawesy. We've still got the option of getting little Jake to look at a photo board line-up, but that's a risky call. Who knows if the court will deem the ID evidence of a seven-year-old as being reliable? If he fingers someone else, it could damage our case. I don't even think he got a good look at the guy's face.'

'Yeah, it's a tough call,' said Dawes, still staring at Ryan's mugshot.

'We'll hold off until we get something back from forensics,' Jarrod decided. 'Besides, the kid has been through enough for now.'

They stood in silence, urging the white board to give them answers.

'What's the latest news this morning?' Jarrod asked.

'Well, plenty has been happening, but we've had no results. We've had the boys in Sydney check out all the last known addresses of Edward Ryan and they had no luck. The SERT boys hit the hottest addresses during overnight raids, but there was no sign of him. Ryan had spent six months in the bin and before that he just seemed to float. He stayed in men's shelters and lived on the street. From time to time he crashed with mates but all of them claim they haven't seen him since just before he got locked up, if you can believe that.'

'What about since he got released?'

'Well, that was four months ago and he's slipped through the cracks since then. A ghost.'

'What about the Department of Corrective Services? Surely they kept tabs on him,' said Jarrod.

Dawes scratched his head. 'Yeah, they were supposed to. Ryan failed to front up for his parole interviews, but they were never able to track him down. He's flagged on our system for breach of parole. And believe it or not, he hasn't come to the attention of the police since he was released from prison. That's the most unbelievable part.'

'What about his parents or family?'

'His mother has been dead for years and his father is doing ten years for armed robbery. No siblings. We're still trying to track down any other relatives, but so far any addresses we've come up with have been raided or are under surveillance.'

'Any links to the Kingstons?'

'That's just it, Jarrod. None. We can't find any reason for him to go after the Kingston family. I don't know. I'm starting to think we're barking up the wrong tree. Maybe we've missed something, maybe we're going after the wrong person? I hope chasing after Ryan doesn't turn out to be a waste of time.'

'So do I, mate. But he does fit the profile and the tattoo is the strongest lead. I still believe Jake was rock solid with his description of the tattoo.'

'Between you and me, Jarrod,' Dawes whispered, 'there are some here who have doubts, Murray Long for one.'

'Yeah, well that goes without saying. I couldn't give a rat's arse what he thinks.'

At that very moment, Long strutted into the MIR. He gave Jarrod an indifferent glance and then approached Benfield, who was receiving a briefing from one of the intelligence officers.

'Any news back from the scientific boys? Did they find anything at the crime scene?' Jarrod asked Dawes.

'I don't know, I haven't heard. I think we're still waiting to hear back from them.'

Jarrod overheard Long and Benfield, who were now caught up in their own private conversation. 'Ross, I think we need to go to the media for public assistance in finding Edward Ryan.'

'I've considered that, Murray. Maybe it *is* time to go to the media. But if we do, we'll reveal all our cards.'

Benfield turned to Jarrod. 'I'm interested in your view. Do you think we should release Edward Ryan's photo to the media, calling for public assistance?'

'Well, Senior, Ryan's tattoo and his personal profile are all that we're going on. We have nothing to link him to the murders. I'm waiting for some information from the Mental Health Unit as to whether Ryan and Clare Kingston were known to each other. My opinion, for what it's worth, is that we don't go to the media just yet, not until we have something more concrete. We don't want to force him into hiding.'

Long interjected. 'Come on, Ross. We have jack shit. If we want to catch this bastard, then we need help from the media. We have no choice. I'm not prepared to sit around and wait for O'Connor to produce the goods for us.'

'Murray, have you seen today's front page? Can we trust the likes of Jim Caxton to do the right thing by us?' Jarrod said.

'Speaking of which, I bet you're just lapping up being the front page glory boy.'

'For fuck's sake, Murray. I'm sure there'll be time for you to cash in on the limelight before this investigation's through. You always manage to.'

'Are you two quite finished?' Benfield cut in. 'Jarrod, get back to me as soon as you hear from the MHU. Murray, I want you to liaise with scientific. They must have found something at the crime scene. We'll hold off from alerting the media until we have a solid link between Ryan and the Kingstons. We'll continue with general appeals for information. That's all. I want a briefing at midday.'

Long's glare said it all. He was pissed and he made no secret of that. He walked off and called to Dawes. 'Liam, let's get out of here.'

Dawes gave Jarrod a questioning look, shrugged his shoulders and followed Long out of the MIR.

Jarrod headed back to his office. Brad had not long arrived. 'How's our mate, Murray, this morning?' he asked.

'Let's just say that the more things change, the more things stay the same.'

Jarrod's phone rang. 'CPU, O'Connor speaking.'

'Hey Jarrod, this is Jerome Johnson from the youth shelter. Sorry to call you like this, but I need to talk to you urgently.'

'What's up, mate?' Jarrod knew straight away from the tone of his voice that something was wrong.

'It's Billy. You remember Billy Mason, don't you?'

'How could I forget Billy? What's he done now?'

'He says he'll only talk to you. I don't know how to say this but...' Jerome hesitated.

'What is it Jerome?'

'We found a gun in Billy's room. A *real* handgun. It was hidden under his mattress. We found it when we did a routine search of his room.'

'Is it loaded?' Jarrod snapped.

'No, thankfully it had no bullets.'

'Who would he have gotten it from?'

'He hasn't said much other than it might have something to do with a murder.'

Jarrod instructed Brad to stay in the office to cover for him.

Within ten minutes he pulled up out the front of the youth shelter. Billy was sitting on a couch in the activities room playing Simpsons Road Rage on an old Nintendo game console. As Jerome led Jarrod inside, Billy looked up and gave him a casual wave. 'What's up, copper?'

Same old Billy.

'You tell me, Billy,' said Jarrod.

Billy just shrugged his shoulders and went back to playing his game. Homer appeared on the flat screen TV, crashing a rocket car into anything Billy could steer him into. That was the exact opposite of the aim of the game, but he seemed to relish causing as much destruction and mayhem as he could.

'Don't you go anywhere, Billy,' Jarrod said, waving an index finger at him.

Jerome took him into the office, where he produced a .38 Ruger six-shot revolver from a locked filing cabinet. It had a weathered wooden handle but was otherwise well maintained, apart from being caked in a thin layer of dry mud. Jarrod flipped open the empty cylinder and gave it a spin before snapping it closed. His mind flashed back to the Kingston murder crime scene and the .38 round casings found on the floor.

'When I asked him where he got it from, he refused to tell me. That's when he said he would only talk to you. I've got nothing else from him,' said Jerome.

'When do you think he found this?'

'He took off for a few hours on one of our bikes early that morning after you arrested him. That's the only time he's been out of my sight.'

'Do you mind if I talk to him now?'

'Go right ahead. I want to get to the bottom of this as much as anyone,' said Jerome.

They joined Billy in the activities room and Jerome switched off the TV.

'So, Billy. Let's get straight to the point. Tell me about that gun in your room,' Jarrod said.

'I found it.'

'Where did you find it?'

'Near that old church on the hill, ya know, just down the road.'

'Yeah, I know the one. What were you doing there?'

'Dunno, I just went for a ride. I sometimes go cray fishin' in the creek just in the bush behind it.'

'Where did you find the gun?'

'I saw that man throw it in the bush. He was aiming for the creek, I reckon.'

'Woah, hold up, Billy. What man?'

'The white fella that was carrying that other white fella out of that church there,' he said, getting frustrated because clearly Jarrod was slow on the uptake.

'What do you mean, Billy? Why was a fella carrying another fella?' Jarrod tried to contain his impatience.

'One fella looked dead. He had blood all over him. The big fella had a big knife in a pouch on his belt. He had blood on him too, but he didn't look hurt. He carried the dead fella to a white four-wheel-drive ute and threw him in the back. That's when I saw him throw the gun towards the creek. He jumped in the car and took off.'

'Where were you? Did he see you?'

'Nah,' he said with a confident smile. 'I'm too smart for that fella. I was hiding in the bush. When he drove off, I went over and found the gun in the mud. The stupid bugger missed the water.'

Jarrod pressed Billy further, but he wasn't able to provide any useful description other than describing the man as "wild looking".

Jarrod seized the gun and called it in. A short time later, he met other units and a forensics team at the abandoned chapel on Drayton Lane on the outskirts of town. It sat on a small rise overlooking Coopers Creek, which meandered through a thicket of bushland at the rear of the church yard.

The quaint granite stone chapel was built many generations ago at the site that used to be the original town settlement. The A-frame wooden roof beams were buckling under the weight of the rusted corrugated iron sheeting. When the local parish built a new church in the main Lockyer township, the chapel was abandoned and fell into disrepair. Despite the high fencing erected by the local council to keep trespassers out, local kids still used it for rock throwing practice and most windows had since been smashed. All but one. Strangely, the only window that had survived was a mosaic of a crucifix encircled by a serpent. Despite years of grime and dust, the mosaic would have been a stunning feature back when the heavy wooden doors of the chapel were opened for Sunday mass. Before now, Jarrod hadn't noticed the sharp blue and red colours of the imagery within the glass. The significance of this image had been lost on him until that moment. It was the same image as the tattoo depicted in Edward Ryan's mugshots. This was becoming a day of uncanny coincidences.

The forensics team established a crime scene. A pool of blood was found inside the chapel, along with drag marks in the dust. Tyre impressions were taken outside in the dirt. Forensics would remain to scour the scene in more detail.

Jarrod returned to the station and lodged the handgun as an exhibit for immediate ballistics testing, along with the recovered shells at the Kingston crime scene.

He had to unravel the mystery of the two men at the Chapel.

TWENTY-FIVE

JARROD doodled on a note pad, scrawling hexagonal shapes and shading them in with his pen. He crossed them out in frustration. He drew a three-dimensional cube and studied it, hoping it would reveal the answers to the puzzle. He visualised the pendant around Clare Kingston's neck and the strange paintings on her walls and ceiling.

He logged onto his PC and Googled keywords "geometric shapes", "hexagon", "prism", "cube". The searches returned hits on hundreds of web pages, and he had no idea where to begin. He found sites on geometry and anthropology and then one caught his eye. It was titled "Metatron's cube and the essence of life". He clicked on the link and waited for the site to open. In the middle of the screen appeared an animated image of Metatron's Cube, a three-dimensional cube rotating on its axis. Within this cube was another, smaller cube. It was identical to the glass cube hanging from Clare Kingston's neck. As the cube rotated, the lines between its corners formed different shapes, the image appearing as a hexagon and then a cube as it turned. Jarrod read the first paragraph of text. *Metatron's cube is a representation of something that exists in a higher state of consciousness. It is the inter-dimensional gateway for reaching higher dimensions of existence. The symmetry and balance of this sacred geometrical shape will resonate with those individuals who have a desire to take their place as a universal being.*

There was reference to the Angel Metatron, so he searched sites relating to angels. He clicked on one link, which took him to a site called "The Fallen Angels". The site explained there were thousands of angels that had been named over history. There was a long alphabetical list of angels and he found Metatron and clicked on the link.

The Archangel Metatron was depicted as a winged, bearded angel wearing a gold crown and holding a stone tablet emblazoned with a gold cross. Seated on the angel's lap was an infant child. Beside this image the text read, *The Archangel Metatron is considered by many to be the greatest angel of all. He has been called Prince of Divine Face, Angel of the Covenant and King of the Angels. He is the direct link between God and humanity and is in charge of the sustenance of the world. He was also the heavenly scribe who recorded all celestial happenings. On the darker side, Metatron is mentioned in Exodus as being identified with Satan. A strange figure, on one hand Metatron is set above Michael and Gabriel, while on the other hand he is depicted as bloodthirsty, delighting in torturing disobedient people.*

The text went into the history of a man named Enoch who it is believed was later transformed by God to the Archangel Metatron. Bolded text on the screen grabbed his attention. *Metatron represents the supreme Angel of Death, to whom God daily gives orders as to which souls will be taken that day. Metatron transmits these orders to his subordinate, Sammael.*

He clicked the link for the angel Sammael. This winged angel was portrayed as a warrior with a sword and shield bearing the insignia of a serpent and cross. The same image that Edward Ryan had tattooed on his neck. *Sammael: it is thought this angel of death was the demon who tempted Eve. Also the prince of air. This is merely another name for Satan. Sammael is also a symbol of the Venom of God. This title refers to his role as executioner of the death sentences ordered by God, and links him to the Angel of Death.*

He searched more sites and found many references to the Angel Sammael. Each represented the angel in various forms, however the Venom of God was consistently referenced.

Jarrod's neck felt hot and flushed when he realised he may have stumbled onto something that gave meaning to Clare Kingston's suicide and the Kingston murders. *Were Clare Kingston and Edward Ryan part of some religious cult? Could some distorted notion of punishment be the motive for the killings? Was it an execution for some perceived sin?* He stared at his computer screen, mesmerised by the image of the angel referred to as the Venom of God.

He was startled when his desk phone rang.

'Hello, Detective O'Connor, my name is Garth Lindsay. I'm a social worker at the Prince Phillip Mental Health Facility in Sydney. Dr Alex Wright contacted me.'

'Ah yes, Garth, thanks for ringing. Do you have any information for us?'

'I understand you were after information about Clare Kingston and Edward Ryan. Is that correct?'

'Yes, that's correct,' Jarrod said with anticipation.

'Alex had his people cross-reference Clare Kingston's files with Edward Ryan's files. They were both admitted here for treatment at the same time early last year.'

Now he had Jarrod's full attention.

'I was the case worker for them both, as it turns out. Alex has authorised the release of any information you might need.'

'That's great, Garth. We need to know as much as possible about them. Any information at all will be a great help.'

'Well, Clare Kingston was transferred here from the local hospital to receive specialist therapy. At that time, Edward Ryan had been regulated after presenting with psychotic behaviour triggered by extensive inhalant use. He was confused and suffered delusions and hallucinations. In particular, Edward experienced grandiose delusions about being a higher being. We curbed the delusions with medication, although we suspected the inhalant abuse had caused irreparable damage.'

'What was his connection to Clare Kingston? They seem like an odd couple.'

'You're right, they were a very odd couple, but for some reason they were drawn to each other. They first met during group therapy sessions and later they spent increasing amounts of time together. I would often see them sitting on the lawns or walking around the grounds together. During the group sessions they were both subdued, but when they were alone, they talked constantly. Their delusional conditions gave them something in common, a similar belief in higher beings. Clare believed she had a guardian angel who protected her, while Edward went through various degrees of grandiose delusions of being all powerful. Together they conjured up stories and they validated the other's delusions as fact. This was hindering their therapy, so they were separated.'

'How long had they been in contact with each other before being separated?'

'They had full contact for about two months. It was during this time they formed this mutual bond and started sharing and acting out each other's delusions,' said Garth.

'How do you mean, acting out?'

'They became so dependent on each other for acceptance that they began to share each other's beliefs. Edward started playing the role of Clare's guardian angel and she accepted him as some all-powerful agent of God. Once they were separated, Clare made good progress with her therapy and soon the delusions ceased. Edward, on the other hand, was suffering from drug-induced psychosis. This kid had been sniffing all kinds of inhalants. The long-term damage was too great for any successful treatment.'

'So, what became of them?'

'Clare Kingston was referred back to the Lockyer Mental Health Unit for therapy, but I believe she never followed up. Edward Ryan was sent to live with a community support agency, but he just dropped off the radar. I heard he went to prison.'

Jarrod explained Clare Kingston's apparent association with Metatron's Cube, but Garth couldn't shed any more light on the subject.

After the call, Jarrod pondered at his desk. *Did Edward Ryan believe he was the angel Sammael? If so, was he acting as an agent for someone else? Did Clare believe she was Metatron and sent Ryan to execute her ex-husband and his new wife? But why go after the kids as well?* It didn't make sense. *Was Clare capable of manipulating the likes of Edward Ryan to commit murder?*

He'd found the connection between Edward Ryan and Clare Kingston, but critical pieces were still missing.

TWENTY-SIX

THE phone on Jarrod's desk rang again. 'CPU, O'Connor,' he answered.

'Jarrod, it's Graham Savage down at the watchhouse.'

'Yeah, mate. What's up?'

'Thomas Barton, he's asking for you. He says it's important. He reckons he remembers the name. Does that make sense to you?'

'I'll be right down,' Jarrod snapped. He slammed down the phone and hurried out of the office.

'Where are you going in such a rush?' asked Brad as Jarrod brushed past him.

'I'll be down at the watchhouse. I'll explain when I get back.'

He flew down the stairs. Heads in the station day room turned as he pivoted around the hand railing at the base of the stairs, sliding on the tiled floor. He raced down the windowless corridor that led to the internal watchhouse door. He pressed the buzzer, looked up into the security camera and the electric door lock clicked. He pulled open the heavy steel door that led into the staging area. Another click and the second internal door unlocked. Graham met him inside the door.

'Can I see him straight away?' Jarrod puffed.

'He's waiting for you.'

'Thanks.' He walked towards Thomas' cell door, trying to control his breathing. Since speaking with Thomas yesterday, he had gotten caught up with so many other things he had forgotten all about him. This one name could well be the associate of Ryan they were looking for, the man who gave him refuge in prison. So far, they had turned over every relative and known associate of Ryan with no luck. A name, just a name, could be the breakthrough they were looking for.

'Hey, Jarrod. You'll need these,' called Graham as he tossed him the cell keys. Jarrod caught them with one hand as they hurtled towards him.

Through the steel mesh he saw Thomas lounging back on his bunk reading an out-dated copy of Reader's Digest, standard watchhouse issue. He looked up and squinted his eyes to see who it was. His eyes lit up in recognition and he jumped to his feet.

'G'day, Mr O'Connor.' Showered, fed and rested, he was back to the Thomas Barton of old. He actually seemed pleased to see Jarrod.

Jarrod jingled the keys as he fumbled with the lock. He worked his way through the triple lock mechanism and heaved the door open. He stepped into the cell and faced Thomas.

'I remember the name,' said Thomas. 'The crazy fucker that was friends with Eddie Ryan in the joint. I remember his name! Do we still have a deal? Are you gonna put a good word in for me, Mr O'Connor?'

'Yes, Thomas, you have my word.'

'His name was Vincent. Vincent Miles,' he said with confidence, looking quite proud of himself.

Jarrod's heart pounded against the inside of his chest at the sound of the name. Vincent Miles. He stared into Thomas' eyes. 'Thomas, are you sure?'

'I swear, that's his name. What's wrong, Mr O'Connor?'

'Nothing's wrong, Thomas, nothing's wrong,' Jarrod lied.

But it was all wrong. Vincent Miles was one of the most violent and unpredictable men Jarrod had met.

A series of images played back in his mind, a grainy movie reel imprinted in his brain. His fingers subconsciously caressed the scar on the top of his hand. He remembered the Holden Statesman station wagon parked in a garage at the back of the house, the V6 engine rumbling as it idled. He remembered the green irrigation hose leading from the exhaust pipe to the driver's side window. The hose was wedged in place by the closed window. At first, Jarrod had seen his own reflection in the window, but when he peered through the glass he saw their faces, ashen and still. What were their names? Yes, Roxy and little baby Jazmin. She was only six months old. The baby was cradled in her mother's arms as though they were sleeping.

He remembered the toxic fumes pouring in from the hose, converting the vehicle into a carbon monoxide gas chamber. The doors and windows were locked. He didn't know if they were alive, so he tried forcing the driver's door and then the window, but it was no use.

He remembered finding a brick in long grass nearby and smashing it into the back driver's side window, glass shattering everywhere. He slashed his hand, blood gushing down his arm. He reached in to unlock the front door but was overcome by fumes. Pulling himself free of the car, he took another breath and thrust his arm into the opening to unlock the door. He reefed the door open and killed the ignition. He remembered the silence. Everything was so still and quiet when the rumbling engine died. Their eyelids were purple and blood trickled from Roxy's nose. Their lips were blue. Roxy was dead and he took the baby from her arms. Her little body was cold and limp. Jarrod fell to his knees, the baby still in his arms. He ran his fingertips over her little face and closed her eyelids.

She never stood a chance, both in life and in death.

'Mr O'Connor. Hey, Mr O'Connor,' said Thomas, waving his hand in front of Jarrod's face. 'You look like you saw a ghost.'

Jarrod emerged from his dazed state and stared into Thomas' inquisitive eyes. He studied every detail of his boyish face. 'No Thomas, I didn't see a ghost. It was far worse than that.'

TWENTY-SEVEN

JARROD'S mind raced when he left Thomas Barton's cell. He assembled the scattered pieces of information, hoping to formulate a theory that made sense. It was nearly midday and he was late for the briefing. All available police personnel had assumed their briefing positions around the conference room. The rabble of tired detectives and uniform officers came to attention. Benfield waited behind the lectern facing the group, with Long hovering at his side. Jarrod slunk into the back of the room as the briefing was about to get underway. Benfield glared at him. 'Glad you could join us, O'Connor. Perhaps next time you'll make the briefing on time.'

'Sorry, Senior, but I've been with an informant. I have some new information.'

Murray Long chimed in before Jarrod could explain, ignoring him completely. 'Okay, listen up people. Shall I start the briefing, Senior?' Benfield gave an approving nod. Long relished being at the podium, the centre of attention. 'The scientific boys have had a breakthrough. Traces of skin were found under the fingernails of Anne Kingston. The DNA Co-ordination Unit helped us out and fast tracked our sample for testing. They found a match.' He paused to maximise the impact value of his news. 'They cross-referenced the skin with a mouth swab DNA sample taken from Edward Ryan when he was last arrested. It was a perfect match. Edward Ryan is our shooter.'

The impact of the news spread through the room, the relief on

172

the face of every officer was evident. Some smiled and others let out a, 'Yeah!'

Someone else said, 'We've got the bastard now.'

'This is excellent news in terms of our investigation,' said Benfield. Almost in the same breath, he shifted his attention to Jarrod. 'O'Connor, please brief us on your new information.'

Long glared at Benfield like a kid who just had his balloon busted.

Benfield had taken Jarrod a little by surprise. Like everyone else, he was still taking in the DNA evidence news and how it related to what he had already begun to surmise.

Jarrod began. 'I've found the connection between Clare Kingston and Edward Ryan.' He cleared his throat. 'They met at a mental health hospital in Sydney last year. It seems they were both quite delusional and formed a close bond. I believe Ryan's tattoo and the pendant worn by Clare Kingston are associated with their delusions about angels and higher beings.'

Long burst into laughter and others joined in. 'What a crock of shit, O'Connor.'

'I know how it sounds but hear me out. I still haven't worked out a clear motive for the killings, but it's possible he's taking orders from someone who he believes is a higher being, someone who decides which souls should be taken. Either he was sent by Clare Kingston,' he paused, 'or someone else.'

Long leaned against the lectern with one hand, the other fidgeted inside his trouser pocket. 'How the hell did you come to this conclusion, O'Connor?' he jeered with a sarcastic smile.

'It's a combination of a lot of things, their profiles, mental health assessments, the tattoo and Clare Kingston's obsession with this object called Metatron's Cube. Ryan's tattoo is the symbol for the angel Sammael, the angel who follows the orders of Metatron. I believe it's pointing towards our motive. Clare Kingston could have had motive to want her ex-husband killed and who better to send to do the job than Edward Ryan.'

'Let's deal with facts and not mystical riddles,' scoffed Long.

'Is that all you have, Jarrod?' asked Benfield.

'No, it's not,' he replied. Long rolled his eyes and let out an impatient sigh.

'Edward Ryan formed a friendship with another inmate at the remand centre, someone we haven't yet associated with Ryan.' His voice sounded shaky in his own ears. He was being scrutinised by his peers and his theory hadn't convinced them. He hadn't convinced himself. Maybe he should have waited until he could find out more instead of blurting all this out like a rambling idiot.

He was attempting to salvage some credibility. 'Vincent Miles. The associate of Edward Ryan is Vincent Miles.'

'Where'd you get that info from?' said Long.

'A reliable informant who was in prison with them at the same time.'

'Go on, O'Connor,' said Benfield.

'Well, think about it. Miles lives right here in Lockyer. Ryan could be hiding out with him right here under our noses.' There was a murmur and whispers among officers. Jarrod continued before Long had a chance to cut him off. 'Miles has a long history for offences of violence and amphetamine dependence. He's been in and out of prison for the last three years since the murder-suicide of his wife and baby.'

'Yes, I recall that case,' said Benfield. 'That was your investigation, wasn't it, Jarrod?'

'That's right, Senior,' he said. 'He's an unpredictable drug addict. The last time I had dealings with him, he was angry at the world and everyone in it. I believe he's capable of anything.'

Benfield pondered for a moment, considering the new information. 'Right, I want the intel team to put together a full profile of Miles,' he said. 'I want a layout of his residence and surrounding property, list of associates, mugshots, firearms history, registered vehicles, criminal history, the lot. Jarrod, you work with the intel team. You know more about Miles than anyone else here. I want to know what his movements have been and I want to know where he is now. We need to establish if Vincent Miles, Edward Ryan and Clare Kingston have been associating.'

He turned to Long. 'Murray, I need you to arrange immediate surveillance of his residence. Activate the SERT team and have them on standby. I want to be moving on this immediately. We're paying Mr Miles a visit. Let's move people!'

Jarrod remembered Vincent Miles' last words to him three years earlier. *I will come for her.*

TWENTY-EIGHT

RETURNING to his office was the temporary respite Jarrod needed. It was quiet. As he had promised, he typed up a bail recommendation and emailed it to the Police Prosecutions office. A deal was to be struck with Thomas Barton's Legal Aid solicitor for him to get conditional bail later that day.

He slid open the bottom draw of his filing cabinet and fingered through old case files stored in alphabetical order. He found the manila folder labelled "Stone / Miles". He pulled the file and just held it closed for a moment. It contained photos he had no desire to ever see again. He took a deep breath and opened it.

Pinned to the inside cover was a photograph of Vincent Miles. He remembered Thomas Barton's description of him. *'He's a real scary fucker, he's got evil eyes.'*

He had to agree with Thomas. It was an apt description. Vincent Miles scowled in his mugshot photo. His shoulder length, greying hair was tied back in a ponytail, his ginger goatee beard had grown wild. His bloodshot eyes squinted, giving him a devilish appearance. Old scars above his left eye and across his right cheek distorted his face into a constant grimace. His eyes projected so much hatred. From his date of birth, Jarrod calculated he would be forty-five years old but his face was battered and aged beyond his years.

He flicked through the file and came across the photos of the scene inside the house where Miles' blood had spilled all over the floor. He couldn't help but think Roxy would have done the world a favour if she had succeeded in her attempt to kill him. Next came the photos of the car, the hose, the smashed window and the dead mother sitting upright in the driver's seat, the dead baby. He closed his eyes and shook his head, trying to banish those memories from his mind, but it was no use. The images would be branded into his brain forever. He read through the coroner's inquest report. It was an open and shut case. There were no mysteries or secret answers to be revealed, just one woman's desperate attempts to end her miserable life. The case had been closed by the coroner – death by suicide.

Jarrod hadn't seen Miles since that day in the hospital three years ago. There wasn't enough evidence to charge him. When he had the strength, he simply walked out of the hospital without a word. He packed up and left town before Roxy and the baby were buried. He couldn't be located for the coronial inquest. Jarrod heard that he surfaced a few months later in Byron Bay, where he was arrested on drug charges.

He gave the file to the intel guys so they could compile their profile of Miles. Soon his photo featured on the whiteboard in the conference room and plans were underway for the raid on his house. Discreet inquiries established that Miles had been released from his most recent stretch in prison three months earlier after serving his time for a string of violent assaults. He last collected his unemployment benefit one week prior at the Lockyer Centrelink office. From all accounts, he was living a hermit lifestyle at the farmhouse where Roxy and their baby had died. The property had been in his family for generations. There had always been mystery and speculation around the demise of Vincent Miles' parents and there appeared to be no other living relatives.

Jarrod remembered the story of the mysterious disappearance of little Tom Baker over thirty years ago. It had become folklore around those parts. Everyone knew the story. Tom lived next door to the Miles farm at the time of his disappearance. He had a nagging feeling there might be some connection, but with a shake of his head he pushed the idea from his mind. That was a question for another day.

Jarrod regularly drove past the property on his way to Sydney, often glancing at the derelict house that harboured such bitter memories. It was a dilapidated, high-set weatherboard house hunched in front of acres of useless, dense bushland about five kilometres from town. The paddocks, where cows once grazed, were now overgrown with lantana and wild clumps of prickly pear. It had become the graveyard for several disused sheds, decaying tractors and car bodies. Rotting fence posts had collapsed under their own weight. The house was as tired as the landscape – dreary and weather beaten. A long, dusty dirt driveway led to the house from the front gate.

The hardwood framed garage at the rear of the house had a rusted corrugated iron roof and doors that sagged from their broken hinges. Sheltered inside was the old Holden which had not moved since that horrible day. Knee-length grass grew around the wheels and rust devoured the door panels. Miles now drove a battered Toyota Landcruiser tray back, which he kept parked at the front of the house. He had made little effort to make repairs during his stints between prison over the last three years.

The MIR was buzzing. A three-man covert surveillance team had been deployed and was hidden in bushland surrounding Miles' house after approaching on foot. They had reported that his vehicle was parked at the front, but there had been no movement or sightings. They relayed information about entry and exit points. Photographs of the layout of the property were sent back to the MIR. These would be used by the SERT team in preparing their initial entry.

Ross Benfield held another briefing at three o'clock. Everything was in place. The six-man SERT team was activated and had made it to town in good time from Sydney. The elite Special Emergency Response Team and their impressive range of equipment and firepower were on standby at the station for immediate deployment in their Bearcat mobile unit. If there were any sightings of Miles, they were to strike first and secure the residence followed by a team of detectives led by Murray Long. Much to Long's annoyance, Benfield had instructed that Jarrod and Brad were to join the lead team.

There was a sense of growing anticipation. Jarrod hoped it would be all over that afternoon, that they would pin down Edward Ryan and Vincent Miles. He was uneasy thinking about a confrontation with Vincent Miles. However, the investigation was falling into place. The connections had been made between Clare Kingston, Edward Ryan and Vincent Miles. The DNA evidence would ensure a conviction against Ryan. There was nothing better than wrapping up a case as a result of old-fashioned good police work. However, they still didn't have Ryan in custody and couldn't be too complacent until they did. Jarrod hoped his assumption about Ryan hiding out with Miles was right, but there were no guarantees.

They lingered in the MIR, assembled and waiting for the go-ahead to launch the raid.

TWENTY-NINE

VINCENT Miles controlled his breathing as he transcended into a deep state of meditation. He sat cross-legged on the bare floorboards, his posture upright and rigid. The palms of his hands faced upwards in an open gesture towards the wooden ceiling. The cool air in the underground cavern lingered with an earthy dampness. A single candle flickered in the darkness, casting a ghostly shadow against the bunker walls. He was entombed in his place of safety, concealing him from the outside world. He closed his eyes. Memories of his distant past projected like an old film on the back of his eyelids in a jumbled timeline. His troubled mind was a cloud of confusion between the past and the present.

It had always been there growing inside him, a darkness in his soul. He was wired differently to everyone else. To him, other living creatures were something he could kill. As a boy he had enjoyed inventing new ways to torture animals to see how long they could endure before the lights faded in their eyes. Devoid of remorse, he showed neither pity nor compassion. It was programmed into his DNA, ingrained deep in his fibres. He didn't pretend to be anything other than what he was and enjoyed the isolation of being different. He was impulsive and had a hollow indifference towards others.

Vincent's chamber was buried beneath the farm where he grew up, a five-hundred-acre property not far from the outskirts of town. His parents had once run over fifty head of Hereford cattle and grew their own veggies. Free range chickens provided all the eggs they needed. It was Vincent's job each morning to milk Helen, their old Jersey cow. Of course, the farm animals were now long gone, as were his parents.

'We thank you Jesus for our home, our meal and our family. We pray for peace and prosperity. We serve you in obedience, Holy Father.' As a boy, Vincent cared little for his father's dinner time sermons. His mind was consumed with deviant thoughts, his fantasies to kill.

His father was the local minister of the evangelistic community church and his mother a devoted wife and Christian role model. Together, his parents worked the land and shared the word of the Gospel to the local farming community in the small hall on the edge of town.

Vincent was not exposed to domestic violence, nor was he sexually abused by a sadistic mother. He was not beaten by a cruel father. There were no other obvious reasons associated with the psychopathic tendencies of killers. He was an anomaly of nature. It was that simple.

His parents struggled to contain his belligerent and violent behaviour, which became worse as he grew into adolescence. They prayed hard for divine help, but none came and their pride prevented them from seeking it. They suffered alone in silence. They wore fake smiles in front of the congregation, however Vincent made their home lives a living hell. To the outside world, they were the perfect family, but it was all a masquerade.

It was through his father's teachings of the bible that Vincent grew fond of parables about angels and demons. He became obsessed with the notion of higher beings, blessed with the fortitude to take lives as commanded by God. Was he a demon? That seemed to be the best explanation for his natural tendencies to kill. He was thirteen when he killed for the first time. The thrill of taking a human life surged through his veins. The adrenaline made him feel invincible. What a rush.

That was back when his life had no direction. A glimpse of his future changed everything; he was enlightened by a premonition so powerful he saw what lay before him with incisive clarity. His destiny had become clear.

However, he still pondered over the memories of his dark past and the journey that steered him to this point in his life. He had embraced his adolescent desire to kill but had since learned to control the urges. He no longer killed just for self-gratification; his actions were now driven by the necessity to achieve final redemption, a peace he longed for. He was working towards a higher plan. Despite this, the souls of those he'd killed in his previous life clung to his consciousness. They were cruel and unforgiving. He'd been tortured by their presence ever since that fateful day he sent Tom Baker plummeting to his death. The little boy invaded his dreams, materialising hand in hand with the ghosts of Vincent's own parents. For twenty-seven years, Tom's remains lay scattered at the bottom of a murky green quarry lake. His spirit was restless. The mystery of his disappearance still haunted the town. He suppressed the urge to smile. The memory of his first kill was the most vivid. No one else alive knew the truth.

There was one other soul that tormented his dreams; its hatred surged through his veins and tingled with bitterness. As he meditated, the whispers of Dillan McAllister's spirit echoed in his skull. 'I'm still here, Vincent. Come join me in the dark place.'

Vincent's mind drifted back to the day he killed his twelve-year-old cousin. He was fourteen at the time. The euphoria of murdering Tom Baker had waned and torturing animals had done nothing to quell his natural instincts. He hated his cousin. Vincent led Dillan to a sorghum grain silo. They climbed the ladder and scaled the domed roof until they reached the summit.

Vincent unlatched the manhole cover and yanked it open. On hands and knees, they peered into the darkness. Seizing the opportunity, Vincent grabbed Dillan by the feet. Losing his balance,

Dillan's upper body and arms dangled inside the cavernous silo. Vincent gripped onto his ankles and laughed as Dillan's dead weight slipped from his grasp. Dillan shrieked.

Vincent savoured the power, the total control. He released his grip and Dillan disappeared into the darkness. His screams of terror, as he sunk deeper into the grain, became muffled echoes after Vincent slammed the hatch closed. He sat aloft the silo as Dillan slowly suffocated to death, alone and in total darkness. When the screaming stopped, Vincent opened the hatch and listened. The thrashing and blood-curdling screams had ceased. Satisfied that Dillan had been swallowed, his lungs crushed and filled with grain, Vincent climbed down the ladder and meandered back to the farmhouse. He concocted a story that Dillan had gone missing when they were playing hide and seek. Hours passed as Dillan's parents frantically called out his name in panic, searching in vain.

Over the next two days, police and volunteers searched the surrounding farms. Rumours were rife that the child abductor had struck again. Old fears resurfaced. The wounds of Tom Baker's disappearance were still too raw. Vincent stuck to his story. It took all his willpower to hold back a chuckle.

Eventually the grain silo was drained and Dillan's body was found. "Death by misadventure" was the determination and the police investigation wrapped up. Vincent and his parents attended the funeral, but his uncle and auntie never spoke to them again. He was glad. He hated them so much. However, Dillan's spirit never left his side and manifested as a dark shadow waiting patiently for revenge.

His mind jumped to another time, to when he was eighteen. Vincent's obsession with the power of taking lives thrust him towards his ultimate act of blind rage and bloodshed. He grew to despise his parents. Their goodness and Christian values were at odds with his natural instincts. His parents disappeared under mysterious circumstances. Vincent stuck to his story that his parents had up and left; he could be extremely convincing. Did his parents just skip town? This didn't seem plausible. Had they met with foul play? No one really knew – except for Vincent of course. He never told a soul. He chuckled to himself before he went to sleep each night in that empty farmhouse. It was his most precious secret.

~

Vincent sensed a faint disturbance above on ground level and his consciousness returned to the present. He was prepared. He knew they would come. For weeks, he and Edward had been making the final preparations. They had completed construction of the underground bunker, hidden in thick bushland in one corner of the property. As a boy, he had stumbled on the abandoned mine shaft and over the years had excavated it by hand. The land had once been an opal mining operation before it was deserted and sold off as farmland. The landscape was pockmarked with carved tunnels and shafts, most of which had since collapsed or been filled in.

His mission in life had become so clear. He was no longer just a man. He and Edward had been reborn. The bunker was to be their stronghold, a place where they could make their last stand if it came to that. They had constructed new support beams and lined the walls with sturdy posts. The bunker consisted of one underground room, four metres long and three metres wide. There was enough head height allowing an average man to stand without stooping. They had widened it to accommodate their equipment and supplies. Entry was by the steel ladder which led up to ground level. The shaft opening was covered by a camouflaged wooden hatch door. The entry was difficult to see, the undergrowth forming a natural cover. The bunker was to serve as their lair until their mission was complete. It had also been stocked with weapons, food, water, bedding and candles and could sustain them for weeks. They could come and go undetected; no one would ever find him there.

He mourned the loss of Clare and Edward, but he knew he

would be with them soon. Together in prison, he and Edward had been reborn. They both had similar interests in biblical higher powers, although Edward's beliefs were erratic. His energies needed harnessing. He needed focus. Together, they studied the New Testament and found a meaning for life where before there had been none. Vincent rose from the ashes of his previous life. In their cramped prison cell, he christened Edward, from that day forward, to take on the name Sammael. Vincent was disappointed in Edward. He had failed his mission and had to die. Clare had already begun her journey to be reunited with her children. He longed to be with her. His heart ached to be with his little baby Jazmin once again.

It was her death that fired up the torment in his mind, the unquenched anger and desire for revenge. But then the blinding madness had subsided and everything became so clear. He knew who he had become and what he had to do. His desire to see his little girl again had driven him to all this. Through Edward, he met Clare and she shared the same pain. They formed a deep connection in such a short time; she believed in him and had taken her first step to be reunited with her children. He'd sworn to keep his promise to her. He would live and die by that vow.

When his mission was fulfilled, he would leave his earthly existence behind and return to her, emerging as the Archangel Metatron. His friend and servant, Sammael, would already be waiting for him. He regretted killing Edward, but he could not afford any more mistakes. He cremated Edward's body the night before. He had to finish what he had started; every breath he drew was for the sole purpose of completing his task. They had all planned this together. This is what it had all come down to. They had made a pact in blood.

Vincent was climbing out of the bunker when he first saw the men, dressed in camouflage gear, carrying police issue radios and R4 Remington rifles. He was surprised they had come so soon, but he was ready for them. The crossbow was loaded and a quiver of arrows was slung over his shoulder. He circled around without making a sound, a shadow hidden within this bushland he knew so well.

It had begun.

THIRTY

THE surveillance officer monitored the rear of the house, crouched on one knee, concealing himself within a thicket of long, dry grass. The arrow whooshed through the air at blinding speed as it left the crossbow. His upper body spun off balance from the force of the dull thud that slammed against the back of his shoulder. The rifle flew from his grip and rattled as it hit the dirt. In the first split second, he thought he'd been struck by a lump of wood, shattering his shoulder. He fell onto his side and grimaced from the intense burning pain, and then he saw the blood. He shrieked in horror at the sight of the sharpened arrow tip that had penetrated his shoulder and pierced the front of his shirt. He tried to find cover by digging the heels of his boots into the ground, pushing with all his might. He drove with his legs and dragged his body across the dirt on his side.

'I'm hit!' he screamed in between desperate screams of agony. The two other members of his surveillance team were positioned thirty metres away in opposite directions, one covering the left side of the house and the other the right. They abandoned their concealed positions and sprinted to the aid of their colleague and friend.

The injured officer had no cover. He rolled over his good shoulder and willed himself to his feet. He heard someone running at him from behind. He turned and saw a man appear, aiming the reloaded crossbow directly at him. With a snap, the second arrow was released and the officer dove to his left as the projectile skimmed through the air, missing his right ear by centimetres. He stumbled onto his hands and knees, the pain of the protruding arrow excruciating. In his peripheral vision, the officer saw the man scoop up his abandoned police rifle with one hand before retreating back from where he had first appeared. In just seconds he was gone.

The officer's colleagues reached him, one assuming a shooting platform in a kneeling position, rifle scanning towards the threat. The other officer slung his rifle strap over his shoulder and heaved the injured man to his feet.

'He's got my rifle. We need cover!'

The rusting carcass of an old tractor, a forgotten relic from years gone by, was their closest cover. They retreated and dropped onto the long grass at the base of its enormous tyre, which offered temporary protection and good visibility.

'Urgent, urgent! Require backup, officer down!' one officer called into his radio.

THIRTY-ONE

OFFICER down. 'That's the surveillance team,' snapped Benfield as the plea for assistance crackled over the radio. Jarrod had never seen him so rattled. 'Deploy the SERT team! We're moving out now.'

Jarrod and Brad were at the rear of the convoy of police vehicles racing out of town towards the Miles property. All units were ordered to pull over at a rally point a hundred metres from the main entrance to the property as the armoured vehicle surged ahead. The matt black SERT tank manoeuvred into the driveway and accelerated towards the house, leaving behind a cloud of dust in its wake. All the rest could do was wait for the call. They would all move in once the stronghold was secure.

So they waited. As minutes passed by Jarrod and Brad sat in silence. Jarrod could see the detectives in the cars ahead moving about and fidgeting. Then a call came from Benfield over the radio. 'Standby all units, awaiting confirmation,' followed by radio silence.

More minutes ticked by. Then the call came Jarrod had been anticipating. 'All units move in, location is secure. Repeat, all units move in.'

Tyres squealed. The cars ahead of Jarrod and Brad sped off and he followed in their slipstream. They approached Vincent Miles' property and the dilapidated old farmhouse came into view. Jarrod could make out the SERT vehicle parked at the front of the house, doors wide open. The first police sedan turned into the long driveway, then the second, then the third. He negotiated the turn at the safest speed he could manage and followed the cloud of dust created by the other vehicles. He skidded the car to a halt behind the others and they all scrambled out, firearms drawn. They spread out, covering the front and back stairs, doorways and windows. Some SERT officers were already inside the house, others remained downstairs, their semi-automatic rifles scanning the immediate area. The SERT team looked impressive in black helmets, goggles and face masks, navy overalls, black lace-up boots and ballistic vests. Their utility belts were equipped with a vast array of equipment and carry pouches. Glock handguns were holstered to their thighs.

The commander calmly walked out through the front doorway of the house and onto the veranda. He pulled his helmet off and announced, 'The stronghold is secure.'

The three surveillance officers had been found safe, hunkered against an old tractor. The injured officer was led to an awaiting ambulance for immediate transport to hospital. The arrow protruding from his shoulder was a ghastly sight. He had gotten a good look at his assailant, who he identified as Vincent Miles from the intel bulletin mug shot.

There had been no more sightings of Miles. Jarrod received this news with mixed feelings. No one else had been hurt, but they were still no closer to locating Miles and Ryan. He hoped a search of the house would provide answers.

The SERT team scoured nearby bushland as the other detectives checked the rooms inside the house. Other officers searched the verandas and the downstairs area. Jarrod moved towards the back of the house where he found the old Holden parked in the garage. He was strangely drawn to it and moved towards the car. The whole scene was as though it had been frozen in time. The brick he had used to smash the window still lay on the ground where he dropped it three years ago. Glass fragments were scattered on the ground and inside the car on the floor and front seats. The long coil of industrial hose lay on the ground. He relived that awful day; the day baby

Jazmin and her mother Roxy had died.

He was aware of someone else's presence. Brad walked up behind him. 'This is where you found them, isn't it?'

Jarrod stared into the car and nodded.

THIRTY-TWO

JARROD'S mind returned to the present as the frenzied police activity around the house kicked into top gear. The other detectives were being divided into search teams under the control of Benfield. Jarrod and Brad paced around the perimeter of the house, surrounded by a cordon of SERT officers. Where the hell was Miles? His four-wheel drive was still parked out the front so he was out there on foot, somewhere. The rear tray of the vehicle was covered in blood. Jarrod peered out towards the surrounding bushland, wondering if Miles was watching their every move.

The SERT team reformed and Benfield called a briefing at the front of the house. A team of city Homicide Squad detectives were ordered to secure the house and commence a thorough search. The rest were to search the bushland. 'We're going after this bastard. He couldn't have gotten too far on foot,' said Benfield.

The SERT officers, with superior firepower and training, were dispersed among the rest of the officers. Wearing protective vests and firearms drawn, they fanned out into a semi-circular formation and moved from the house towards the adjacent bushland. Benfield, Dawes and Long joined the formation. Jarrod breathed hard under the weight of his protective vest, his Glock heavy in his hands as he scanned the fringe of bushland through the gun's sights. His heart pounded against the walls of his chest. He stepped into the long undergrowth and moved forward through the trees. Brad walked alongside to his left about five metres away. They shared a glance and a nod and then proceeded forward. To Jarrod's right was a hulking SERT officer whose name he didn't know. He held his rifle up in the firing position, his eye trained on his front foresight as he surged forward.

What the hell were they doing? They were hunting for an armed madman in a vast area of thick bushland, walking blind. The line of police was spread thin to cover the land area and they had no idea where to concentrate their search. The strategy was to begin with a broad sweep to secure as much area as possible. They were trying to flush out Vincent Miles, who had the advantage. He knew the land like the back of his hand. They weren't going to just stumble upon Miles hiding in the bush. It was more likely he was observing them, tracking their movements.

But what choice did they have? They had to take the fight to him. A dog unit and the police chopper from the city were a long way off.

Jarrod thought about the officer who had been picked off with a crossbow. The fact that Miles was able to hunt them in broad daylight frightened the hell out of him. They continued forward regardless, deeper into the thick scrub. He couldn't see any worn tracks or marks that might indicate someone was there before them. Their semi-circular formation spread wider, each man separating further apart with each step forward. Jarrod's eyes scanned from side to side as he kept pace with the other detectives and SERT officers, but he soon started losing sight of them.

It was then that he saw it, a dark object up ahead in a clearing. As he moved forward, he could make out the singed grass circling a ring of large stones. The mound of charcoal and burnt logs in the middle of the stones suggested the remnants of a bonfire. Thin wisps of smoke still rose from the mound, however the fire had long since burnt itself out.

What he saw next horrified him. Lying within the charcoal and burnt logs was a scorched body. It scarcely resembled a human being, but there was no mistaking the skull and jawbone. Below the skull, the charred remains were a molten mass of burnt flesh. The blackened arm and leg bones, feet and hands were still recognisable. The pungent odour hit him as a slight breeze blew through the trees. He stopped in his tracks a few metres away from the body. Brad and the SERT officer saw what he had discovered and rushed over for a closer look.

'Is that what I think it is?' asked Brad.

'Yep. I wonder who the poor bastard is.'

The SERT officer pulled off his headgear and hurled where he stood.

'You right, mate?' asked Brad.

The giant man looked up. His face was pale and he wiped his mouth with his sleeve. He nodded and stared at the charred body.

Jarrod then noticed the other stones. He stepped to his left and circled around so that he was standing in front of the protruding charred bones of the victim's feet. Six round stones had been placed outside the bonfire on the ground in the shape of a hexagon. Lines had been drawn in the earth, connecting each stone to form the complete shape. It was the symbol that was emerging as the key behind the rising death toll.

It all seemed so surreal. The breeze whispered through the tree branches above. There was an eerie silence as they gazed at the burnt corpse. Jarrod could hear the faint echo of boots stomping and branches crunching as the other officers continued forward on both flanks, oblivious to their discovery.

Jarrod's attention was drawn towards a darting movement just ahead of them in the thicket on the far side of the clearing. He raised his firearm and trained it in that direction. He couldn't see anyone. The scrub was too thick.

'What's the matter?' asked Brad.

'I don't know, I thought I heard...'

The gun shots were deafening. They boomed relentlessly, one

after the other. The SERT officer on Jarrod's right spun around and was thrown backwards onto the ground from the impact of a bullet that smashed into the chest plate of his protective vest. Jarrod dived and rolled in the dirt. The gunshots continued. He turned and looked for Brad. Jarrod's heart sank. Brad had been hit. He was hunched behind the pile of burnt logs. Jarrod crawled over to him, the remains of the bonfire providing some cover between them and the gunman. Blood gushed from a gaping wound in Brad's thigh.

'I'm shot. The bastard fucking shot me, can you believe that!' he yelled, panicking.

'Just hold on, mate, and for Christ's sake, keep your head down,' Jarrod ordered.

Brad nodded, writhing in agony. Jarrod removed his folded handkerchief and pressed it against the wound. Brad cried out in anguish. Jarrod took hold of Brad's hand and placed it over the handkerchief. 'Keep the pressure on it if you can.'

Brad grimaced, gritting his teeth.

Jarrod holstered his Glock and fumbled to undo Brad's belt. It came loose and he slid it out and fashioned a tourniquet, pulling the belt tight to stem the bleeding. Brad wailed in agony as Jarrod looped the end into a knot and gave it one last tug.

The SERT officer clutched his chest, winded and gasping for air. Jarrod crawled over to him, exposed. He no longer had cover.

'I. Can't. Breathe,' the big man wheezed with short shallow breaths. The round hadn't penetrated his chest, but Jarrod suspected he had broken ribs from the impact that shattered the plate.

They were still out in the open. Jarrod grabbed the man's vest and pulled him with all his strength. He was a heavy bastard, but Jarrod dragged him about ten metres across the dirt. He pulled with every ounce of remaining strength until they were behind the pile of burnt logs. The gunshots didn't let up, one after the other. The booming echoes reverberated in Jarrod's ears. A semi-auto. He guessed that about fifteen rounds had been fired. The three of them lay in the dirt against the pile of burnt logs, the charred body just above. Bullets whizzed through the air, some splintering the logs.

Jarrod heard the cries of their fellow officers. 'Get down, get down! Where's it coming from?' He prayed there were no more casualties.

The gunshots fell silent. He took a deep breath and peeked out above the corpse to see if he could see the gunman. Nothing.

A screaming voice pierced the silence. 'You can't stop what has already begun. No one can stop our union in paradise.'

Jarrod recognised the voice. It was Vincent Miles. He then saw Miles leaning out from behind a tree about twenty metres away. For a moment their eyes met, Miles' gaze intense and full of hatred. He aimed a police issue R4 rifle at Jarrod who ducked behind the logs bracing for more gunfire, but none came.

He heard the dry fire click of the rifle trigger. 'Damn it!' Miles cursed.

Jarrod took the risk and peeked over the logs. The R4 was jammed and Miles was trying to clear the round that must have stove-piped in the chamber. Jarrod took his chance and balanced himself in a kneeling position. He levelled his Glock, controlled his breathing and fired a string of five shots. Chunks of bark splintered near Miles' face as he ducked back behind the tree. He threw the rifle to the ground and darted off into the shadows, crashing through the thick scrub. Jarrod scanned his Glock, salty sweat stinging his eyes as it dripped from his brow. Miles had disappeared, but Jarrod could still hear the muffled stomping of boots through the dry undergrowth. He leapt out from behind cover and pursued him, adrenaline taking over.

As Jarrod hurdled rocks and logs, low tree branches scratched his face and arms. Ahead of him, Miles surged ahead. Jarrod lost his bearings. His head spun, his breathing erratic. He stumbled but regained balance and kept running, however he'd lost sight of Miles. The dense bushland had formed a blanket closing in around him. He couldn't see very far in front of him and had no idea which way to go. As he was about to run into a patch of lantana, he stopped in his tracks to avoid their stinging stems. The vegetation hadn't been disturbed. Miles hadn't come that way. Jarrod tried to control his breathing. Footsteps crunched in the undergrowth to his right. He cautiously moved towards the sound and as he stepped into a small clearing, a figure emerged from the trees. Jarrod levelled his Glock. A man aimed a handgun at him. Their eyes locked in recognition. Murray Long lowered his gun and bent down with his hands on his knees, panting for breath. 'You can put your gun down now, O'Connor,' he wheezed as he hunched over.

To the left of the clearing lumbered Dawes, struggling to catch his breath. Then to Jarrod's right, Benfield ran out into the clearing. The four detectives stood looking at each other in dismay, guns at their sides. They'd all come from different directions, but somehow Miles had slipped past them.

He was gone.

THIRTY-THREE

VINCENT Miles was hyped, every nerve in his body fired in overdrive. He sat on the planked bunker floor and savoured the aroma of the moist earth encasing his underground refuge. He'd slipped into his hiding place, pulling shut the camouflaged hatch behind him as he slid down the ladder.

He tried to meditate however the exhilaration of his attack on the police scum had heightened his senses.

Wax dripped from the candle, light from the flickering flame danced across the walls of the cramped chamber. He removed his sweat-soaked shirt, exposing his muscular body, toned from years of pumping iron in prison gyms. Dragons, serpents and grim reapers bulged on his biceps and forearms.

One image had been tattooed with reverence over his heart. Metatron's cube and its intricate matrix of three-dimensional shapes were inked into the skin. He drew in deep, slow breaths through his nose, filling his lungs with cool air. He held and then expelled through his mouth. He did this over and over until he regained focus. He tightened the rubber strap under his left bicep and flexed, tapping the vein in the crook of his arm. The white powder dissolved on the spoon as he waved it over the candle. With precision, he drew the warm liquid into the syringe, pierced the vein with the needle and slowly squeezed the amphetamine into his bloodstream. Euphoria.

He relished his victory over the police scum. He hoped to take out more before it all came to an end. The thought of their suffering gave him strength. They had caused so much pain in his life, now it was payback time.

All his preparations were complete. His quest was nearly over.

The children must die.

They must die soon.

Memories of Clare's face were becoming distant. How he missed her. He longed to be with her again. He knew he had to be patient. Just one more thing remained; it had to be done so that he could put closure on his pitiful existence. Soon he would transcend into a new realm.

He could hear the distant murmur of police somewhere up on ground level. It would be dark outside soon. He would slip away into the night, away from there. He would find the children and from the darkness he would emerge, then they would die. And then he would bring them to her. Clare would be so happy, so grateful. Then he would come to her and in her arms she would hold his little baby girl. He would be with her again for eternity. On his journey he would take revenge on his little girl's mother, Roxy. In the form of the Archangel, he would hunt down her soul and cast it into eternal suffering. He knew how it had to be done.

He prepared his weapons and equipment.

Nothing or no one would stand in the way of his destiny.

No one can stop our union in paradise.

THIRTY-FOUR

DARKNESS was setting in over the harsh landscape surrounding Vincent Miles' property. A flock of white cockatoos screeched and argued as they nestled in trees overhead. The vibrant orange glow of the setting sun faded as it dipped beneath the horizon, replaced by the dim early night sky.

Crime scene officer Larry Carson and the scientific officers from Sydney established a crime scene around the burnt corpse. The weather was clear so there was no threat of rain damaging physical evidence. Portable floodlights cast an oasis of artificial light in the sea of encroaching darkness. Up at the farmhouse, Benfield marshalled the little manpower he had at his disposal, but more officers were needed.

It was impossible to lock the place down entirely. SERT officers provided security, positioned at key points around the crime scene and up at the house. The deafening shrill of chirping cicadas pulsated in the air. A band of insects joined the chorus to welcome in the new night. The ruckus reverberated in Jarrod's ears.

Two paramedic units had arrived and were treating Brad and the SERT officer. Jarrod paced impatiently near the back of the ambulance in which Brad lay. He peeked through the gap in the doors at the two paramedics working on Brad's injured leg. He had lost a lot of blood but was stable. He lay semi-conscious on the gurney with an oxygen mask strapped to his face, an IV tube inserted into his forearm.

The young paramedic working on Brad's bandaging turned to Jarrod with a reassuring smile. 'Your friend here will be fine. We've doped him up with morphine so he'll be out of it for a while. It's a clean wound. The bullet just missed the femoral artery. He was very lucky. We'll get him to the hospital and they'll look after him there.'

'Thanks, mate. That's what I needed to hear,' Jarrod replied with relief.

The paramedic nodded and the rear doors closed. The ambulance pulled away and negotiated its way out the dusty driveway past the tangle of hastily parked police vehicles, turning onto the road heading into town. Jarrod looked up at the police helicopter that had arrived from Sydney, circling above to get a sighting of Vincent Miles. A powerful searchlight beamed towards the ground, scouring the bushland. Trees swayed and a dust cloud formed as the aircraft hovered and then circled, the thud of rotor blades reverberating.

A heavy hand rested on Jarrod's shoulder. Long was beside him. Jarrod turned his head towards him. Long's eyes were locked onto the chopper as it flew out of sight.

'How you holding up, O'Connor? The word has gotten around that you were a bit of a hero this afternoon,' he said, no sarcasm in his voice this time.

'Is that what they say, hey? That's all bullshit. I had my chance and I let the bastard get away. I had a clear shot and I missed. Some hero.' Jarrod was exhausted and overwhelmed by the madness of these last few days. Everything had been turned upside down. People had died. Things were out of control and he had done nothing to stop it.

'Well, O'Connor, you did what you could. You kept your head when it counted. In fact, I guess I owe you an apology. It turns out your theories were spot on. I know I haven't been very fair to you lately and given you the credit you deserve. And for the record, I'm glad that Harding is okay.'

Jarrod just nodded. He wasn't in the mood for sentiment.

'And one more thing, there's someone who wants to talk to you.' Long pointed towards the remaining ambulance vehicle. Come on, I'll introduce you.

Inside the ambulance lay Bob Thorn. Jarrod now had a name to associate with the hulking SERT officer he'd dragged behind cover as all hell opened up on them. Thorn tilted up his head and offered his hand. Jarrod reached in, Thorn's huge hand engulfing his. It was an effort for Thorn to speak. His breathing was short and laboured. 'Thanks man, I owe you one. I was a sitting duck out there.'

'Don't mention it. Besides, we're on the same team. Sometimes we lose sight of that.' Jarrod glanced at Long. The irony wasn't wasted on him. His eyes squinted and he allowed himself a smug smile.

Jarrod turned to the paramedic who was watching a cardiac monitor hooked up to Bob. 'What's the verdict? Is this bloke going to live?'

'Yep, looks like a few broken ribs. The chest plate inside his ballistic vest shattered from the impact of the round, but it saved his life. He'll be sore, but he'll live.'

Bob took another painful breath and wheezed. 'Go and catch that crazy bastard. He's gotta be stopped.'

'We'll do our best, mate,' was all Jarrod could manage.

Miles had to be stopped.

Catching him was what worried Jarrod.

As they stepped away from the ambulance, a Dog Squad van pulled in. Jarrod and Long jumped as police dog 'Jed', a fiery German Shepherd, lunged at them from behind the wire mesh in the rear of the vehicle. The dog snarled viciously.

Long's expression was thunderous. 'That dog will be the end of me one of these days. Don't trust the crazy mutt, he'll go for your balls. The bloody dog doesn't know the difference between good guys and bad guys. He's a pretty good tracker though, just don't get in his road.'

The van parked and the dog handler, Sergeant Glenn Marcus, jumped out of the cab wearing tactical trousers and black military boots. His Glock was strapped around his leg in a thigh holster. Hands on hips, he let out a boisterous laugh. 'My boy got you again, Long. When are you gonna learn?' he chuckled to himself.

'Just keep that man-eating monster away from me, Marcus,' replied Long.

Glenn gave a wink and a grin. 'Righto then, but if you get in his way, your arse is his. So, who's running this rock show anyway?' he said eagerly.

~

Benfield assembled all available officers for another briefing on the fly. The detectives who had searched the house gave their update first. They explained Miles was living a meagre existence and the house was furnished only with essentials. Non-perishable food had been stockpiled in the pantry. Hunting knives and camping equipment were packed in duffle bags ready for deployment. Miles was preparing for something, maybe his version of the apocalypse. There was very little else in the house. It was a stark and hollow space. It was no stereotypical madman's lair. There were no grotesque drawings of demons, dismembered body parts in jars, or biblical ramblings covering the walls. There was a sense of order and methodical preparation. Jarrod had been inside the house once before. On that day, the floor was covered in Miles' blood and the place was in total disarray. There were now no signs of the cluttered mess it once was. All remnants of his previous life with Roxy had been erased.

However, in the bedroom, bundled among Miles' few personal effects, a stack of letters and poems were found, written by Clare Kingston. On the crumpled pages, she pledged herself to Vincent.

The words spoke of her love for her "archangel" and revealed some of the missing pieces of the puzzle. She vowed to be with him until the end. She would do whatever he asked of her. There was reference to Edward Ryan in the letters. She referred to him as her shining light, the one who brought her to Vincent. She wrote about her dreams of having her revenge against her ex-husband. This was the first direct evidence they uncovered of a motive for the Kingston murders. However, it didn't explain everything.

Inside another bedroom lay a mattress and bedding alongside bags of clothing. Documentation and personal effects belonging to Edward Ryan were found.

Somehow, Vincent Miles and Clare Kingston had persuaded Edward Ryan to go after the Kingston family. There was no sign of Edward Ryan. *Were those his charred remains out on that bonfire?* Soon they would know for sure. *If so, what had caused his demise? A double-cross maybe?* He was a perfect scapegoat to take the blame for the murders. That didn't explain why Miles hadn't properly disposed of Ryan's body. Instead, it had been ceremoniously cremated. *Was all the paranoia about angels and mystical symbols just evidence of how deluded these people were, or was it something more?* There was no telling what Miles' next move would be.

Theories and assumptions cluttered Jarrod's mind.

THIRTY-FIVE

THEY gathered around with torches as Benfield used a black whiteboard marker to draw a rough mud map on the bonnet of a marked police vehicle. 'Now listen up,' he said. 'I don't want any stupid heroics out there. I've called in the dog to try and locate the suspect's scent and establish his last direction of travel. If we can work out how he gave us the slip, we may be able to narrow down his escape options. If the dog gets a hit, we'll concentrate our searches on a more defined area so we can direct the chopper. The SERT commander has given us some of his men. We've had to spread ourselves thin to cover the entire area. Long and O'Connor, you'll be team leaders. Are you two up for this? If not, I'll send someone else.'

Jarrod and Long looked at each other and then back at Benfield. 'O'Connor and I are good to go,' said Long.

Jarrod was glad at least one of them was confident.

'That's it then. I want you to remain in radio contact at all times. Good luck,' said Benfield.

Glenn, the dog handler, Long and Jarrod vested up. Two SERT officers, fully equipped with night vision goggles and the usual firepower, were ready to go. They had torches fitted below their rifle barrels. Glenn attached the tracking lead to Jed's collar and released him from the dog van's holding cage. Jarrod found himself taking a cautious step away as Glenn led Jed past. The German shepherd was now quite docile, easily mistaken for a family pet. Jarrod knew better

205

though. He had seen the psychotic police dog turn on people for no apparent reason. He had once bitten a uniform officer on the thigh, tearing his trousers and resulting in the poor bloke needing stitches. Glenn always kept him on a short and very secure lead, but on that one occasion the dog had taken everyone by surprise. His tracking and offender take-down skills were superior to most police dogs, hence the forgiving attitude to his indiscretions.

They led Glenn and Jed to the vicinity of the burnt corpse where scientific officers still worked under the artificial lighting. The helicopter flew overhead to provide aerial observation. The noise of the aircraft was deafening. Its powerful spotlights circled around them, providing enough light as they made their way through the scrub. Their Mag light torches were their only other source of light. A SERT sniper armed with a long-range rifle was aboard the helicopter. The crew were also using thermal imaging, scanning for heat signatures. As the light shone through the trees, the landscape around them bore no resemblance to its daytime appearance. Dark shadows behind the trees created an eerie backdrop.

They circled around the cordoned area of the cremation site and followed their torch beams through the trees. Jarrod led the others to where he had seen Miles emerge from behind the tree. He shone his light in the direction he had fled. Glenn and Jed pushed ahead and took the lead. The SERT officers were at the rear of the group, scanning from side to side with semi-auto rifles and night scopes. Jed looked disinterested and trotted alongside his handler.

In a soft voice just above a whisper, Glenn gave the dog instructions. 'Where is it Jed? Get it Jed, get it Jed.' This triggered the dog's interest. His tail wagged and he knew the game was on. This was what he lived for. Glenn released more length on the retractable lead and the dog sniffed the ground precisely on the spot where Miles had stood. Jed's interest was piqued and he took off, his nose working overtime, sniffing along the ground. Glenn gave him more lead for freedom of movement and followed, maintaining tight control of the lead.

Jed moved with purpose. He had located the scent and followed it with pinpoint accuracy. The others jogged to keep up with Glenn and the dog. Jarrod was retracing the steps he had taken earlier while pursuing Miles, however he soon lost his bearings. The landscape was unrecognisable, each tree, log and rock looked like the next. They shone their lights ahead, more for their own benefit. Jed didn't need their help. He knew exactly where he was heading. Soon they came to a spot Jarrod recognised, the lantana patch he had almost stumbled into. As they came upon it, Jed deviated to his right and followed a path in a different direction. It was there that Miles had evaded Jarrod. They were now following the path he had taken.

The helicopter was also on the move, thudding above at low altitude. Jed led them on a winding path through dense scrub, his pace becoming more urgent.

'Good boy, good boy. Where's it at, where's it at?' Glenn asked in a high pitch voice.

Glenn pulled Jed back to a walking pace, the dog pulling hard on his lead, urging his master to go faster. The others were following at a good distance and quickened their pace to catch up.

Jarrod froze when Jed started barking. Glenn pulled hard on the lead, stopping Jed from going any further. Glenn drew his firearm. Using his spotlight, he scanned the immediate area up ahead. Jarrod and Long were alongside him now, firearms also drawn. The SERT officers knelt on either side of them and took up their firing positions.

'You boys better get ready. The scent is strong here. We're getting very close,' whispered Glenn. The helicopter circled above, its lights creating a large circle on the ground. It reminded Jarrod of a theatre spotlight that followed the actors around the stage.

The excitement in Jed's bark intensified. He pulled at his lead, eager to continue after the scent. 'Whoa, Jed, settle down boy,'

Glenn instructed, but the dog continued to bark. Glenn and Jed held their position.

'We've located a good scent and we're close. Do you have a visual?' said Long into his radio handset. 'Copy that, we have visual of your location,' replied the helicopter co-pilot. 'Negative on thermal imaging. We're not seeing anyone.'

'It's your call, Murray. What now?' asked Glenn.

'We hold our position.' Talking into the radio, he gave further instructions to the chopper co-pilot. 'We're holding our position. Concentrate your search on the vicinity directly in front of us.'

'Copy that.' The helicopter circled ahead, its spotlight scanning the bushland below.

Jarrod was relieved. It was suicide to go any further. The darkness was their greatest enemy. He didn't care for walking straight into another ambush.

Jarrod then saw something metallic glistening on the ground as the helicopter spotlight circled past it. He shone his light where he had seen it but there was nothing.

'What is it?' asked Long.

'I don't know, something's over there. It could be nothing.'

Jarrod then saw it again, a small object reflecting the light. 'Over there,' he pointed. Jed had stopped barking, but was still intent on following the scent. Jarrod edged towards the glistening object but couldn't make it out. They closed in, step by step. Jed barked, wanting to move straight toward the metallic object. They panned out and approached from different angles. They were now in a small clearing. Jed was almost right on the object. Glenn pulled him back.

Jarrod stepped closer and bent down, shining his light onto the object. It was a metal handle. There was a square shape around it in the dust, covered by twigs and leaves. He jumped back, realising what he had discovered. It was a wooden hatch door. They were standing over some sort of underground compartment. The others also understood, not saying a word. They aimed their firearms at the hatch door, half expecting Vincent Miles to lunge out. *Was he waiting down below?*

Long called it in on the radio. They may have cornered Vincent Miles.

THIRTY-SIX

LONG directed the helicopter to maintain its spotlight on them. Glenn and the dog kept back. They'd done their bit for now. Jarrod took a deep breath and gripped the metal handle. Above in the helicopter, the SERT sniper had his weapon fixed on the hatch. The SERT officers on the ground were in kneeling positions ready to make their move. They both gave Jarrod the thumbs up and then a nod. It had to be one smooth motion; there was no room for mistakes. Jarrod heaved the handle and swung the hatch door open. Without hesitation the SERT officers moved, the first scanning his rifle into the opening as the other slid down the ladder. The second quickly followed. The others shone their torches into the dark underground cavern. Out of sight, they yelled, 'Armed police, don't move!' There was shuffling of boots and then the call came. 'Secure. Area secure. There's no one here.'

Jarrod and Long made their way down the metal ladder through the narrow opening. They were in a dark, tomb-like bunker with wooden floors and thick timber beams and posts supporting the walls and ceiling. Jarrod was surprised there was enough head height, however the room was quite narrow. Stored on wooden shelves sat rows of tinned food, survival supplies and a Polaroid camera. A crossbow hung from its shoulder strap from a hook on one of the vertical posts. A burnt-out candle stood on the floor in a hardened puddle of wax. Beside it lay a used needle and syringe. Jarrod bent down and touched the wax that had dripped down the sides of the candle and onto the floor. It was just starting to set and was still warm. 'Christ, we must have just missed him,' he said.

'You blokes better have a look at this,' said one of the SERT officers. He pointed his rifle torch at something at the far end of the bunker. Jarrod hadn't noticed it in the partial light of flickering torches. He shone his own torch onto a small cork board that hung on the wall. Pinned to it were photographs. At the top was an old family portrait. The heads of a man, a woman and two children had been cut out of the photograph. Below it, the cut-out heads of Olivia and Jamie were pinned to the board. He followed his torch down the corkboard, the light reflecting off a Polaroid photo of a male corpse lying on a pile of logs. It was the nearby bonfire before it had been ignited. He looked closer at the photo, focusing on the face of the young man dressed in blood-soaked clothing. It was Edward Ryan.

The next photo horrified Jarrod. It was a Polaroid of Clare Kingston, hanging by her neck from the tree on the hilltop where her body had been found. The photo had been taken when it was still dark, the flash of the camera illuminating her pale, naked body against a pitch-black background. Pinned over the top of her head was her smiling cut out face from the family portrait. The symbolism was clear, in her death she found happiness. But what shocked Jarrod was the photo itself. Miles must have been there when she committed suicide. He'd photographed her hanging, lifeless body as a keepsake, a record of her death.

Pinned to the board below the other photographs was a Polaroid of a smiling Vincent Miles, his eyes staring out from the photograph. To the right of this was the cut out head of Stewart Kingston. The image was attached to the cork board by two pins that pierced Stewart's eyes.

Jarrod adjusted his torch lens and widened the light beam. The photographs had been pinned to the board in a deliberate order. The faces of the children, Edward Ryan's body, Clare Kingston's body, Vincent Miles and Stewart Kingston formed the six exterior points of a hexagon. Woven between the pins was thin black cotton which formed the exterior sides of the hexagon. The cotton ran from each exterior corner across to other corners, forming a web of lines and shapes within. It was Metatron's cube, the essence of life.

'Well, Murray,' said Jarrod. 'It's not the cold hard evidence you were after, but it is one of those riddles you had referred to. I think you called it a crock of shit, but it may well explain what is going on in the messed-up mind of Vincent Miles.'

'I'm hearing ya,' muttered Long. 'Let's get the hell out of here and secure this place until morning.'

'No arguments from me,' said Jarrod.

'And none from us,' chimed in one of the SERT guys. They were the first to climb back up into the light of the hovering helicopter.

Jed was soon onto the fresh scent, leading Glenn on a trail that headed back into the tree line down a hill towards a gully. They all followed as they had done before. Jarrod's anticipation of a possible final confrontation with Miles was growing. Water trickled along a stream that flowed over smooth rocks and pebbles. Jed stopped at the bank of the creek. The scent had led him to the edge of the water.

'Let's go, boy, come on,' said Glenn as he coerced the dog to cross the shallow creek. On the other side, Jed paced up and down sniffing the sand bank. He'd lost the scent.

'Our boy is a smart lad. He's used the creek to stop us tracking his scent. He's gone one of two ways, upstream or downstream. Any of you blokes wanna take a punt?' said Glenn.

Long scratched his head. 'We don't have enough men to split up. The chopper's our best bet.' He spoke into the radio. 'Portable to aerial unit, we've lost the suspect's scent at the creek. Can you take a run up and down the creek for a few kilometres?'

'Roger that,' crackled the radio. It became quiet as the helicopter circled and flew upstream, its lights and the throbbing noise of its rotor blades fading as it disappeared over the hill. They stood in silence as the water trickled over the rocks. Beyond the reach of their torchlights, the darkness formed an impenetrable black sheet around them.

They held their position, realising it was pointless splitting up or taking a gamble on the direction Miles may have headed. The helicopter flew by again, heading down stream this time, its spotlight carving its way through the dark landscape. They waited but too much time slipped by.

The helicopter co-pilot radioed back. The aerial search had been unsuccessful. Still no hits on thermal imaging. The chopper had to turn back for refuelling. By now Miles could be anywhere. Even in daylight, it would be difficult to coordinate a search over such a vast area with the limited manpower they had.

The search had to be scaled back until first light. Traipsing around the bush under torch light was futile and dangerous. They'd be easy targets for an ambush. Jarrod considered the possibilities – Miles could have gone to ground, holed up in another bunker. Maybe he was on the move. *Where would he go?*

Benfield scrambled the few crews available and dispatched them to warn residents of neighbouring farmhouses. The last thing they needed was a hostage situation.

Jarrod tried to put himself in Miles' shoes, to think like him, anticipate his next move. *Was evading capture enough? Or would he want more? Would he be brazen enough to come after the kids again?* Surely not. Not with so much heat bearing down on him. But Miles was a man on a ledge – erratic, desperate. Nothing to lose. He was capable of anything. *Would he hide in plain sight and emerge where they least expected?* One thing for certain, he was working to a plan, a master scheme. Only Miles knew what would come next.

Jarrod's thoughts returned to Olivia, Jake and Jamie. The idea of harm coming to them sickened him. He retrieved his mobile phone and made a call. He confirmed the kids were still safely tucked away under police guard at the safehouse. Knowing they were safe for now, did little to quell his growing unease.

He felt helpless being one step behind, with Miles calling the shots.

THIRTY-SEVEN

IT hadn't taken Vincent Miles long to circle around the police and make good his escape.

'The arrogant bastards thought they could hunt me down like an animal, but they don't know what they're dealing with,' he muttered aloud. He'd hiked through the familiar bushland and across farm paddocks until he reached the outskirts of town, then skulked along the dark back streets like a shadow. He was a spiritual being awaiting his final metamorphosis.

He stood below a streetlight, gazing towards the house. The front porch lights were on. Someone was home. His silhouetted figure moved stealthily across the lawn towards the front door. A canvas duffel bag was slung over one shoulder, the hunting knife in hand.

He knocked at the front door and the hallway light came on. *Someone was coming.* As the door swung open, Vincent Miles thrust his hand forward and held the throat of Jim Caxton, the freelance journalist. With his other hand, he held the point of the knife against Caxton's abdomen. 'Say one word and I'll spill your intestines, right here on your doorstep.' He moved the knife blade up to Caxton's lips and whispered, 'Shhh, not a sound. Is anyone else with you?'

Caxton shook his head, his eyes terrorised.

'Good, then let's go inside, Jim. We have a lot to talk about.'

Miles, still holding Caxton by the throat, led him back inside the house, kicking the door closed behind them.

Miles led Caxton to the lounge room and shoved him down onto a couch.

'Don't hurt me,' whimpered Caxton. 'What do you want from me? I have money. Is that what you want?'

Miles offered a sinister smile and sat on the couch beside Caxton. 'Money? No, my friend, I have no need for money, not where I'm going. What I need from you is information. You're the local big shot investigative journalist, aren't you? You're the man who's in the know, the man on the spot when news is breaking. You see, Jim, what I need from you is information that might save your life.'

'Who the hell are you?' croaked Caxton.

Miles punched Caxton in the sternum. He reeled over in pain, air thrust from his lungs. Miles lounged back, making himself comfortable, casually holding the knife. He saw a packet of Horizon Blue cigarettes and a lighter on the coffee table and helped himself. He lit the cigarette and inhaled, then blew the smoke towards Caxton.

'Here's the thing. I need to know where the Kingston children are. You seem to have a special connection with them. I saw your front page photo and headlines. I'm sure you have the resources to find out where they are,' said Miles, taking another drag and blowing a cloud of smoke.

Caxton heaved, still recovering from the blow to his chest. 'It's not that easy…' he panted. '…the police will have them hidden away somewhere, probably a safe house.'

'Well, Jimmy, you don't mind if I call you Jimmy? Let me make it simple for you. Either you find out for me where the Kingston children are hiding or you die.'

Caxton scratched his head and considered the proposal. 'Why do you need to know? Are you responsible for the killings?'

'Don't ask questions you don't want to know the answers to, Jimmy. You should know that.'

Miles took another hit of the cigarette, staring intently into Caxton's eyes. 'Everyone paves their own destiny. The Kingstons were responsible for their own deaths.'

Miles slid across the couch and pressed his body against his prisoner. He leaned forward so their faces almost touched. The cigarette dangled from his lips, its smoke making Caxton blink, irritating his eyes. Miles held the tip of the knife against Caxton's throat and whispered into his ear. 'I can see you need some motivation.'

Caxton's eyes widened.

Miles grabbed Caxton with a pincer grip at the base of his skull and reefed him forward, pinning his hand flat on the coffee table, fingers splayed. Caxton struggled, but he was outmuscled. Miles gripped Caxton's wrist. With the other hand, he raised the knife above his head, threatening to strike.

'No! No! I'll do it, I'll do whatever you say!' Caxton pleaded.

'That's what I like to hear, but just so you know I'm not to be messed with...' He thrust the knife down hard, the blade penetrating Caxton's hand. His scream pierced the air. Miles moved his hand over Caxton's mouth to muffle his cries. Caxton stared in disbelief at his bloodied hand nailed to the tabletop by the knife.

'Now, Jimmy, I don't have much time. You better get to it. You've got some calls to make. You'll need this hand.' Miles yanked the knife free. The journalist screamed as the blade slid out through mangled bone and flesh. Miles went to the bathroom and found a towel. He threw it at Caxton, who fumbled with shaking hands, wrapping the towel clumsily around the bloody wound.

Miles picked up the cordless telephone and passed it to Caxton. 'Let's see how good you are. Remember, this may save your life.'

THIRTY-EIGHT

SARAH Morgan sat alone watching television, as she did most nights. She was surprised when the phone rang. Who would ring her at ten o'clock at night? As the phone continued to ring, Sarah grumbled and pulled herself free from the cosy blanket. She slid her feet into her slippers and eased herself up out of the reclining chair. She shuffled over to the phone hanging on the wall in the kitchen.

'Hello?' she answered.

'Um, ah, hello, Sarah. This is Jim Caxton,' said the trembling voice on the other end.

'What do you want? Why are you ringing me at home?'

'Um, Sarah, I need a favour. You have to understand, this is important. I need your help,' Caxton paused.

'What is it, Jim?' She didn't trust him and the tone of his voice made her uncomfortable. He sounded desperate.

'The thing is, I need to know where the police have placed the Kingston children. It's important for my follow-up story.'

'You know I can't tell you that. I'll lose my job at Children's Services if they find out I've given out confidential information.'

'Sarah, I'm sorry to put you in this position. It's important,' he said with a strange urgency in his voice.

'What could be so important? Those kids are under protection.'

'Sarah, I give you my word my source will remain confidential. I just need some more photographs and the chance to clarify some information about the murders.'

'You've got to be kidding, no way,' she said, about to hang up the phone.

'I didn't want to force your hand, Sarah,' he snapped. 'But I need this information. You've got a lot to lose.'

'What the hell is that supposed to mean?'

'Our arrangement, Sarah.'

'Go on,' said Sarah. He had her attention and she was scared.

'I'm sure you haven't forgotten about that information I uncovered during my research into your department. Let me spell it out for you. You know the one where departmental staff destroyed records during a cover up? I still have the backup disc containing the data you wiped from your departmental system. I still have copies of the documents you shredded and claimed didn't exist. These were all leaked to me, remember?'

Sarah fell silent. She knew he had the evidence. He could use it against her at any time. He hadn't handed her into the authorities. Where was the benefit in that for him? No, he was biding his time until he needed to cash in a return favour. He had backed her into a corner with blackmail.

'Sarah, I need that information, otherwise I will blow the lid off the whole scandal. You and your colleagues will be hung out to dry. It will destroy your career. You could even go to prison. I just need the address where the Kingston children have been placed, just the address. In return, I'll destroy the evidence and this whole thing goes away forever. Just the address, Sarah, that's all I need. No one will get hurt, I promise. It will be our secret. No one will know how I found out and I promise I'll tell no one where the children are.'

Sarah considered the proposal. 'Do you give me your word that you will give me the disc and the documents and that no other copies will be made?'

'Yes, yes, Sarah, I give you my word. I've hidden it somewhere safe. No one else will get their hands on it.'

Sarah closed her eyes. It made her sick knowing what she was about to do. 'Twenty-seven Hamilton Drive, Lockyer. They are staying with Mrs Wilson at that address. Now leave me alone.'

'Thank you, Sarah. You've done the right thing. You've just saved my life.'

'What?' said Sarah. 'What the hell does that mean?'

The telephone clunked in her ear. Caxton was gone.

Sarah slid down the wall and slumped to the floor with the telephone still in her hand. Something was horribly wrong.

What have I done?

THIRTY-NINE

JARROD cruised dirt roads, shining a spotlight out his window, chasing shadows. He'd ignored Benfield's order to go home for a few hours' sleep. The CIB guys and scientific officers were still working the crime scene at Vincent Miles' property. The house and the underground bunker were being guarded by SERT officers in case Miles returned. The remaining crews were manning roadblocks or out patrolling. When Jarrod nodded off at the wheel and nearly swerved into a tree, he decided it was time to pull the pin. He headed back to the station.

When he arrived at his office, he turned on the lights and his heart sank when he saw Brad's jacket hanging over the back of his partner's chair. The latest news was that he was in a stable condition in hospital. Jarrod felt light-headed. He didn't know if it was from the insanity of the last few days, the lack of sleep or a combination of both.

A brown paper exhibit bag sat upright on his desk. He sat down and was about to open the package when his feet came to rest on something under his desk. It was a skateboard. He placed his feet on it and rolled it from side to side. He opened the package and pulled out a fluffy Paddington Bear teddy, complete with yellow hat and red raincoat. Next, he found a Nintendo game console and he smiled. The guys at the Kingston murder crime scene had remembered to collect the children's belongings, the precious items they had requested.

Something rattled at the bottom of the package. He reached in and pulled out a silver necklace. Olivia's heart-shaped locket dangled from the chain. He opened the locket. The tiny photograph of Olivia's and her father's smiling faces beamed up at him. He held the open locket in the palm of his hand, a thousand images racing through his mind. He thought of Olivia, Jamie and Jake having to deal with their loss alone and it saddened him, weighing heavy on his conscience. The last few days had been madness and he needed sleep. Most of all, he needed to spend time with his own family.

He placed the items back in the packet and grabbed the skateboard and his keys, flicking off the lights with his elbow as he left the office. He would drop in on the Kingston kids in the morning, hoping their precious possessions would cheer them up. He also looked forward to seeing them again. They were a reminder of why he kept doing this bloody job. It was special kids like Olivia, Jamie and Jake that made it all worthwhile.

He padded across the car park and climbed into the Forerunner. His mobile phone vibrated in his pocket and he jumped. He was still on edge. 'Hello, this is Jarrod O'Connor.'

The female voice on the other end was hysterical. 'Jarrod, you were the only one I could think of to call, the only one I trust.'

'Sarah, is that you?'

'Yes. Jarrod, I can't believe what I've done.'

'Sarah, calm down. What is it?'

'Jim Caxton just called me. He sounded desperate. He's blackmailing me.'

'Go on.'

'Somehow Caxton obtained a computer disc and copies of documents from our department. Oh my God, I stuffed up. I destroyed records and he found out.'

'Why would you do a thing like that? What's this all about, Sarah?'

'I've seen people in my department dragged over the coals

222

because of decisions they made. The same thing would happen to me, I knew it. I made a recommendation to leave a child in care, but she came out later with allegations of being sexually abused by her foster father. How could I have known? I was the girl's case worker. She told me she didn't want to stay there anymore but she wouldn't tell me why. When she later came out with the allegations, I deleted the database entry and shredded my notes of what she had told me. I was scared they would blame me for not getting her out of there. I've seen it happen before.'

'Hold on, Sarah. I don't understand,' Jarrod interjected, losing patience with her ramblings. 'Why did Caxton call you tonight? What did he want?'

'He wanted to know where the Kingston kids are being kept.'

'Oh no. Did you tell him?'

There was no reply, just Sarah's muffled sobs.

'Sarah, listen to me. Did you tell Caxton where the children are?'

'He promised that he'd tell no one, that he just wanted to do a follow up story about the murders. He threatened to go public with his evidence if I didn't help him. I didn't know what to do. I panicked.'

'Did you tell him?' Jarrod demanded, desperate for an answer.

'Yes. I told him.'

'Sarah, what have you done?'

'Jarrod, you have to believe me. I regret telling him. I feel sick because of what I've done.'

'You did the right thing telling me. I have to go.'

'What about me? What should I do?'

'Nothing, talk to no one about this. Do you understand?'

'Yes, I understand.'

Jarrod hung up and ran back into the station and headed straight for the communications room. Maggie, the radio operator, tapped away on her keyboard as she monitored multiple communications and mapping systems displayed across three computer screens.

Wearing a telephone headset, she listened to emergency services radio channels chattering in the background.

'Hey Maggie, I need the address and mobile phone number of Jim Caxton, the journalist. Can you get that for me please?' he said, still trying to catch his breath.

'Oh, I'm fine thanks, and you?' she said without looking up.

'Sorry, Mags. Something's just come up, it could be important.'

She turned and tilted her head as she peered over her reading glasses. She sighed and shook her head. 'Sure, hold on,' she said, pulling the database up on screen. Within seconds, she gave Jarrod the details.

'You're an angel, Maggie. I'm heading over there right now. I'll get back to you from my mobile phone. Thanks.'

'Wait, what's going on?'

There's been a leak to the media about the location of the Kingston kids. Are any other crews available?'

'The uniform crews have just been diverted to a serious traffic crash on the highway. All other units are still tied up out of town at the Miles property. With all that's been going on we're stretched thin. The place is a bloody madhouse.'

A jittery feeling rose in his belly. His instincts told him something was off. 'Shit! Who's guarding the kids at the safe house?'

'Constable Kirsty Loudin is still there.'

'Can you call her for me? Tell her that journalist Caxton might be snooping around and she is not to open the door for anyone. I'm heading out to find him, to see what he's up to.'

He dashed out of the coms room leaving Maggie with a stunned look, her mouth falling open. Jarrod was soon back in the Forerunner, its chunky tyres squealing as he swung out of the police station driveway. He called Caxton's number but there was no answer.

He raced along the quiet streets. Thankfully, the late evening traffic was light. He soon entered the prestigious housing estate where Caxton had built his impressive new home. Freelance journalism must pay well, thought Jarrod cynically. He pulled up out the front of the house, a two-storey brick rendered home with a long driveway and exotic tropical gardens. The front porch light was on, as well as other lights in the house. The double garage door was closed. He assumed Caxton's silver Porsche was parked inside. He'd often seen him cruising around town in the sports car, full of self-importance. Jarrod knew he also drove an old Nissan Patrol four-wheel drive.

As he approached the front door, he noticed it was ajar. He knocked and waited, but there was no answer. He knocked again and then pushed the door open. 'Hello, Jim, it's Detective Jarrod O'Connor. Anyone home?'

No answer.

He moved in through the open door and made his way down the hallway. Something was wrong. As he entered the lounge room, he saw a pool of fresh blood on a coffee table. He drew his Glock and scanned the room. His heart pounded, his palms sweaty. He fought to control his breathing, his senses heightened.

Droplets of blood on the lush carpet created a trail into Caxton's home office. There was a large desk with a computer screen and scattered notepads. A cordless telephone lay in another small pool of blood that had formed near the edge of the desk. A bloodied handprint gripped the phone.

Jarrod climbed the carpeted staircase, crossing one foot over the other as he took each deliberate step. He locked his arms out straight, his eyes focused just beyond the front sights of his Glock. He drew in long breaths, held for a few seconds and exhaled, slowing his heart rate. Room by room, he checked the bedrooms and bathroom. No one was there. He hurried back down the staircase and checked the rooms again including the laundry, but they were all empty. It was then that he noticed the faint humming sound for the first time. He followed the dull sound into the kitchen where it grew louder. There was a closed door, which he assumed led into the adjacent double garage. He realised the humming sound was an idling car engine. Panicking, he pulled open the door and gagged as he gulped a mouthful of exhaust fumes.

The engine of the old Porsche idled. The four-wheel drive was gone. Through the gassy haze he made out the silhouette of a man sitting inside the Porsche. A length of industrial hose led from the exhaust pipe and into the driver's window. He'd seen that kind of hose before, at Vincent Miles' house. A rolled-up blanket was shoved into the window gap forming a crude seal.

He re-holstered his Glock and shielded his face from the fumes with the crook of his elbow. He reached for the driver's door of the car; it was unlocked. He opened it and was nearly overcome by the fumes. He held his breath and turned the ignition off as a grey cloud of toxic exhaust poured out. Caxton was sitting upright in the driver's seat. Jarrod then saw why. Several layers of grey duct tape were wrapped around his forehead, his head bound tight to the headrest. Another row of duct tape was wrapped around his chest and the seat. His entire upper body was pinned. His hands were bound at the front with more tape. A bloodied towel hung from his left hand, exposing a deep wound.

His motionless body resembled a prisoner on death row, strapped to the gas chamber chair. His skin was pale, his lips blue and there was no sign of breathing.

Jarrod coughed and choked. He stumbled over to a window, slid it open and gulped the sweet fresh air as the exhaust fumes billowed out. He pushed the electric garage door button and it hummed as it slowly opened. The cool night air flowed in as the fumes escaped. He needed something to cut the tape. He hurried back into the kitchen and found a small carving knife. He raced back to the Porsche and sliced through the tape. As he was cut free, Caxton slumped forward and Jarrod caught him, supporting his upper body in his arms before pulling him from the car. He laid him on the concrete and felt for a pulse. Nothing. No sign of life.

Jarrod remembered CPR from first aid training. He rolled Caxton onto his side and checked his airway and then placed him onto his back, tilting his head. He blew into Caxton's mouth twice, watching his chest rise and fall. Jarrod measured down the sternum using his thumbs and forefingers like he had been taught. Using the ball of his right hand, gripping his wrist with the other, he compressed Caxton's chest thirty times. He listened for a pulse, but there was nothing. He repeated this cycle, but there was still no pulse. He went through the process again before pulling out his mobile phone and dialling triple zero.

'Which emergency service do you require, police, fire or ambulance?' said the operator.

'Ambulance!' he snapped. He was connected through and soon he had identified himself and given directions. An ambulance was being dispatched, but would be about ten minutes. He hung up and persisted with the CPR, but Caxton's limp body showed no signs of life.

Jarrod kept going – breaths followed by compressions – sweat dripping from his forehead. He was light-headed from the fumes. Time stilled. He couldn't help but think that Caxton's unscrupulous methods had finally caught up with him, but the poor bastard didn't deserve this, no one did. Jarrod was determined not to give up. He continued his attempts to resuscitate him and yelled out in frustration, 'Come on, Jim, hang on. Come on. Breathe, just breathe!' Jarrod's arms felt like lead weights and his back muscles ached. His knees burned from the unforgiving concrete floor.

Jarrod slowed as he realised his attempts to revive the man had failed. He stood, exhausted, and gazed down at Caxton's lifeless body. In the stillness, it hit him.

Vincent Miles had been there. He'd used Caxton to find out where the Kingston children were. Jarrod feared he'd wasted too much time.

The wailing ambulance siren grew louder. Jarrod flagged them down on the street and briefed them on what had happened. He recognised the faces of the paramedics as the same guys who had taken Brad to the hospital. He directed them to where Caxton lay, although he knew there was little they could do for him.

They hurried into the garage with their resuscitation equipment. Jarrod climbed back into his Forerunner and dialled the police station. As it rang, he planted his foot, screeching the tyres as he accelerated away.

Maggie answered.

'Maggie, it's Jarrod O'Connor. I need your help. I've just left Jim Caxton's place. He's dead. You need to get onto Kirsty Loudin immediately. You need to warn her. I'm on my way to the safe house. Miles is coming after them. Do you understand, Maggie? I need urgent backup!'

'Yes, Jarrod, I understand. But the uniform crews are still tied up on the highway, traffic is backed up for miles and it'll take them a while to get back into town. There's no one else nearby. I'll do my best to get hold of some of the officers out at the Miles property. I have no one else in town. You're on your own, I'm sorry.'

'Damn it! Get onto Benfield for me. Ring me back as soon as you get hold of Kirsty.'

Jarrod ended the call, throwing the phone on the passenger's seat in sheer frustration. Their resources had been stretched to the limit over the last few days, spread far too thin.

He had to focus on what lay ahead. He steered the heavy truck through the back streets of town. It would take at least ten minutes to get to Mrs Wilson's house. As he drove, he had the sensation that he was floating out of his body, observing from above. His body was numb. He wasn't a religious person, but in desperation he prayed. He asked God for the strength and courage he needed to stop Vincent Miles. Jarrod feared he was no match for him. He feared he couldn't stand in his way and didn't have what it would take to protect the children. He was no hero.

His mobile phone rang; it was Maggie. 'Jarrod, Mrs Wilson's phone rang out. There was no answer. I can't reach Kirsty on her mobile either.'

'I'm nearly there, I've got to go,' he said, hanging up the phone as he wrestled the truck into a sharp left-hand turn.

The truck slid wildly across the bitumen as he turned the last corner into Hamilton Drive. He recognised Jim Caxton's Nissan Patrol parked in the street a few houses down from Mrs Wilson's house.

Jesus Christ, Miles was there.

FORTY

JARROD screeched the truck to a halt at the front of the house, mounting the curb in the process. As he jumped out, he drew his Glock. He sprinted towards the house using the fence line as cover, concealing himself in the shadows. The lights were on but there was no movement. He had no time to waste casing the place out – he needed to get inside.

He took a deep breath and dashed straight up to the front door. The jamb was pulverised, the splintered door ajar. It creaked as he pushed it open with his shoulder. He crossed the threshold and stepped inside, exposed in the doorway. He headed down the hallway, scanning through the sights of his Glock. As he stepped into the kitchen, he found Mrs Wilson slumped on the floor in a half sitting position, her plump shoulder leaning against a cupboard. Her hair was matted with blood, a cut in her scalp gaping. Jarrod knelt at her side. She was dazed but conscious.

Jarrod was startled by a loud clatter and thumping coming from the next room. The blood drained from his face. He scrambled to his feet and stepped through the doorway into the lounge room. Kirsty Loudin was lying prone on the floor, her hands handcuffed behind the leg of a heavy couch. Her police shirt was covered in blood from a gash over her right eye. She winced in pain as she wriggled and stomped, trying to free herself from the handcuffs, the last of her strength draining. For a split-second, shock registered on her face, then relief.

'Jarrod! He's here, Miles is here.' Her words slurred as she strained with every breath. 'He's got Olivia and Jamie. He's got my gun.' Bleary-eyed, her head slumped to the floor and she drifted into unconsciousness.

Jarrod cocked his head towards a noise in the garage, his senses heightened. The engine of Mrs Wilson's car fired up and revved. He headed for the laundry which led to the internal garage door. As his fingers were about to take hold of the handle the door swung open towards him. Vincent Miles' imposing frame filled the doorway. For a millisecond, they stared into each other's eyes in surprise and then recognition. Miles was right on top of him. What happened next seemed to occur in slow motion.

As Jarrod squeezed the trigger, Miles grabbed his hands and twisted them upwards, pointing the muzzle of the Glock towards the ceiling. With a deafening boom and muzzle flash, the gun discharged and chalky drywall fragments showered from the ceiling. Miles grappled with Jarrod's hands, trying to twist the gun free from his grasp. Jarrod fought against his powerful grip, their arms entangled in a wrestle for the gun. Jarrod knew if he lost the gun he was dead.

Their eyes locked and Miles smiled, his sour breath hot against Jarrod's cheek. Jarrod slammed his knee into his abdomen but Miles didn't buckle, it had little effect. Miles sneered, lifted his chin and thrust his head forward, glancing Jarrod's forehead with a head butt. The blow stunned Jarrod, blinding him from the impact. Jarrod fell backwards free of Miles' grip, his back slamming against the wall and sliding to the floor in a daze. As his hand hit the ground, the Glock came free and clattered across the floor, coming to a stop just out of reach.

Jarrod mustered the strength to clamber onto his knees towards the gun. His vision was blurred, but his brain quickly processed the sight of Kirsty's police firearm tucked into Miles' belt.

Miles took a menacing step towards him. 'O'Connor, tonight you die. I've waited a long time for this moment. I won't show you the same mercy I showed those two women.'

His fingers slid down to the protruding handle of the gun. Jarrod's primal "fight or flight" instinct took over. Jumping to his feet he dived at Miles, driving his shoulder into the other man's chest. Jarrod tackled him against the wall, leaving a dent in the gyprock the shape of Miles' back. Jarrod swivelled and then punched his abdomen with his remaining strength. Miles arched forward from the blow. Jarrod slammed his other fist down hard against the side of his face and heard his jaw crack.

Miles shook off the blow with a shake of the head and reacted swiftly. He came back at Jarrod and grabbed him by the throat. Jarrod stumbled back as Miles drove forward with the power and fury of a madman. Jarrod slipped his hands up between Miles' arms and prised his hands free. Miles slammed his forehead into the side of Jarrod's head and his legs crumpled under his own weight, falling to the floor.

Jarrod knew the fight was lost.

Miles stared at him with contempt. 'You thought you could stop me, O'Connor. This isn't about you. It's about revenge and salvation. You see, I've discovered the glory of who we can become. I'm not what you think I am. I'm more than you. I don't expect you to understand.'

He stepped closer. Jarrod propelled himself backwards along the floor with the heels of his shoes, scrambling to get up. His head throbbed and all rational thinking was consumed by the incessant ringing in his ears. Miles took a long stride and slammed his boot down hard on his chest, pinning him under his weight.

'The likes of you, O'Connor, will never understand. You spend your time persecuting people like me, and Clare... and poor Edward. But now is our time for revenge. Soon we will reunite in paradise and I am bringing my Love a precious gift. I will deliver the children back to her. It's over, my friend. They have begun their journey. And now I'm sending you to hell where you belong.'

Miles gripped the gun handle, freeing it from his belt. Jarrod's sight was blurred, the edges of his peripheral vision an array of flashes of light and dark blotches.

He knew he was about to die. His hand lay outstretched on the floor; his body sprawled helplessly. Miles was in no rush to kill him – he was enjoying his moment of glory, toying with him. He took his foot off Jarrod's chest and gripped the gun with both hands preparing to fire, the muzzle aimed at his head.

Jarrod turned his face away and closed his eyes. He then heard the shuffle of little feet and his eyes shot open. Jake emerged into the hallway, out of sight from Miles who had his back to him. He was like a little angel sent from God.

Jake scurried behind Miles and bent down for Jarrod's gun, pushing it along the floor towards him. It slid and spun and came to rest against Jarrod's outstretched hand. In one movement he grabbed the gun, raised it towards Miles and fired.

Time slowed. Jarrod heard the click of the trigger, the clunk of the hammer and the explosion as the firing pin tapped the primer of the brass bullet casing. He saw the bright flash of exploding gunpowder and the shockwave in the air as the lead projectile spun from the muzzle and hurtled through the air, colliding into Vincent Miles' shoulder. He heard flesh and bone mashing together as the bullet tore its way through his body. Miles was thrown backwards from the impact. Jarrod fired again, his hand shaking. The shot missed Miles but exploded into the window behind him. Glass shattered and Miles stumbled backwards, crashing through the remaining jagged glass that clung to the window frame. He disappeared into the darkness as he fell backwards out the window and onto the ground outside.

Jarrod's concept of time returned to normal. Little Jake stood beside him, reaching under his armpits, trying to lift him up. Jarrod dragged himself up and staggered back onto his feet. He stepped towards the opening of the window. Smashed glass lay scattered on the floor. He thrust his Glock forward and scanned his sights through the opening. He expected to see Miles lying on the ground and he was prepared to kill him, right there and then.

But he was gone. Jarrod slung his legs out through the window. Fragments of glass crunched under his shoes as he hit the ground. He searched the darkness with his Glock, but he couldn't see Miles.

Hurried footsteps faded away towards the road, then a car fired up out the front and tyres squealed. Jarrod ran down the side of the house and saw Jim Caxton's four-wheel drive swerving off down the street. God damn it, he'd gotten away.

Little Jake screamed from inside, 'Olivia and Jamie, you have to help them!'

Oh god, the children! Jarrod climbed back into the window and burst through the garage door. Mrs Wilson's Toyota Corolla was idling in the garage. Two little people sat in the back seat.

Jarrod smelt the fumes and saw the hose.

'No!' he screamed. This couldn't be happening again.

Jamie's face pressed against the car window, then Olivia's. *They were alive!* A hose attached to the exhaust pipe poked in through the small gap of a partially opened window. The kids sat upright, their hands bound behind them with duct tape. They screamed and coughed, tears streaming down their faces. 'Help! Help! Please get us out of here.'

Jarrod tried the doors, but they were locked. He pulled the hose from the window and dropped it onto the floor, fumes spewing out into the garage.

The kids were still trapped inside the gas chamber. A fog of exhaust fumes floated inside the car. Jarrod looked around in desperation. A hammer hung on a rack alongside a complete set of well organised spanners, screwdrivers and household tools.

Jarrod grabbed the hammer and made eye contact with Olivia and Jamie. He yelled, 'Get away from the glass!' He raised the hammer above his head and Olivia and Jamie understood. They

234

shuffled across to the far side and huddled together, tucking their heads into their knees.

The hammer came down hard onto the driver's window. Glass shattered into a million tiny fragments. Opaque fumes billowed through the opening from the belly of the vehicle, dissipating into the garage in light wisps. Jarrod gagged and covered his mouth with his forearm as he reached in, killed the ignition and unlocked the back door. He reefed open the door and climbed into the back seat, grabbing hold of the kids' clothes. He dragged them from the car, their little bodies toppling on top of him as they crashed in a heap onto the concrete floor. He needed to free them from the duct tape. A pair of scissors hanging on the tool rack did the job.

They both coughed, their faces pale. Their eyes were red and glassy.

'I feel sick,' slurred Jamie.

Olivia stroked his hair. Still gasping air into her lungs, she looked up at Jarrod with wide eyes as a new fear took hold. 'Where's the man? He's trying to kill us. Where is he?'

'It's okay, sweetheart, he's gone. You're safe,' Jarrod whispered.

Jake was standing in the doorway and he ran over and they all embraced.

Olivia looked up at Jarrod with a pained expression. 'Mrs Wilson, Kirsty! Are they alright?'

'They're pretty beaten up. Come on, let's go and help them,' said Jarrod.

They negotiated the glass fragments and headed back inside the house. Jarrod told the kids to check on Mrs Wilson. Kirsty was still lying on the floor, bound to the couch leg by the handcuffs. Jarrod fished around in his pocket and found his keys. They jingled as he shuffled them clumsily. He found the universal police handcuff key and removed her shackles. He sat her up against him. She was breathing steadily and her eyes opened. She uttered an incoherent jumble of words.

'Don't speak, just rest. Everyone is okay. Hold tight, help will be here soon.'

Kirsty nodded and closed her eyes again. Jarrod laid her down and rested her head on a cushion, making her as comfortable as he could.

He went into the kitchen, where the children were sitting on the floor beside Mrs Wilson. Olivia was sponging the blood from the old woman's face with a damp hand towel. Mrs Wilson sat upright against the cupboard, still groggy. She looked up at Jarrod. 'Don't worry about me, detective. It takes more than that to keep a tough old stick like me down. Now don't make a fuss.'

'You just stay where you are, Mrs Wilson, you're in good hands. The kids will take care of you, hey guys?'

The kids nodded and Olivia said, 'You bet, Mrs Wilson, we'll look after you.'

Mrs Wilson grimaced in pain and then gave a determined smile. 'You sweet children, you truly are my little angels.'

FORTY-ONE

JARROD was relieved when the backup crew arrived. He'd been hunkered down inside the house behind locked doors and windows with Mrs Wilson, Kirsty and the children in case Miles returned. Miles was injured, but still armed and desperate. The uniformed officers positioned themselves inside the front and back doors, standing guard until more units arrived.

The ambulance arrived soon after, the same paramedics who had come to his aid at Jim Caxton's house. Jarrod met them at the front door and they looked equally surprised when they saw him. With a deadpan look on his face the senior paramedic said, 'Bloody hell, mate, we're busy enough without you drumming up business for us. What have you got for us this time?'

'They're inside. The two older kids were exposed to exhaust fumes, the little one is in a bit of shock and there are two ladies who've copped a fair beating.'

'Jesus, man, what the hell is going on? The town has gone nuts,' the paramedic replied as he brushed past and headed inside lugging a medical kit.

The second paramedic hesitated in the doorway, something weighing heavily on his mind. 'I'm sorry, but your friend back at the house didn't make it. We kept him ventilated until we arrived at A & E but there was nothing they could do. He was pronounced deceased on arrival.'

'He wasn't my friend. I didn't even like the guy. He didn't

deserve to die though. The poor bastard was tortured. It was the same arsehole who attacked the women and children here.'

The paramedic placed a reassuring hand on Jarrod's shoulder. 'We'll look after the patients inside, detective.' With gloved hands, he examined Jarrod's forehead. 'You look like you could do with a patch up yourself.'

Jarrod put his hand up to his face. Blood crusted around a gash on his forehead. 'I'll live. See to the others first.'

He followed the paramedic inside. He walked past a mirror hanging on the wall just inside the front door. He stopped and studied his reflection. He barely recognised the man looking back at him. Bruising was starting to appear under both eyes and there was a protruding lump on the side of his head. Blood smeared across his face and his neck was striped with red finger marks. He looked an absolute wreck.

He was lightheaded. He needed fresh air so went outside and sat on the top step of the porch looking out across Mrs Wilson's front yard. He realised how weak his legs were as they ached as soon as he sat down. He pressed a hand towel against the gash in his head to stem the flow of blood. It was such a relief to take the weight off his feet.

A streetlight down the road radiated enough dim light for him to make out the features of Mrs Wilson's quaint cottage garden. Daffodils lined the paved pathway, their petals closed as they slumbered in the moonlight. Climbing roses and honeysuckle, various herbs, simple daisies, marigolds and annuals were in abundance. The tangy scent of pollen filled his senses as a cool breeze drifted through the night air. Out on that porch there was no hint of the violence that had erupted inside. The gentle beauty of the garden remained resolute. For a moment he was lost in a daze. He rested his head in his hands, his elbows supported by his bent knees.

His head was still spinning and he tried to focus on Vincent Miles. *What was his next move? What did he plan to do next if he had succeeded in killing Olivia and Jamie?* He was now motivated by the desire to reunite with Clare. That's what made him so dangerous. He didn't fear death. He had nothing to lose and nothing to live for.

Jarrod was deeply troubled. *It wasn't over.* Miles wouldn't stop until he knew the children were dead. Vincent Miles would be back. He would soon find out the children escaped and he would come after them. Again and again, until his destiny was fulfilled. He wouldn't stop.

Jarrod tried to get inside the head of Vincent Miles, to somehow piece it all together. He feared him just as much as ever, but he needed to know the man's weaknesses if he had any chance of bringing him down. Miles had been consumed by grief and fury when his baby girl was taken from him. His already violent and unstable character had been tipped over the edge. He no longer saw the world in a rational way. Jarrod pictured him trying to cope in a world that had fallen apart around him. He went on a campaign of self-destruction, more violence, more drugs and ultimately prison. It was then that he met Edward Ryan.

They formed a bond and saw themselves as something powerful. *Had they manufactured the delusion to escape their meaningless lives?* They fuelled each other's delusions until reality was confused with fantasy. They probably shared the same paranoia. They'd built their own underground fortress. Maybe they wanted to go out in a blaze of glory.

Then Clare came along, the final member of the unstable trio. She was needy and teetering on her own path of self-destruction and paranoia. Jarrod guessed it wouldn't have taken long for her to be drawn in by Vincent Miles' dominance and charm. He must have promised her everything, even eternal happiness.

Another irony was that Miles had so much anger towards Roxy, the woman who killed herself and their child. In his delusional state, Miles was prepared to perform the same act – he was willing to take innocent lives to accommodate Clare's selfishness. She couldn't live without her children, so they wouldn't live without her. The realisation infuriated Jarrod. At what stage does a person cross that line where they can justify the murder of their children? He would never understand that. He had given up a long time ago trying to understand human nature.

He could see there was no point trying to understand or rationalise the actions and thought processes of Vincent Miles' delusional mind. Whatever his mindset was, he truly believed in his own cause. How else can a person justify murder?

Jarrod forced himself back up onto his feet. He needed to get back inside to check on the others. As he limped inside the house, he was afraid of how all this was impacting the kids. They had endured more terror and heartache than any child should. He found them inside with the paramedics, Jamie and Olivia taking turns at breathing in oxygen from a face mask attached to a small canister.

Mrs Wilson was telling the younger paramedic to stop fussing as he patched up her head wounds. Kirsty was still groggy with concussion. She was being taken care of by the senior paramedic, who went about stabilising her. The paramedic saw Jarrod standing in the kitchen doorway and came over to him.

He spoke in a low voice. 'The kids are okay for now, but they need to get to hospital to make sure there's no damage to their airways. Carbon monoxide poisoning is serious. We also need to get both ladies to hospital for observation.'

'Um, yeah sure, but can I ask a favour?' Jarrod asked.

'Yeah, what is it?'

'This will sound a little crazy.'

'Try me.'

'The kids were the target. If word gets out they survived, he'll come after them again. We need to make him think we didn't get to them in time, that they didn't make it.'

'Are you serious?'

'I'm dead serious, mate. Will you help me?'

The paramedic glanced at the kids and then looked back at Jarrod. 'This bloke won't stop, will he?'

'No, he won't.'

'What do you need us to do?'

'Get the ladies to hospital. Once the other police get here, we'll slip the kids out the back and we'll race them straight to hospital. We'll explain it to the hospital staff when we get there. If anyone asks, you just need to say the kids didn't make it and the police have taken over.'

'It sounds bloody crazy, but yeah we can do that,' said the paramedic. 'We'll have enough on our hands with the two ladies here. That'll be enough distraction to buy you some time.'

'I know it sounds crazy but this might be our last play to stop this lunatic.'

'You got it. Count us in. Anyway, we best get these ladies to hospital.'

They were joined by the younger paramedic. 'I'm not leaving until I patch up that wound to your head. I'm not taking no for an answer. Sit down.'

Jarrod sat, too light-headed to argue. He flinched as the paramedic cleaned the cut, a sharp sting biting hard. He then applied Steri-Strips and a gauze bandage. 'That should close the wound and stop the bleeding, but you could do with some stitches.'

'I'm fine, really. Thanks.'

'Take these. You'll be needing them,' said the paramedic, handing Jarrod a sleeve of painkiller capsules. He nodded and shoved them in his pocket.

Jarrod went inside and explained his plan to the women and they understood. They would not make any mention of the condition of the children. If asked by hospital staff, they were to act confused and claim they were unsure of the children's fate. He was confident they would remain tight-lipped. They understood the part they had to play.

The women were lifted onto gurneys and wheeled out to the awaiting ambulance. From the rear of the ambulance, Mrs Wilson gave a defiant grin and double thumbs up. Kirsty closed her eyes as an oxygen mask was placed over her face. The doors closed and the ambulance drove off, the taillights fading into the distance as it rounded the corner.

The uniformed officers remained on guard inside the doors, peering out through the windows. Jarrod flopped down onto the couch in the lounge room. Jake tiptoed over to him and without hesitation he climbed up onto his lap. Jamie and Olivia sat on either side of him and snuggled under his arms.

A car screeched to a halt outside, doors slammed and then footsteps pounded onto the front porch. 'O'Connor?' Jarrod heard a familiar voice.

'I'm in here!'

The uniformed officer gave a nod as Murray Long and Liam Dawes lumbered in with matching puzzled looks, staring at the children and Jarrod huddled together on the couch.

'What the hell's going on, O'Connor?' asked Long.

'I don't have a clue where to begin. We don't have much time. We need to get these kids out of here.'

FORTY-TWO

WHEN Ross Benfield arrived at the house, Jarrod briefed him on what had occurred. He explained the phone call he received from Sarah Morgan that led him to Jim Caxton's house and the discovery of his murder. Next came the account of what had happened there at the safe house, how Miles had come so close to killing Olivia and Jamie. Jarrod explained that it was all about Olivia and Jamie, that he believed Miles' rampage would not stop until he had succeeded in killing them.

They didn't know where Miles was or what his next move would be, but Jarrod believed the playing field was now even; in fact they had some advantages. They knew what car he was travelling in; he was wounded and he had nowhere to go. He wouldn't let up until he knew the children were dead. Miles was committed to his cause and desperate. He was capable of anything.

Dawes occupied the children in the lounge room while Long, Benfield and Jarrod sat at the kitchen table discussing their next move. They went back over the events of the last few days until the inevitable question was asked by Long. 'So, what now?'

'The thing is,' Jarrod began, 'Miles wants Olivia and Jamie dead. The whole plan means nothing unless he can bring them to Clare, that's what he believes. While the children are alive, he'll continue to hunt them.'

'Alright, let's get these kids checked out at the hospital and into high-level protection,' said Benfield. 'Sooner or later, we'll get Miles.

He's running out of luck. We'll corner him.'

'How many people have to suffer in the meantime?' said Jarrod. 'We saw what lengths he's prepared to go to. He used people for leverage and he'll do it again. More people will die. He's out of control. Let's give him what he wants. He wants the kids dead, so let's make him think they are.'

'How do you figure that?' asked Long.

'Miles doesn't know the kids made it out of the car alive. When he got away they were still trapped in the car. He doesn't know I got to them in time. After all, he succeeded with Caxton.'

Benfield pursed his bottom lip and nodded. 'Alright, I'm with you on this, but how do you suggest we pull this off? Do you think the media will swallow that story?'

'Why not? If we play our cards right, they have no choice. We create the illusion the children were murdered. Meanwhile, we get them away undetected. I've spoken to the ambos. They'll keep it under wraps for the time being. If the media come sniffing around, Boss, you'll have to confirm the kids have died. We need to get the undertaker out here as soon as possible so the cameras can get their pictures of the bodies being taken from the scene. They love that sort of stuff. It won't be long before the cameras arrive.'

'Bloody hell, Jarrod, this could blow up in our faces if it goes wrong. It's a big gamble,' said Benfield.

'That's why we have to do this quickly,' Jarrod urged.

'Okay then, let's do it. I'll need to make some phone calls. I know the ambulance commander. I'll square that end away. Can the undertakers be trusted?'

'Leave that to me, I know the guys down there pretty well,' said Long. 'They can be trusted. I'll arrange that side of things.'

Outside, car doors slammed. Long jumped up and peeked out through the curtains. 'Our friends from Channel Eight are right on cue.'

'We've got to get the kids out of here,' said Jarrod. 'I can take them out through the back and cut through the neighbour's yard. Dawes can take a car and drive around the block and pick us up on the other side.'

'I'll go and piss in the pocket of the news crew to buy you some time,' said Benfield. He headed out the front door, where he cut off the attractive news reporter and her cameraman as they scurried up the front path. He escorted them back out onto the footpath. Long was already on the phone to the undertaker.

Jarrod joined Dawes and the kids in the lounge room. 'Righto gang, we have to go for a little walk. We need to stay very quiet.'

The kids didn't question it. They stood up and were ready to go.

Jarrod threw Dawes his car keys. 'Take my car and drive around the block to the back street. We'll cut through the yard behind and meet you there.'

'Okay, I'll see you around the corner in five.' Dawes dragged his big frame off the floor where he had been reading picture books to the kids. He had two kids of his own and was a natural, although he wouldn't admit it.

Jake reached up for Jarrod's hand and their fingers locked. Olivia put her arm around Jamie and took hold of Jake's other hand. She was still playing the protective big sister and Jarrod's admiration for her grew.

'Let's go, Jarrod. We're ready,' she said.

Jarrod led them out through the laundry and around the shattered glass littering the floor. He quietly slid open the sliding glass door and they crept out into the dark backyard. The fence at the back was only quite low. Jarrod picked Jake up and placed him over the fence. Olivia and Jamie easily scaled it on their own. Jarrod's body was still aching and he let out a groan as he swung his leg over the fence and then stumbled. Olivia grabbed his arm just enough to help him regain his balance. He whispered, 'Thanks, Liv.'

'You're welcome, Jarrod,' she whispered back.

There were no dogs or obstructions and they hustled along the side fence line towards the street out the front. It was just after midnight and the neighbouring houses were in darkness. Residents had lingered in their front yards after the earlier commotion, but it seemed most had lost interest and gone back to bed. They approached the front yard and opened the gate. It squeaked and clunked as Jarrod pushed it. Jarrod looked at the kids and held a finger up to his lips. No lights came on, no one came rushing out to investigate.

They made it to the footpath and took cover in the darkness beside a bushy shrub. From around the corner came a set of headlights. Jarrod recognised the hum of the Forerunner engine as it approached and pulled over. Dawes reached over and opened the passenger door and smiled. 'Need a lift?'

Jarrod lifted the kids into the car, got them belted up and gave Dawes the nod to drive off.

'Where to now, Jarrod?' Dawes asked.

'Head straight to the hospital. We'll sneak the kids in through the staff entrance.'

Jarrod then remembered the package sitting at his feet. He reached down and grabbed it and turned to the kids. 'I have something special for you guys.'

In that moment, they were just normal little kids again as their eyes lit up in excitement. He reached into the bag and produced the soft fluffy teddy bear and held it up.

'Paddington!' said Jake happily.

Jarrod passed it back to him and Jake cuddled it against his chest.

Jarrod then produced the Gameboy and handed it over to Jamie who said, 'Cool.'

'Your skateboard is in the back,' Jarrod said.

Jamie smiled.

Finally, Jarrod pulled out the locket and chain, allowing it to dangle for Olivia to see. She smiled as he passed it to her. She undid the latch and hung it around her neck. She clicked open the locket and stared down at the photos of her and her father. She looked up through teary eyes and said in a soft voice, 'Thank you, Jarrod.'

He smiled and turned back towards the front. They drove in silence. There was not much left to say. Soon they were at the hospital, parking in a secluded parking bay. Jarrod pivoted his aching body towards the back seat. 'Now guys, we'll get the doctors to take a look at you. We'll stay here with you. You'll be safe.'

'Do you promise?' asked Jamie.

'I promise.'

He had let them down before. Miles had come after them and he hadn't been able to protect them. He wasn't going to let it happen again.

Dawes slid across the car park, remaining in the shadows to stay out of sight. He pressed a buzzer outside a door. A sign read Authorised Personnel Only. He held up his badge and a hospital orderly opened the door. They were locked in conversation and Dawes pointed over to the car. The orderly directed his gaze their way and then gave an awkward smile and wave. He turned back to Dawes and they shook hands. Dawes gave a thumbs-up and waved Jarrod over.

'Let's go kids, you can bring your things with you,' he said. 'Follow me.'

Jarrod scurried across the car park with the kids and the door closed behind them. They were met by a friendly female doctor who took the kids into a private examination room away from the public seating area of the Accident & Emergency ward. Dawes and Jarrod waited in a nearby staff tearoom.

'Make yourselves at home, gents,' the orderly said with a knowing smile. 'Help yourself to tea, coffee, bickies. Whatever you need.'

The satchels of coffee and sugar were a godsend. Jarrod found fresh milk in the bar fridge and Dawes made them a strong brew.

They sat down at the table, sipping their bitter coffees, each lost in their own thoughts as the caffeine kicked in. They crunched on biscuits which served as Jarrod's meal for the night. Jarrod's eyelids were heavy, but he fought the urge to doze. He swallowed two pain killers and closed his eyes, trying to clear his mind. His brain pounded inside his skull; the wound above his eye throbbed.

He needed fresh air. He stepped outside into the cool night and dialled home.

'Hello,' answered Jayne sleepily.

'Hello, sweetheart, it's me. I'm sorry I haven't called. It's been mayhem.'

'It's okay, I heard about what's been going on, the media have been all over it. It's been on the TV all day. Are you alright?'

'I'm fine,' he lied. 'I had a close call tonight, but I'll be fine. I'm just a bit battered and bruised.'

'My God Jarrod, what happened?'

'We're tracking a lunatic called Vincent Miles who's on the run. He came after the Kingston children.'

'What happened? What did he do? Jarrod, are you alright?' she said, her voice high with panic.

'I'm fine, I'm fine. It's okay, really. I'm safe. The kids are safe too.' His tone was hardly convincing.

'You said Vincent Miles? I know that name,' said Jayne.

'What do you mean?' Jarrod's stomach dropped.

'He came into the hospital late last week. I'll never forget that name, or that face. He just walked into A & E off the street bleeding all over the place, arms stretched out like he was some holy man. I remember he had self-inflicted cuts to his arms. He was off his head – on something. We had to call security. He was getting agitated and started ranting like a mad man.'

'He *is* a mad man. You didn't tell me about that, Jayne,' he said, trying to mask his alarm.

'Yeah, well you were having a bad week and I didn't think I

needed to tell you about it. I didn't want you to be worried about me at work.'

'Did he hurt you?'

'No, Jarrod, he didn't hurt me.'

'Did he say anything?' he urged.

'I don't really remember. He was rambling about Heaven and Hell.'

'Please, Jayne, think. What did he say?'

'He was irrational, saying he would be reunited with his angel soon. I remember he said it was all coming to an end real soon. I didn't know what he meant by that. He was a scary man. We bandaged him up, but then he did the strangest thing.'

'What did he do, Jayne?'

'He saw my name tag and just stared at me. He took my hand, not aggressively, he was gentle. He just said, "Soon he will understand". He then got up and walked out. It was pretty unsettling.'

'Did he threaten you? Did he say anything else?'

'No, Jarrod. He didn't threaten me. I was fine, really.'

He took a deep breath and tried to control his anxiety, speaking as calmly as he could. 'Look sweetheart, there's a lot I can't tell you right now. I just wanted you to know that I'm thinking of you and the kids and that I'm okay.'

'I understand, just please be careful,' she pleaded.

'How are the kids?'

'They're fine. I have them both in bed with me right now. I guess they miss their daddy. We all miss you.'

'Give them a kiss for me and whisper into their ears that I love them. Will you do that for me?'

'Yes, Jarrod. When will you be home? It's late.'

'I don't know, I'm sorry sweetheart, I really don't know. I'm in the middle of something right now. God, I miss you and the kids. I have to go, sweet dreams.'

'Hold on, someone has just woken up and wants to talk to you, hang on…'

'Hello, Daddy, watch ya doin?' said Katie through a yawn.

'Oh, not much baby, I'm just a bit busy. Are you being a good girl?'

'Yes, of course. When are you coming home?'

'I'll be home as soon as I can. I miss you very much.'

'I miss you too.'

'You better go back to sleep, sweet dreams,' he said sadly.

'Sweet dreams, Daddy.' There was a rustling at the other end.

'You still there, Jarrod?' said Jayne as she fumbled with the phone.

'Yeah, I'm still here. You go back to sleep, I'll let you know when I'll be home.'

'Okay, just be careful. Good night. I love you, Jarrod.'

'I love you too.'

He hung up the phone and his heart ached.

FORTY-THREE

IT was 1:30AM and Jarrod leaned back on an uncomfortable chair with his feet up on the table. The doctor had given the kids the all clear; they had been very lucky. They were now asleep in a private room right next door. Dawes was taking his turn guarding the room from out in the corridor. A hospital chair laboured under his heavy frame as he sat checking his emails on his phone. Jarrod jumped when his mobile phone rang. He answered it.

'Where are you guys, can you get to a TV?' said Murray Long, impatient as ever.

'Yeah, we're still at the hospital. What's up?'

'Turn the tube onto channel eight.'

Jarrod inspected a relic of a television in the corner of the tearoom, balancing the phone between his shoulder and cheek. Dawes ambled into the room when he heard Jarrod talking. Jarrod turned on the TV and found the right channel. A blonde news reporter was standing outside Mrs Wilson's house announcing the breaking news.

The reporter delivered her on-scene report, enunciating each sentence with exaggerated infliction and pauses for added drama. 'Tragically, two children, believed to be those of murdered couple Ann and Stewart Kingston, were found dead earlier tonight in this house behind me.'

Jarrod recognised Mrs Wilson's house in the background.

'Police are reluctant to provide details at this stage, but we are led to believe the children had been under police guard when the incident occurred. There are reports that a third child somehow survived, however details are sketchy. A female police officer and an elderly woman have been taken to hospital in a stable condition with head injuries. Police investigations are continuing and a manhunt is underway. Karly Tierney, Channel 8 News.'

In the background, the camera panned over to the grim sight of two body bags being wheeled from the house by the undertaker and flanked by Murray Long and Ross Benfield. For greater effect, the camera then zoomed to the blue and white chequered tape cordoning off the crime scene.

'Bloody hell, they bought it,' Jarrod said into the phone. 'You even got your ugly mug on camera. They'll be playing that all day tomorrow during prime-time bulletins. Well done.'

'Yeah, the undertakers were great; they got right into the whole masquerade. We brought in a couple of CPR training dummies and they wheeled them out in the body bags. They played the role beautifully. The media ate it all up; they loved it. It'll be national headlines for sure.'

'Good. Now what?' Jarrod asked.

'Ah, this is the best part, O'Connor. Ross Benfield got onto the Detective Inspector at Witness Protection. He's on his way on the police chopper from Sydney to collect the kids as we speak. We'll bring him to you, just hold tight. We've got a few loose ends to sort out. We need to cover our tracks to make sure no one leaks any information.'

'Righto, come around the back of A & E, ask for us,' Jarrod said. He felt sick to the stomach. It could go awfully bad if there was a leak.

'No problems. See you soon, O'Connor.'

~

Later, there was a quiet tap on the tearoom door. In stepped Murray

Long, Ross Benfield and a tall, distinguished man wearing jeans and a sports coat. Jarrod was introduced to Detective Inspector Graham Crawford of the Witness Protection Program. He seemed like an affable man, in his late fifties with greying hair and handsome features.

He spoke with assurance. 'I'll be taking the children to a secure location. We'll be able to integrate them into one of our programs so we can get them back into some type of normality. I'd like to get acquainted with them, but we need to be on our way immediately. We have a placement ready for them. They'll be kept together and most importantly they'll be safe. I can personally guarantee that,' explained the Inspector.

The children were fast asleep, top and tailing in the same bed. It broke Jarrod's heart to have to wake them. They sat upright in the bed, all bug-eyed and fluffy haired. At first, they seemed a little overwhelmed by the group of policemen in the room. Jarrod introduced the Inspector and he sat down on the bed near them, just close enough to create a personal touch without being overbearing.

'Hello kids, I'm Mr Crawford. I'm also a policeman. I'll be taking you away for a while. I suppose you could call it a little holiday. It's just so that we can take you to a safe place. It may not be safe for you here in Lockyer right now, so that's why I've come to collect you.'

Olivia and Jamie both looked at Jarrod for reassurance.

'It's okay guys, it's better this way. I'm sorry, you can't stay here. We need to take you somewhere safe. There are nice people that will look after you. Will you go with Mr Crawford for me?'

Olivia and Jamie looked at each other and then back at Jarrod. They nodded. Jake looked confused. 'I want to stay here with you, Jarrod, and with Mrs Wilson and with Kirsty. Why can't we stay?' Tears welled in his eyes.

A lump the size of a golf ball formed in Jarrod's throat. He fought against the threatening tears. 'Mrs Wilson and Kirsty will be in hospital for a while, my little mate. I wish you could stay here with me, but I still have a lot of work to do. I'm sorry, I know it's hard, but I need you to be brave. Olivia and Jamie need you to be brave as well. Can you do that for me? I'll see you again soon, I promise.'

'Do you really promise?' Jake asked, his eyes staring into Jarrod's.

'I promise. Are you ready to go?'

Jake leaned forward and hugged Jarrod around his neck. After a long embrace, Jake let go and Inspector Crawford took his hand. Dawes opened the door and checked that no one was about. At that time of the morning the ward corridors were quiet. The children were led out to an awaiting van and they slid into the back seat. The poor little buggers had been ferried from one police car to another, from one place to the next yet they still did so without complaint. Ross Benfield sat at the wheel. Inspector Crawford sat in the front passenger seat.

As the van drove out of the car park, Jarrod saw the three sad little faces staring back at him. Jake held up his Paddington Bear teddy and pressed it against the window, waving its furry paw.

Jarrod was sad for them as they had lost so much and experienced more heartache than could be imagined. They would experience more hard times as the sorrow of their loss sunk in, but he knew they had the resilience to stay strong. They were special children – so courageous. They would help each other through this ordeal.

The car lights disappeared around the corner and Jarrod stood alone.

Long and Dawes emerged and stood next to him.

'I guess that's that then, nothing more for us to do tonight,' said Long. 'We've got other units patrolling. They'll let us know if there's a sighting of Miles. Let's go home and get some sleep.'

FORTY-FOUR

JUST before 3AM Jarrod tip-toed through the house. As he always did, he popped his head in to check on the kids. They weren't in their beds and he remembered they were sleeping in his bed with Jayne. He found them – with Jayne pinned in the middle between Matty and Katie. Delirious from exhaustion, he sat at the end of the bed and flicked off his shoes. Resisting the temptation to just flop onto the bed, he stood and trudged to the bathroom. The hot shower was a godsend. It was revitalising to wash away the grit and grime from the last twenty-four hours. He changed into a pair of boxer shorts and a t-shirt and slid into the bed beside Katie. She murmured and rolled onto her side facing him. Her arm curled around his neck and her soft breath tickled his cheek. Jayne lifted her head and smiled, wedged in by Matty, who lay with his head on her shoulder.

Despite being kicked and shoved by Katie in her sleep, Jarrod drifted off in minutes. The quarry lake ghosts were not far away – they seemed destined to haunt him forever. He fought them off as they tried to pull him deep into the abyss once again. It was futile. He drowned in their hatred and endless need for revenge and retribution.

At 6AM he woke feeling just as exhausted as ever. His spirits were lifted during his morning cuddles and kisses with the kids before they went off to watch Play School while waiting for breakfast. Jayne slid across and put her head on his chest and hugged

255

him. She gazed up at him and smiled. 'I'm glad you finally made it home. You sleep in for a bit longer. I'll get the kids organised.' She climbed out of bed and the morning ritual began.

He lay there staring at the ceiling, disappointed at the stark reality that the last few days hadn't all just been a bad dream. They were all very real. Everything had all really taken place; there was no escaping that. His scrambled mind was in a place it had never been before. He wished it was all over. The Kingston children were safe, but Vincent Miles was still out there. He hoped their deception had worked, that Miles had seen or heard a news broadcast. But the man was wounded and had gone into hiding, he was hardly going to go to the newsagent to buy the daily paper. If he suspected the children were still alive, he would come after them again. Jarrod hoped they could maintain the cover story of the fate of the Kingston children. It was a long shot but also their best chance of Miles giving up his pursuit of the children and finishing what he had to do – ridding the world of himself.

From the bedroom Jarrod heard the children's program interrupted by a news broadcast. The bulletin confirmed two children had been murdered overnight. Jayne rushed into the bedroom, her face pale. 'I'm so sorry, Jarrod. I had no idea.' She sat on the edge of the bed.

He took her hand and smiled. 'The kids are safe. It's a cover story. We fed the media some lies to buy some time so that we could get the kids to somewhere safe.'

'But why come up with this story? Why say they were murdered?'

'Vincent Miles is still out there. He won't stop coming after the children, ever. We had no choice.'

'Are you sure you know what you're doing?'

'Not really.'

Jayne let it go. As usual, she seemed to know when not to probe. 'I've made some bacon and eggs. Want some?'

Jarrod's growling stomach reminded him that he hadn't eaten much in the last twenty-four hours – he was ravenous.

'You bet. I'd love some.'

Breakfast was chaotic as usual. Matty sat in his highchair spitting out food as fast as Jarrod could shovel it in. He smiled and tapped his spoon on the food tray. Katie chatted about her life's dramas. Two boys in grade two liked her and she couldn't decide which one she was going to marry. Then there were the arguments she had with the other girls because they thought the boys liked them. Katie continued with her stories, hardly stopping for a breath. Jarrod listened and just smiled.

He showered, shaved and dressed in fresh clothes. After getting the kids dressed, teeth brushed, toys picked up and dishes washed, it was time to head into the station. Jayne was dropping Matty off at day care and then taking Katie to school before going to work herself.

Jarrod said his goodbyes and shared more hugs and kisses. Katie blocked his path as he was about to leave and wrapped her arms around his waist. She looked up sadly and said, 'Daddy, I miss you when you're not here.'

'I miss you too, baby. I'll try and be home more often, I promise. It's just that...'

Katie interrupted, dejected. 'Yeah, I know Dad, you get busy at the police station.'

Jarrod knelt down beside her so they were at eye level. 'I'm sorry I'm not here as much as I would like, but I promise I'll make some changes. Things will get better, you'll see.'

'Okay, Dad,' she said with a lovely smile. 'Have a good day.'

'I will sweetheart, you have a good day too,' he said, giving her one more kiss on the nose.

He couldn't remember the last time he'd had a good day.

FORTY-FIVE

AT eight-thirty, Jayne carried Matty into the day care centre while Katie waited in the car. As soon as they entered the child-locked gates, he strode off like he owned the place, ready for a big day of adventures, digging in the sandpit and fraternising with other toddlers. There were no tears, he was having a good day and was bursting with excitement. After unpacking Matty's Lightning McQueen backpack and wiping his nose one last time, Jayne left him in the care of the competent and friendly staff. Spending all day, every day, with other people's babies and toddlers wasn't her idea of a career choice. It made her job at the Accident and Emergency ward seem like a cakewalk. Katie was busily playing with her iPad when Jayne returned to the car and they set off for school.

Along the way they chatted about the usual girly things and discussed the day ahead. Jayne would normally drop Katie off in the school car park, allowing her to walk into the front gate of the school grounds on her own. However today the car park was full so she had to find a park on the street and walk Katie up to the school.

Eventually Jayne found a park down the street. Katie lugged her school bag from the back seat and chatted away as they walked along the pavement towards her school. Jayne heard unusual sounding footfalls and glanced over her shoulder. A man in a coat limped behind them. His hair and beard were matted, his face sickly pale. The hood of his coat covered his head, partially concealing his face. One arm hung in a crude shoulder sling under the heavy overcoat.

As Jayne nervously glanced over her shoulder again, the man quickened his pace and drew closer. A wave of panic rushed through her. She grabbed Katie's hand, hurrying her pace.

'Ouch, what's the matter, Mummy? You're hurting my hand,' complained Katie.

The man started running after them.

Jayne snapped at Katie, 'Run!'

It was too late. He was on them. He grabbed Jayne's shoulder and spun her around.

'Mrs O'Connor. Or is that, Sister O'Connor? Do you remember me?' the man said with an ugly smile.

'What do you want?' she said, trying to mask her fear.

'It's time your husband learned the meaning of pain, then he will understand. He needs to understand.'

Jayne had no chance to duck the lightning-fast blow to her face. She lurched backwards and dropped to the pavement. Katie froze. Vincent Miles bent down and rummaged through Jayne's handbag. He found her mobile phone and slid it into his coat pocket. Miles pounced on Katie and scooped her up using his good arm. He slung her over his shoulder and scurried away from the school. Katie squealed, legs kicking.

Other parents and children arriving at the school looked on in shock.

'Someone help!' Jayne screamed.

Dazed, her head screaming, she stumbled as she tried to get up. One father ran over to her. Norman Beasley, an overweight real estate agent dressed in a suit, yelled for someone to call the police. He pursued the kidnapper on foot, disappearing into the next side street.

Jayne dragged herself to her feet and staggered as a wave of dizziness took hold. She willed one foot in front of the other until she rounded the corner.

Standing there, grimacing in pain, was Vincent Miles. He glared at Norman, who approached with his hands out in a calming gesture.

Miles lowered Katie to the ground. He slid his injured arm from the sling, grabbing hold of Katie's ponytail. She squealed.

He yanked her hair. 'Shut up, child.' His words floated in the air, sinister and cruel.

Katie whimpered.

Jayne stopped alongside Norman, her hand covering her mouth to stifle a gasp. Her little girl stared back at her, eyes wide with terror.

'Mummy,' Katie sobbed, her face smeared with tears.

Panting for breath, Norman wheezed. 'Come on mister, let the little girl go. Just let her go. Let her walk over to me. I won't follow you…'

He stopped mid-sentence when Miles gripped the handle of a gun and removed it from his belt.

Norman's mouth gaped.

Miles raised the gun and aimed at Norman.

Jayne flinched at the deafening boom and muzzle flash of the gunshot. Norman looked down in shock as a bright red circle of blood seeped through his white shirt in the centre of his chest. He stumbled backwards, holding his hand against the wound, blood seeping through his fingers. The second shot struck his abdomen. He looked up in disbelief and Vincent Miles' eyes of pure evil stared back at him.

Norman's knees dropped to the bitumen and he exhaled in a whisper. 'Why?' He slumped forward onto the roadway, falling heavy. Norman Beasely, the unlikely hero, exhaled his last breath and died where he lay.

Katie screamed and Miles yanked harder on her hair. She gasped and fell silent. The shrieks of hysterical mothers bounced off the school buildings and echoed in the street. Miles' eyes met Jayne's and he aimed the gun at her. He squinted to focus on her, his body shaking. The gun wobbled in his hand.

Jayne shook her head, pleading. 'No.'

He lowered the gun and turned, coldly dismissing the man he had killed in the street. He placed the gun in the pocket of his coat and scooped Katie up, balancing her on his hip as he strode towards the four-wheel drive parked in a loading zone. Katie struggled and kicked out, but this only infuriated him more. He threw her into the back seat and slammed the door. Within seconds he was in the driver's seat and accelerating away, the tyres screeching as the vehicle skidded around the corner.

Jayne sprinted after them, screaming, 'No! Stop!'

As the vehicle pulled away, she lost her balance, concussion taking hold. She stumbled to the bitumen and tried to get back up, but her legs were jelly.

In an instant, they were gone.

Jayne clutched at herself, rocking back and forth. 'He took my little girl,' she whimpered.

FORTY-SIX

WHEN Jarrod arrived at the station, he sat at his desk and telephoned the hospital. He spoke to the charge nurse. Brad was doing well. He'd had surgery and was stable. Mrs Wilson was being released later that morning after the final all-clear by the doctors. She agreed to stay with friends while her house remained a crime scene. All part of the ruse. Media were still camped out the front of the "scene of the horrific murders of the Kingston children".

Kirsty was in worse shape and would be staying in hospital for observation with a suspected fractured jaw and concussion. The nurse assured Jarrod she would be fine. He asked to speak to his wife but was told Jayne hadn't arrived at work yet.

His mobile phone rang. Jayne's caller ID flashed up on the screen. 'Jayne, is everything all right? They said you haven't arrived at work.'

'Your wife will live. But I have your little girl.' A man's voice, raspy, pained. Vincent Miles. 'It's time for your reckoning, O'Connor.'

The floor shifted beneath Jarrod's feet. His fear boiled into burning anger, seeking to inflict harm. His jaw clenched. 'What have you done? I will hunt you down! Do you understand me?' His words seethed through gritted teeth.

'You listen to me!' Miles retorted. He paused, controlling his tone. 'Your daughter is still alive, but for how long depends on you.'

Jarrod swallowed and took a deep breath. 'What do you want

262

from me? You've taken the Kingston children. Isn't that what this is all about?' The muscles in his neck and shoulders tensed.

'Yes, I heard you couldn't save them. The guilt must be killing you. But don't feel bad, it was their destiny to be returned to their mother. I took them painlessly. They're now in paradise.'

'Don't feel bad? You cold-hearted bastard!'

Miles sniggered. 'Now, now, *Jarrod*. Don't go getting all self-righteous on me. Emotion is lack of self-control, weakness.'

'Killing innocent children is demented, you sick fuck.'

The phone muffled. A squeal, a cry. Katie.

'Watch your tongue! I have a gun to your little girl's head.'

Jarrod bit his lip until he tasted blood. He'd lost control. *Focus. Think.* Katie was still alive for a reason. He had to play Miles' game. He swallowed the rising panic and calmed himself.

'Tell me what you want. It's all over, isn't it? Didn't you accomplish what you'd set out to do?'

'It's not over,' Miles mocked. 'Not even close.'

'What then? Explain it to me. Make me understand.'

'All you need to understand is that we don't make the rules. There's a higher power at play. You have to quieten your mind. If you listen hard enough, you'll hear them, the whispers and the echoes. They're out there, guiding us.'

'And what are these whispers telling you now?'

'That it wasn't your time to die, not yet anyway. You should be dead, but clearly the gods had other plans. I would have killed you, back at that house. You know that, don't you?'

Jarrod remembered the coldness in Miles' eyes, his finger on the trigger, the muzzle pointed at his head. 'You should have taken that shot when you had the chance.'

Sickly coughing stifled Miles' laughter. He wheezed, his words laboured. 'That little boy,' he said, panting. 'He was your guardian angel. We all have a part to play, no matter how small. That was his. The beautiful chaos of it all, the wisdom. Even now, it still surprises me. It was meant to be, all of it. Shooting you in the face would have been too easy, quick and painless. You won't get off that easy. It's funny how things have turned out. Wouldn't you say? It has a, what's the word for it? … Symmetry. Yes, symmetry.'

'My little girl, she's got nothing to do with any of this. Let her go. Please.'

'No! I can't do that. I won't. She's the key.'

'The key? To what?'

'To unlocking the gates of heaven. It all makes sense now.'

'Unlocking the gate for who?'

Heavy breathing on the other end of the phone, gasping.

'Tell me!' Jarrod yelled.

'Tell you?' Miles chuckled. 'No, you wouldn't understand. You need to *feel* it, live it. Fear, that deep, dark terror that crushes all hope, it needs to flow through your veins. Only then will salvation come.'

'Salvation for who?'

'Both of us.'

'I don't understand!'

'I know. You will. Come find us, and you'll see.'

'Where are you?'

'The Remembrance Gardens Cemetery. Come to the front gate and I'll call you. I'll be watching. Come alone or your little girl dies.'

'Let me speak to her. I need to know she's alright.'

'Not until you give me your word. You come alone. No tricks, no cop bullshit. No heroes hiding in trees, no surveillance, no snipers, no back up. I can smell you pigs for miles. If I get the slightest sniff of another cop, I will blow a hole in this sweet little girl's head. Search your heart. You know I will. Time is ticking.'

Jarrod had no doubt. Miles wouldn't hesitate to kill Katie. He was too far gone, too deranged to care.

'You have my word. I'll come alone.'

'A man's word is his bond. In your case, your daughter's life

264

depends on it.'

'I said you have my word. Now put Katie on the phone.'

Silence at the other end until a timid voice spoke. 'Daddy?'

Jarrod closed his eyes at the sound of her voice. 'I'm coming baby, just hold on. I'm coming for you.' His gut wrenched. It broke his heart to hear his little girl so scared.

'Where are you, Daddy?' she whimpered.

There was a ruffling in the background as the phone was snatched from her. The call ended and the handset beeped. Katie was gone.

Jarrod sat at his desk frozen with disbelief, shivering in a cold sweat. He tried to focus, plan his next move. His mind went foggy and panic set in. He had tried to force Miles' hand with a deception about the Kingston children but had grossly underestimated him. He wasn't finished yet. Instead, he'd taken the initiative and the tables were turned. Jarrod was suffocating, his lungs contracted in his chest, his ribs tight. A deranged killer had his child.

His mobile phone rang and he jumped. Caller ID unknown. He answered it. 'Yes, who is this?'

'Jarrod, he's taken our little girl. He's got Katie,' cried Jayne in desperation.

He was overcome with relief to hear her voice. 'I know, the bastard just rang me from your phone. What happened?'

'He snuck up on us outside the school. He punched me and knocked me down. He snatched Katie and drove off with her. He shot a man.'

'What? Are you alright?'

'I think I have a broken nose,' she said between sobs. 'Poor Norman is dead.'

'Oh no. What about Matty? Where is he?'

'He's fine. I'd already dropped him off at day care. That's where I'm ringing from, I've come back to collect him. I wasn't thinking straight. I needed to get to him.'

'That's good, sweetheart, you've done the right thing. Stay there, alright. I'll send police around to you.'

'Some police have just arrived. Someone called them. Are you coming? We need to find our little girl. We have to get her back.'

Jarrod hesitated. 'I... I can't. He wants to meet with me. I spoke to Katie on the phone just now.'

'Oh God! Is she okay?'

'She's scared but she was okay. I'm meeting him. I need to go alone.'

'No, Jarrod, don't go alone. Get help. You can't do this alone,' she pleaded.

'Jayne, listen to me. I can't risk it. He says that if anyone else comes, he'll kill her. He'll do it! Do you understand?'

'Just get our little girl back, Jarrod.'

'I will, I promise. I'll get her back.'

He hung up and trembled uncontrollably with rage.

FORTY-SEVEN

AS Jarrod sped out of town towards the cemetery, he ran all possible scenarios through his head, however he didn't have a single plan of action. He was bumbling in blind, towards a certain trap. A monster had his little girl. He had to control his rage or things could go horribly wrong. He had to let it play out with a cool head. Miles could have killed Katie by now if he had wanted it that way. He lured Jarrod out there to that lonely place for a reason. He was toying with Jarrod. Miles loved being in control. Making people suffer was the ultimate power.

Jarrod drove up the long dusty road that led from the highway towards the cemetery entrance. He drove through the black iron gates hanging from sandstone pillars, the weathered faces of angel statues locked in an eternal gaze towards the heavens. He stopped and waited for the dust cloud to settle. *Now what?* He got out and walked around the car, scanning the cemetery landscape in a full circle. It was deserted. He was surrounded by hundreds of souls, but the only heartbeat was his own. Nothing but endless rows of headstones. A scattering of trees gave partial shade to the graves below. Hedgerows represented the perimeter of the cemetery which nestled on a small plain surrounded by rolling hills of bushland. The ground was dusty and dry.

A breeze whistled and swirled around the headstones. A lone crow, black eyed and menacing, perched on the outstretched hand of an angel statue, squawking with contempt. He waited. His mobile phone rang. Jayne's caller ID. He answered. 'Where are you?'

'Follow the main road in,' Miles said in a raspy voice, short of breath. 'Stop when you get to a large white cross,' he wheezed. 'Get out of your car, turn right and follow the path down to the end. When you get there look at the headstones until you find a name you recognise.' He hung up.

Jarrod did as instructed and drove down the road, taking him deeper into the cemetery. He came across a white marble cross mounted above an elaborate headstone. He killed the engine and climbed out, drawing his firearm. He followed the path to the right, taking cover between rows of headstones.

He came to the end and studied the headstones. He didn't know where to start looking. So many names. Men, women and children of all ages, their remains buried deep in the earth beneath him. Some headstones bore the scars of time, the engravings worn from the elements. Others were more recent with bare soil and fresh bouquets. Many had decayed with neglect, others maintained with loving care. One after the other, he read epitaphs.

His eyes snagged on a name he recognised and he read the simple inscription. His heart sank. He understood why Miles had led him there. The grave was tiny and plain, the headstone a drab grey granite stone. *Baby Jazmin Miles. In god's loving care.'* A cherub playing a harp was engraved below. It had all the hallmarks of a pauper's grave.

Jarrod heard movement. He swung around, following the front sight of his Glock. Vincent Miles stepped out from behind a tall headstone two rows away. His hand covered Katie's mouth. She looked terrified. Miles crouched behind her, using her as a shield. He held a police service Glock to Katie's head. His finger hovered over the trigger. Katie was frozen with fear, her cheeks glistening with tears. Her eyes darted to Jarrod, pleading for him to rescue her. He fought the urge to run to her.

'It's okay, sweetheart. I'm here now,' he called.

Miles stared at him with a sinister scowl. 'It's time I teach you about suffering, O'Connor,' he yelled, pressing the gun against Katie's temple.

His voice echoed around the tombstones and a crow squawked from afar.

FORTY-EIGHT

KATIE remained frozen with fear, her arms rigid by the sides of her navy and white chequered school dress. Her shiny black buckled shoes and frilly white socks were soiled by the cemetery's red dust. Blood trickled from a graze to her knee. Miles knelt behind her, pulling at her collar. The heavy overcoat hung from his shoulders. He held her with his injured arm. His shirt was blood soaked from the gunshot wound to his shoulder. His other hand gripped the gun, the muzzle pressed against the side of Katie's head. His index finger caressed the trigger. Jarrod prayed he wouldn't squeeze it, that somehow his daughter's life would be spared.

He aimed his Glock at Miles. He wanted so badly to fire but his hands were shaking, his arms jelly. He couldn't take the risk. If he missed, he could hit Katie. Or Miles could react and pull the trigger. The playing pieces were set. It was Miles' move.

Miles released Katie's collar and grabbed her ponytail, coiling the hair in his grip. She cried out in pain as he pulled harder, her head tilting back towards him.

'Leave her alone! Let my little girl go!' Jarrod pleaded. 'What do you want with us? It's over, isn't it? Everything you set out to do, it's done. You've won. How many more people need to die?'

'Just one more person needs to die, O'Connor, and then it's over,' said Miles in a controlled tone. 'You need to understand my suffering, to share my pain.' Miles was pale and perspired heavily, his hair wild. He swayed and wiped sweat out of his eyes with his coat sleeve. A fever seemed to have taken hold. He was growing weak. Yet he still had Katie in his grasp and had enough strength to pull that trigger. Jarrod had to keep him talking to buy time.

'I'm trying to understand, Vincent. I understand you've suffered and you long to be with your little girl and Clare. That's what this is all about, isn't it?'

'You know shit, O'Connor. Don't tell me you know how I feel. No, not until you have suffered like I have will you truly understand.' His words laboured through his pain.

Jarrod fixed the aim of his gun at Miles' head, waiting for the right moment to take a shot. Miles held Katie against the front of his body, the gun still pressed against her temple.

'I know about the cube of life and the Archangel Metatron,' said Jarrod. 'It's you, isn't it? And Edward Ryan, he was a believer. I know Clare took her own life to be with her children. She made her sacrifice. It's over Vincent. Let my little girl go, please. Is this what Clare would have wanted?'

Miles gazed at him but the injured man was losing his focus, his chin dropped and his eyelids drooped. His balance was unstable, beads of sweat dripped from his forehead and splashed onto the dust at Katie's feet. Yet he held his grip of her hair.

His voice was low. 'Get away from my baby's grave.' Then he screamed, 'Get away from her! Step away now or by Christ I will spread your daughter's brains all over the ground. Drop your gun on the ground. Move back now!' There was a desperate intensity in his eyes. Jarrod saw Miles' knuckles whiten as he squeezed the grip of the gun.

This was his last chance. He had to take the shot now or throw down his gun. He had to take a huge gamble either way. It was a gamble that would determine whether his little girl lived or died. If he wanted Jarrod to see his daughter murdered in cold blood, then why hadn't he pulled the trigger by now? Miles was trying to tell him something. He had Jarrod's full attention.

Jarrod couldn't chance taking the shot. He threw his gun on the ground out in front of him and stepped back.

Miles rose to his feet, staggering. With each backwards step Jarrod took, Miles stepped forward, leading Katie forward with him, still gripping her hair. She whimpered but didn't cry out, his little girl was being so brave. He was heartbroken to see her like this. They were now at the mercy of Vincent Miles, a killer. Jarrod hinged his hopes on there being some humanity or shred of mercy left inside him.

'Keep moving,' he ushered as Jarrod stepped backwards along a row of headstones. Miles halted beside his daughter's grave. He stared down at the headstone, tears smudging his dirty face. He read out the inscription. 'Baby Jazmin Miles. In god's loving care.' His voice was raspy and he cleared his throat.

'She was taken from me. My baby was taken from me!' The bitterness in his voice rose. He looked down at Katie and stroked her face with the back of his hand. 'Your little girl, she's so full of life. My baby had her life stolen from her. How is that fair? Why did God do this to me? Soon I'll have my revenge.'

'Think of your little girl, baby Jazmin. She's looking down on you. Is this what she wants her daddy to do? Would this make her happy? I don't believe that. Do you?' Jarrod pleaded.

'Don't you dare speak her name.' He looked down at the gun, his index finger teetering on the trigger, threatening to squeeze. 'Do you now feel my pain? I can smell your fear. What do you fear most, O'Connor? Do you fear death itself or do you fear the death of someone you love?'

'I would gladly give my life right now if it meant saving hers,' said Jarrod, staring Miles in the eye.

'Could you make that choice?'

Jarrod opened his stance with outstretched arms, palms facing upwards. 'Yes, I could.'

Miles turned the gun towards Jarrod, aiming it at his chest. His voice wilted to a whisper. 'You fear the death of your daughter, but can you ever imagine how you would live your life if she was taken from you? What sort of person would you become? Would you kill to have revenge? What I have done has allowed me to transform into something powerful. I gave Clare her children and now I have been rewarded. What I need you to understand, O'Connor, is that I am not the devil. I am the Archangel, the highest of all angels. I have deceived God, just as he deceived me. I will take my revenge against God just as the fallen angels had tried to do. Though I will not fall, I will succeed. God will pay for his cruelty.'

He stared at Jarrod and flashed a maniacal smirk. His eyes narrowed. 'You have no idea what's coming. *He* is ready. He will set the world on fire – and you will wish I had killed you.'

He took a deep breath and pushed Katie to the ground. She fell on her hands and knees in the dust. Jarrod motioned to go to her but thought better of it. He held his ground. Miles stepped onto his daughter's grave and stretched his arms out, showing no pain from his wound. He looked up to the sky and screamed. 'I'm coming God. I'm coming for you!'

Without hesitation, he put the gun against the side of his head and fired. The gunshot echoed through the tranquil cemetery and surrounding hills. Birds squawked and fluttered from their tree top perches. Vincent Miles' lifeless body slumped onto his daughter's grave. He lay sprawled on his back, arms still outstretched. The gun slid from his hand and came to rest in the dirt. Blood gushed from a gaping head wound and pooled beneath him, oozing bright red around the base of the headstone.

The eyes that once held so much venom stared vacantly towards the sky.

Jarrod ran over to Katie and swooped her up off the ground. He held her tight, cradling her in his arms. She held her little arms around his neck and cried. She felt so tiny and frail. His shirt soaked up her tears.

'Daddy, please don't let me go. Please don't leave me,' she whispered in between sobs.

'No, my baby. I will never leave you.'

As he embraced his daughter, raindrops fell. It was a light, unexpected shower and the cool droplets soothed his face.

He looked up to the heavens, thanking God and the angels for protecting his little girl.

The rain fell like tears from the sky, as though the angels were weeping.

EPILOGUE

IT was time for Jarrod to face his demons. He reconciled his thoughts as he drove along the dirt road, cutting a straight line through the never-ending expanse of the pine forest. *How does one face their demons? What do you say to them?* The nightmares had continued, haunting his sleep without mercy. His demons were relentless, seeming to enjoy the torment they were inflicting. He was desperate to find peace.

He decided to take the fight to them and it seemed to be the most logical place for it. A new gate had since been erected at the site where Jamal Lewis and Douglas Blair plummeted to their deaths. He parked the car and climbed the gate, making the remainder of his journey on foot. He followed the sandy track and came to an opening carved out from the dense forest.

He peered out over the quarry lake. He stepped closer until his shoes teetered at the edge of the cliff. Small stones fell, bouncing and clattering against the jagged rock walls until they plopped with a loud echo into the milky green water below. Ringlets formed and disrupted the mirror-like surface of the lake. He hadn't been back there since that awful day when the Mustang, containing the lifeless bodies of those two boys, was hoisted from the depths of the water.

On the horizon, the sun was setting, shimmering in a haze of slate clouds smeared across a darkening canvass. The sky was a palette of crimson red and orange. A breeze gently blew across the surface of the water and rose from the cliffs below. He savoured the peacefulness of that lonely place. He outstretched his arms and tilted his head back, closing his eyes. The gentle rustle of leaves in the trees and the chirping of birds nestling in preparation for the oncoming darkness were the only sounds. He breathed, calmed his mind and listened for the echoes and whispers.

He opened his eyes. 'What do you want from me?' he whispered. His voice sounded strange in his own ears. He took a deep breath. 'What do you want from me?' he yelled. His words echoed across the lake, bouncing off the cliffs. The birds shrieked and fluttered and a light wind swirled.

'What do you want from me?' he yelled. 'Answer me!' Anger rose from his gut. He waited.

'If you want your revenge, then take it!' he shuffled closer to the edge of the cliff.

'Come on, now's your chance. You want revenge, then take it!' His fading echoes were replaced with silence. He looked down at the lake surface which was once again flat as a sheet of glass. The setting sun and the blood sky reflected perfectly on the surface. There were no signs of the demons in the water, no ghastly corpses reached out beckoning him into the abyss.

'It's over. You've tormented me long enough, set me free!'

A gust of wind blew across his body, causing him to step away from the edge. Then it was gone. The sun dipped below the horizon and all fell quiet. There were no answers to be found. He turned and walked away. He felt hollow inside.

However, with each step he took away from the cliff's edge, the quarry ghosts beckoned louder in his head. They were restless. He stopped and looked back over his shoulder towards the edge of the cliffs. A cold trickle seeped through him as an unsettling shiver bristled the hairs at the back of his neck. He was struck by a sense of uneasiness, followed by a strange feeling of vertigo. As a wave of dizziness came over him, he dropped to one knee and closed his eyes. He rubbed a hand over his face, the coarse stubble of his jawline prickled against his fingertips.

He clenched his eyes shut as a vague image materialised in his mind. Was it a dream, a premonition or just his imagination? It appeared far off into the deep recesses of his mind, too far to make out the detail. The shadowy face of a small boy became clear. Something lodged in his chest and he swallowed, his throat dry. The image faded and then slipped away. He opened his eyes, confused. He rose to his feet and kept on walking, haunted by the image. Something, a kind of unseen force, willed him to return to the edge of the cliffs. Traces of untold secrets clung to his subconsciousness like smoke. He fought against an invisible pull that drew him back. With each laboured step, the force weakened and he broke free of its grasp. He walked away and didn't look back.

Nightmares haunted his sleep once again that night.

ABOUT THE AUTHOR

Jack Roney is a member of the Queensland Writers Centre, Australian Society of Authors and Australian Crime Writers Association. He lives with his family in Brisbane, Australia. His writing is inspired by over thirty years in law enforcement where he gained experience as an investigator, tactical skills and firearms instructor, police academy instructor, strategic policy writer and media officer.

Jack draws on his experience as a former detective to bring authenticity and realism to his writing. He was a police consultant for the ABC television series Harrow. *The Angels Wept* is book 1 of a three-book series and reached the Wattpad Awards shortlist. He has completed writing courses with Curtis Brown Creative and Brisbane Writers Workshop and was selected for the Queensland Writers Centre residency program. His novel, *The Ghost Train and The Scarlet Moon*, was the runner-up in the Hawkeye Publishing Manuscript Development Prize.

www.jackroney.com.au

Book reviews can make or break a book. If you liked what you read today, please do consider posting a review on Goodreads or your favourite forum.

The Angels Wept (second edition) is available at www.hawkeyebooks.com.au and all good bookstores and libraries.

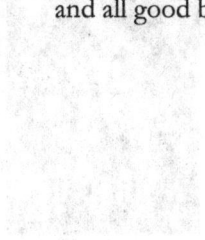

BOOKS BY
JACK RONEY

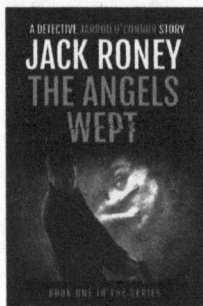

**THE ANGELS WEPT
(JARROD O'CONNOR #1)**

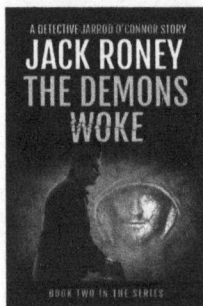

**THE DEMONS WOKE
(JARROD O'CONNOR #2)**

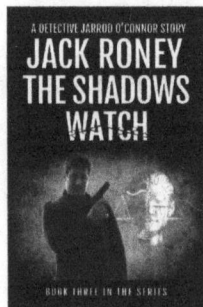

**THE SHADOWS WATCH
(JARROD O'CONNOR #3)**

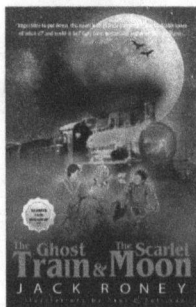

**THE GHOST TRAIN AND
THE SCARLET MOON**

www.ingramcontent.com/pod-product-compliance
Lightning Source LLC
Chambersburg PA
CBHW011829020426
42334CB00027B/2986